Tube Flies Two
Evolution

Mark Mandell & Bob Kenly

Color Plates by Craig Wester

TABLE OF CONTENTS

INTRODUCTION, 6

CHAPTER 1 ◆ **John Alevras, USA,** 8

CHAPTER 2 ◆ Rex Andersen, Denmark, 14

CHAPTER 3 ◆ Graydon Bell, UK, 21

CHAPTER 4 ◆ Bill Black, USA, 25

CHAPTER 5 ◆ **Ken Bonde-Larsen, Denmark,** 29

CHAPTER 6 ◆ **Bart Chandler, USA,** 32

CHAPTER 7 ◆ **Abraham Concepcion, Costa Rica,** 38

CHAPTER 8 ◆ **David Croft, UK,** 42

CHAPTER 9 ◆ **Mike Croft, USA,** 46

CHAPTER 10 ◆ **Rudi Heger, Germany,** 51

CHAPTER 11 ◆ Peter Hylander, USA, 54

CHAPTER 12 ◆ Martin Joergensen, Denmark, 60

CHAPTER 13 ◆ **Tim Johnson, USA,** 64

CHAPTER 14 ◆ **Bob Kenly, USA,** 68

CHAPTER 15 ◆ **Nick Kingston, Ireland/Australia,** 73

CHAPTER 16 ◆ **Skuli Kristinsson, Iceland,** 76

CHAPTER 17 ◆ **Mark Mandell, USA,** 80

CHAPTER 18 ◆ **Sergio Marchioni, Brazil,** 86

CHAPTER 19 ◆ Dag Midtgård, Norway, 90

CHAPTER 20 ◆ **Richard Murphy, USA,** 95

CHAPTER 21 ◆ Bernd Nickoleit, Germany, 100

CHAPTER 22 ◆ Håkan Norling, Sweden, 103

CHAPTER 23 ◆ **Tony Pagliei, USA,** 109

CHAPTER 24 ◆ Sacha Puetz, Germany, 114

CHAPTER 25 ◆ **Tanya Rooney, USA,** 118

CHAPTER 26 ◆ **Derrick Rothermel, Canada,** 122

CHAPTER 27 ◆ Masahito Sato, Japan/USA, 127

CHAPTER 28 ◆ **Darren Scaife, USA,** 132

CHAPTER 29 ◆ Jurij Shumakov, Russia, 136

CHAPTER 30 ◆ **Cam Sigler, Jr., USA,** 144

CHAPTER 31 ◆ David Skok, USA, 148

CHAPTER 32 ◆ Alec Smith, UK, 154

CHAPTER 33 ◆ **Anil Srivastava, USA,** 158

CHAPTER 34 ◆ Gerrit van Ee, Netherlands, 164

CHAPTER 35 ◆ **Tom Wolf, USA,** 168

APPENDIX, 173

INDEX, 174

INTRODUCTION

In 1995 Les Johnson and I wrote *Tube Flies*, the first book-length examination of the tying, history, and fishing of flies tied on tubes. It explained the advantages of using a tubular platform, and covered basic tying procedures for freshwater, Atlantic salmon, and saltwater tube patterns. In the decade that has passed since *Tube Flies* was published, thanks to the invention and artistry of many talented tiers around the world, the advances in materials, technique, and aesthetics have been considerable.

At this writing, new products abound, including fly tubing of very small outside diameter; interlocking tubing sets; colored hook sleeves; cone heads and machined metal tubes of varying shapes, anodized finishes, and sink rates; and specialty tube-fly hooks. It is not an exaggeration to say the new fly designs and tying techniques that co-evolved with these products have expanded the horizon of fly-tying.

Flip through the color plates of this book and you'll find flies that cannot be duplicated on a hook. You'll find flies designed to fish the "unfishable" places. You'll find new modular applications for fresh and salt water, from tube nymphs to striped bass patterns. You'll find Atlantic salmon tube flies that perfectly match the hook-tied versions' proportions, but with better action and survivability.

This book's organization differs from the 1995 work. It features 213 flies and 35 fly tiers from 14 countries, each with his or her own chapter. The contributors are commercial tiers and fly developers, as well as guides, artists, and talented non-professionals — with more than a thousand years of combined tying experience. Bob Kenly and I did our best to tease out the reasoning behind and inspirations for their patterns. Our goal from the start was to provide as much takeaway as possible, not just precisely how these "second generation" tube flies are tied and fished, but how they came into being.

Bob and I hope you enjoy learning from some of the masters of the form. As with *Tube Flies*, only if what follows tickles your imagination, only if it makes you want to stretch the envelope will we consider it a success.

Mark Mandell
Port Townsend, Washington
2006

JOHN ALEVRAS
Sequim, Washington/Chandler, Arizona

I've been fly tying for 47 years. My interest in tube flies was first stimulated over 20 years ago by British salmon fly-fishing authors. All of my tubes are meant for steelhead; most are large flies, used in the late fall and winter when rivers are usually high, cold, and off-color. In the winter and summer months, I focus on the rivers of Washington's Olympic peninsula. In the fall I head north to the Skeena river system in northern British Columbia. I fly-fish for steelhead an average of 75 days a year.

The Atlantic salmon fly tiers of the Victorian era helped define my goals for fly quality, but my models for style were Poul Jorgensen, Keith Fulsher, and especially, Syd Glasso. The stinger style, Intruder flies developed by steelhead fishermen Ed Ward and Jerry French have influenced my tying large patterns for winter conditions. I'm a strong believer in the effectiveness of the Irish grub (shrimp) style salmon fly. I've altered the basic design by using extra-long, soft, flowing hackle. Tubes are an integral part of these grub patterns, which I tie in 3- to 5-inch lengths on 1 1/2- to 2-inch aluminum tubes. The long, flexible hackles, marabou, rhea, and herl, a touch of glitter, and a sparse body combine to produce a fly with both movement and translucency.

The high river and roily conditions of winter push fish into the shallows, into as little as a foot of water. I use a 3 1/2- to 4-foot leader, and fish a Spey rod with a variety of tips. I carefully cover short stretches of holding water, taking advantage of the fact that winter steelhead close to spawning are generally aggressive even though the rivers are cold with strong flows.

Seventy-five percent of my tube flies are tied on aluminum stock. To fish deeper, faster water, such as plunge pools, I switch over to the heavier brass, either machined bottle tubes or Rooney (See Chapter 25: Tanya Rooney) light brass tubes. Bottle tubes have a machined collar in front and a thinner back end to fit the hook sleeve. The Rooney tubes aren't lined with plastic; instead, the ends are highly polished, and the mouth opening is flared, which creates fish-attracting air bubbles as water rushes through. In order to minimize the casting difficulties created by increased weight, I don't use brass tubes longer than one inch. To these short tubes I tie long, soft materials that vibrate in the current.

Since these tubes are thick in diameter (1/8 inch) compared to a hook shank, the bodies of my flies are usually made of tinsel to reduce bulk. This also provides some glitter, and by reflecting back through the wing materials, enhances the pattern's translucency. When I use fur in the body of the tube it is usually to create a small bulge behind the hackle to keep the wing from matting. I like to incorporate two or three colors into a fly's design. I am partial in winter to black/blue, red/orange/yellow, black/purple/blue and occasionally fuchsia/pink shades. I believe that multiple colors make a fly appear more alive and help trigger a take.

Fly Plate: Clockwise from top left: Cold Wind; Winter Storm; Aurora; Warm Fire; Winter Sunset.

A question that I feel needs to be answered is why bother to tie and fish a pattern on a tube? For me tubes provide one significant advantage: they allow me to use hooks that have much better hooking and holding qualities than most salmon/steelhead style hooks. I believe this is particularly true in the case of larger hooks, size 1/0 and up. I don't keep records of fish hooked versus fish landed, but I do know I lose too many on large hooks especially if the shank is long. Since I started using tubes on large patterns my landing ratio has increased dramatically. A short shank, wide gap, slightly curled up, offset point — see my hook recommendations in the fly recipes — simply sets and holds fish better.

COLD WIND

Tube: Aluminum, 1/8-inch O. D., 1 1/2 inches long
Thread: White UNI-Thread 8/0 for the body
Rear wing: Royal blue Arctic fox tail, purple marabou, black marabou
Body: Large silver holographic Mylar tinsel
Front wing: Royal blue Arctic fox tail, purple marabou, black marabou, natural Amherst pheasant tail fibers
Head: Black Danville 6/0
Finish: Head cement, several coats
Hook: Partridge Kevin Maddock Boilie size 2; Daiichi 3111 Beak Point/2x short size 1/0; Partridge Nordic Tube Fly size 2

Step 1: Mount the 1 1/2-inch aluminum tube on your vise with an attached silicone hook sleeve. Tie 8/0 white tying thread on the tube in front of the sleeve. After making a 3-inch dubbing loop, advance the tying thread in wide turns to the front of the tube. From a royal blue Arctic fox tail cut a piece of fur close to the skin that is 2 to 2 1/2 inches long. Only use enough fur to achieve two full turns around the tube with the dubbing loop. Do not pull out the short fibers at the base of the fur. They help spread out the marabou, allowing it to move freely in the water. Insert the butt ends of the fur into the loop 1/4 inch and tightly spin the loop. Wrap the first turn against the face of the sleeve and a second turn in front of that. As you wind the loop around the tube, stroke back the fur back so the long fibers are not trapped beneath it. Bring the tying thread back from the front and secure the loop with three or four turns, one in front of the other. Trim the excess loop. Stroke through the fur with your bodkin to separate any clumped fibers.

Step 2: Select a purple marabou plume with a long, thin stem and sparse, long fibers. These make the best hackle and leave the least bulk when tied off. Working from the tip of the feather, stroke the fibers perpendicular to the stem until you have enough long fibers to make two or three turns of hackle. Cut the stem just above the fibers, leaving a small stub that will be used to attach the marabou to the tube. Strip off the fibers at the base of the stem. Tie the marabou tip in front of the blue fox fur. Bring the tying thread forward. Attach hackle pliers to the butt of the stem and wind on two or three turns, depending on the thickness of the marabou. My preference is for less rather than more material. Each turn should be tight against the previous turn. Secure the stem with four or five firm turns of thread, and trim the excess. Use your bodkin to spread the fibers.

Step 3: Select a black marabou plume with a long stem and fibers. Repeat Step 2, but don't trim away the excess butt after winding on the feather. Instead, wrap the thread forward over the stem with smooth, close, non-overlapping turns to about 3/8 inch from the front of the tube. The stem should be secured in a straight line along the tube and not allowed to spiral around it. Trim stem.

Step 4: Cut a 12-inch piece of large silver holographic Mylar. Cut an angle in one end and attach that end of the Mylar at the nose of the tube in front of the stem end. Using very firm turns, wrap the tinsel back to the black marabou, edge to edge, with no overlap. When the tinsel reaches the marabou, reverse direction, applying extra pressure so the desired angle is achieved — the Mylar will stretch. Wind tinsel forward to the tying thread. Unwrap the turns of thread used to attach the tinsel, then secure it with four turns. (Optional: coat the tinsel with hard, high-gloss head cement to add durability to the fly.)

Step 5: Repeat Step 1 with a slightly thicker piece of fur that will produce a little bulkier foundation. This flares out the front wing wider than the rear. The tips of the fur should reach back to the start of the rear wing.

Step 6: Repeat Step 2 with another purple marabou plume.

Step 7: Tie in black 6/0 thread over the white thread that secured the purple marabou, trim ends. Repeat Step 3 but don't be concerned with the long stem this time. After two or three turns of the marabou, secure the stem and trim.

Step 8: Cut 24 fibers from an Amherst pheasant tail. The fibers should be at least 2 inches long. Divide the fibers into three bundles and trim the butts even. With soft turns of thread attach each of the three bundles spreading the fibers evenly around the front of the black marabou. Tie down the fibers with several more turns of the thread. Trim the butts.

Step 9: Form a small neat head and whip finish. Leave a small (1/16-inch) section of tube exposed in front of the head to minimize the chance of thread slipping off the tube. Apply three coats of head cement to form a smooth hard finish. I use diluted cement for the first coat so it soaks deep into the thread.

WINTER STORM
(CREATED BY DAVID BUSH)

Tube: Aluminum, 1/8-inch O. D., 1 1/2 inches long
Thread: Black Danville 6/0
Body: Royal blue Flashabou, 8 to 10 strands wrapped as tinsel in two layers, front to back and back to front. Apply a small clump of black fur at the front.
Wing: Fifteen strands of black ostrich herl spread around the fur ball and extending 1 to 2 inches beyond the end of the tube. Wrap two turns of royal blue marabou over the ostrich. The length of the marabou should reach the end of the holder. A dozen strands of royal blue holographic Flashabou tied over the blue marabou and spread evenly around the tube. Wrap two slightly shorter turns of black marabou in front of the blue.
Head: Black thread
Finish: Head cement, several coats

Hook: Partridge Kevin Maddock Boilie size 2; Daiichi 3111 Beak Point/2x short size 1/0; Partridge Nordic Tube Fly size 2

WINTER SUNSET

Tube: Rooney 1-inch Light Brass with silicone hook sleeve
Thread: White UNI-Thread 8/0 for the body
Wings: Each of the four wings is an equal combination of Arctic fox tail fur and burnt goose Spey hackle of the same color, 2 inches long. The color sequence from rear to front is yellow, orange, red, and purple. The yellow wing starts directly in front of the sleeve. Wings are all the same size/length; they do not taper from front to rear, or vice versa.
Body: Between the wings are three 3/8-inch sections of medium oval silver tinsel.
Head: Black Danville 6/0
Finish: Head cement, several coats
Hook: Partridge Kevin Maddock Boilie size 2; Daiichi 3111 Beak Point/2x short size 1/0; Partridge Nordic Tube Fly size 2

WARM FIRE

Tube: Brass bottle, 3/4 inch long, with liner and hook sleeve
Thread: Black Danville 6/0
Body: None
Lower wing: Orange Arctic fox, 4 inches long and sparse
Mid wing: Three or four strands of fine gold holographic Mylar tinsel
Upper wing: Flame orange Arctic fox, 4 inches long and sparse
Hackle: Long reddish-orange saddle
Cheek: Jungle cock dyed red
Head: Black thread
Hook: Partridge Kevin Maddock Boilie size 2; Daiichi 3111 Beak Point/2x short size 1/0; Partridge Nordic Tube Fly size 2

AURORA

Tube: Aluminum, 1/8-inch O. D., 1 1/2 inches long
Thread: Claret 6/0 Danville
Body: Hot pink Polar chenille tied in a 1/4-inch section behind the rear wing and in a 1-inch section between the rear and front wings. Make a bulge with the chenille immediately behind the wings.
Wing: Rear and front wings are fuschia rhea fibers, 3 to 4 inches long, fronted by large fuschia Guinea.
Head: Claret thread
Finish: Head cement, several coats
Hook: Partridge Kevin Maddock Boilie size 2; Daiichi 3111 Beak Point/2x short size 1/0; Partridge Nordic Tube Fly size 2

TUBE FLIES: A MURKY HISTORY

Today, tube flies can be found in the fly boxes of most salmon, steelhead, and saltwater anglers around the world. Despite the widespread acceptance of the tube-fly concept, its early history is poorly understood. To give you a picture of its possible origins and evolution, John Alevras has assembled the following excerpts from both celebrated and obscure angling writers and historians he uncovered in his 700-title fishing library.

Author Thomas Clegg, in *Modern Tube Fly Making* (a self-published pamphlet, 1965), states that tube flies "probably came to Britain from America, where anglers got the idea from North American Indians who used hollow bird-bone lures which emitted a string of bubbles." Although this proposition may be plausible, Clegg presents no evidence to support it.

The first published mention of the tube fly appears to be in *The Angler and the Thread Line* (1932) by British writer Alexander Wanless. In the tube concept, Wanless saw a solution to the loss of what he considered an unacceptable number of fly-hooked salmon. Along with several photos of fish caught on tube patterns he writes: "The lure…has a hole through the centre of it so that it slips up the line when a fish is being played. That is to prevent the small hook from being levered out of the fish's mouth by the body of the fly." He tied the standard patterns of the time — "mixed wing and palmered body - fully dressed"— on lead tubes (See Chapter 32: Alec Smith).

Although the photos and writings of Wanless suggest the tube concept originated in the British Isles in the early 1930's, two highly respected angler/historians, the late Joe Bates in his *Streamers and Bucktails* (Alfred A. Knopf, 1979) and Andrew Herd in his *The Fly* (The Medlar Press, 2001), have credited Ms. Winnie Morawski with the invention of the fly on a tube. A fly tier for the firm of Charles Playfair & Co. of Aberdeen, Scotland, Ms. Morawski began tying her flies on sections of hollow turkey quills around 1945. There is no evidence that she was aware of the work of Wanless. Her tube-fly patterns were the first in northern Scotland and the first to be sold commercially.

In *Successful Modern Salmon Flies* (1989), Peter Mackenzie-Philips says the use of treble hooks for salmon fishing in Britain was started by John Parker, who began producing his Parker tube flies in 1947, about the same time Richard Waddington's first book *Salmon Fishing: A New Philosophy* was published. Author Philips speculates that Parker's tube flies didn't catch on because their long, hair wings and shaggy appearance were "less attractive to human eyes" than the slender Waddington shanks. According to Philips, "Parker used starling wing quills, and other bird quills to form tubes on which to dress flies and a mount of wire running through the quill with a treble on the end, rather like a Devon Minnow (See Chapter 8: David Croft) mount." To add extra weight for high-water fishing, Parker wound lead wire around the mount.

Neil Graesser writes in *The Finer Points of Fly Fishing for Salmon* (The Boydell Press, 1989) that the Parker tube flies "with heavily leaded, spinner type mounts and lighter, smaller (plastic) tubes" became available almost immediately after the appearance of Waddington shanks. Graesser says these first tubes were often tied "more like a bottle brush than a fly which would have masked any body as the hair wing completely encircled the tube. They looked like nothing on earth, but did kill fish all the same." Evidently, the lack of a hook holder on these flies caused the treble to foul repeatedly on the cast. According to Graesser, the most popular of the Parker heavy spinner-type flies were the standard patterns of the day: Garry Dog, Hairy Mary, Shrimp, and Akroyd.

Although Thomas Clegg does not attempt to identify the inventor of the tube fly in his 1965 publication, he provides a rationale for its appearance in post-war Britain: economy. Hooks and exotic feathers were in very short supply at the time. "When a fish was hooked," Clegg writes, "the free tube, containing all the important feathers, slid up the cast (leader). Fish teeth had less chance to fray and disrupt the dressing, as often happened with standard flies. Broken treble hooks were easily replaced for a few pence, whereas a salmon hook casualty meant scrapping the whole fly." Clegg goes on to cite the many functional shortcomings of these early tube flies. Leaders frayed against rough metal edges, unaligned or fouled trebles caused missed strikes, and water poured through too large tube bores. In slack water he says that the hooks pulled the leader down, so the tube fly fished at one level and the treble at another, somewhere beneath it.

Clegg credits the late Fred Hill, bailiff on the Strathallan Castle water of the river Earn in Perthshire, with two critical developments in tube fly history in the 1950s: the invention of the "Stoat's Tail" fly and the use of very small diameter, hard plastic tubing. Apparently Mr. Hill clipped a small ermine (stoat) tail from a necklace belonging to his wife, then tied it around a piece of tubing taken from an empty ball-point pen. When he attached a tiny treble hook, his creation caught salmon and sea trout in quantity. Hill's Stoat's Tail became a classic low, summer-water salmon fly on Scottish rivers.

According to Clegg, subsequent advancements in tube design by engineers, model makers and professional fly dressers were a direct result of the "unique efficiency of the Stoat's Tail." Gone were the bird quills. Plastic lining was added to aluminum and brass tubes to prevent leaders from fraying. Lined metal tubes allowed any depth or flow of water to be fished, with or without quick-sinking lines. When duplicate dressed tubes are added to the leader, Clegg writes, the fly's overall size can be increased, making "larger meat-hook salmon flies" no longer necessary. He restates a belief, widely held at the time, that tube flies are most productive in summer low-water conditions. He recommends summer flies be dressed on "molded plastic tubes, beveled at the ends to prevent the dressing slipping off and with a cavity at one end to accommodate and align the treble."

While all this was happening in Britain, the only published evidence of early tube-fly evolution in the U. S. appears in Bill Blade's *Fishing Flies and fly-tying* (Stackpole, 1951). In this book Blade showcases tube-fly patterns he developed for hoppers, nymphs, crawfish, hellgrammites and minnows and states: "this method is not new; it has been used on feathered jigs for many years" and "possibilities are great." Blade provides no description of the construction of these "feathered jigs" or information about their history. Unfortunately, his tube patterns did not catch on with anglers and fly tiers in the States.

In *Tube Flies* (Frank Amato Publications, 1995) Mark Mandell and Les Johnson filled in some of the gaps in the history of tube flies in the Pacific Northwest. In the late 1940's, Lloyd Peters of Port Angeles, Washington commercially tied bucktails on high-pressure plastic tubing which were used from Alaska to California by salmon fishers. Twenty years later, John Gort, also of Port Angeles, supplied trollers and sportfishers with his own tube bucktails, some as small as three inches long. In the 1970's, around the time the Washington State Department of Fisheries began releasing hatchery silver salmon into south Puget Sound, innovative tiers Joe Butorac, Garry Sandstrom, Dave Wands, Brian Steel, and Bruce Ferguson began producing tube flies intended solely for fly casting to these fish.

In 1959 an article in *Trout and Salmon* magazine stated: "Tube flies are perhaps the most important advance which has occurred in Atlantic salmon fly-fishing since Woods introduced the grease line method." Forty-five years later, the advance, largely unheralded, is still unfolding.

CHAPTER 2

REX ANDERSEN

Vejle, Denmark

The fjord to the east of my hometown has some of the best sea trout (sea-run brown) fishing in Denmark. The Vejle AA River empties into the fjord after cutting through a valley lined with farms, forest, small communities, and feeder streams, and holds trout up to 20 pounds and the occasional Atlantic salmon.

From March through June, I fish for trout in the fjord, mostly from the beach. By the beginning of summer, increased water temperatures shift the most productive angling from the daytime to the evening and night. In June, trout begin to migrate upriver. During the day, fish in the river prefer small tubes (one inch and shorter) and salmon flies tied on size 2 to 8 hooks. At night, bigger tubes (2 inches long) with massive hair wings work best. Even a three-pound trout will attack these big tube flies — an average fish is six to seven pounds. By the end of September most of the fish have run upriver to spawn. Sea trout can reproduce four times, and trout mamas with egg-filled bellies are usually released to ensure the next generation. The spawners begin to return to the fjord in December. In winter, the fjord holds plenty of small trout between one and three pounds, as well as bigger ones that chose not to migrate upstream. About ten percent of the population of sexually mature trout stay in salt water; some stay for up to four years and return as trophy-sized fish. They are nature's reserve of sexually mature trout, capable of re-establishing a population if disaster strikes the spawners. Winter fishing continues during January and February, stopping only if the fjord freezes over.

I started fishing when I was four years old. By the age of 10, I had tried fishing with bait for cod, flounders and eels, and more rarely encountered brown and rainbow trout, perch and pike. I had also learned how to swim — a must for overly concerned mothers whose sons wander the streams, piers, and beaches. By the age of 12, I was old enough to become a junior member of the local fishing club that owns angling rights to the river. But before I was released on the streamside, I first had to attend a course in fishing, ethics, and fly-tying. On April 1, 1982, after the longest school day ever, I had my first solo fishing trip on the river. In a deep pool I caught my first sea trout. I wasn't able to kill it by hand — the neck was too thick and powerful for my fingers to have any lethal effect. The tail and rear part of the body wouldn't fit into the small fishing bag I carried, so I stumbled downstream towards my bicycle with my rod in one hand and a firm grip on the tail of that grand prize. From that day on, my primary targets have been salmonids, although killing fish has long ceased to be

Fly Plate: Clockwise from top left: The Golden Fox; Lady Amherst; Straw Shrimp; Easy Silver Doctor;
Ten-Armed Straw Squid; Red and Black Lodge; Flickering Ember; Too Easy

the main purpose. I only harvest the *interest* from nature's *capital*. My portion of the interest adds up to about ten killed sea trout per year.

Local sayings like, "The big trout bite when bats are flying" tickled my young imagination. Vejle's night-shift anglers taught me that "bigger is better" and "dark is beautiful" when it comes to after-sundown flies. In our slow-flowing river, big trout aggressively defend territory in the shallows. Only flies with a large wings trigger strikes, but they are difficult to tie on the required small, light hooks. A big fly tied on a plastic tube is very light and the hook sits at the rear, which makes for better hook ups. In difficult conditions, with just 10 to 20 cm of water flowing above the weeds, I use single carp hooks size 2, or I use the Loop double tube fly hook fixed with points up like a Clouser Minnow. If there is 50 cm of water depth, or when I fish deeper pools, I like a Kamasan B990 treble. Today, half my flies are tied on tubes — both smaller tubes for evening fishing, and bigger, darker ones to challenge night trout. Tubes also found their way into my saltwater fly box in the shape of smaller shrimp imitations in a variety of colors for sea trout from the beach. The possibilities for choosing a suitable silhouette/weight ratio on a tube is far beyond any selection of wet-fly or salmon hooks — at least for bigger flies.

I carry many types of tube flies in my box, but they all have something in common. They are meant for big trout and salmon! Most of the wings are made of bear hair or fox tail dyed in different colors. My box holds tube conversions of the classic Atlantic salmon flies: Akroyd, Black Doctor, Silver Doctor, Thunder & Lightning, Dusty Miller, and Lady Amherst. The latter is the exception to the hair-wing-only rule. I carry conversions of modern flies and tubes that evolved in Mörrum, the famous Swedish river. Mörrum has produced three basic fly styles, all popular in Denmark: big tubes fished at night in August/September when sea trout migrate upriver; hairwing-dressed brass bottle tubes fished in early spring when water conditions are high and temperatures are low; and much smaller summer flies tied on 1-cm (25/64-inch) aluminum tubes, in standard salmon patterns or grub-style patterns like "Uldsok" — the name means "wool stocking"— tail: red wool yarn; body: three sections of black yarn divided by brown hackles tied wet fly style with one hackle in front. I also tie tube-zonkers and small-fish imitations.

I often wonder why a freshwater trout takes an imitation of a squid, a creature not found in the river. I also wonder why a sea trout or salmon that doesn't feed in fresh water vigorously attacks a fly or takes a bait? But then again if there are no riddles to ponder why bother to fish at all? Without questions that tax understanding, without trial and error, and persistence in the face of frustration, fishing would just be another boring way to gain weight — as easy as opening the fridge.

LADY AMHERST TUBE FLY

Tube: Plastic, 1/8-inch (3 mm) O. D., 2 inches or shorter, with silicone hook sleeve
Thread: Black UNI-Thread 6/0 or 8/0
Tag: Silver wire (very thin, silver oval UNI-French can be used as a substitute) and yellow floss
Tail: Gray mallard fibers and a golden pheasant crest feather
Butt: Black ostrich herl
Body: Double layer, flat silver tinsel, UNI-Mylar, 1/16 inch
Rib: UNI-French Medium, oval silver tinsel
Palmer hackle: Badger
Throat hackle: Gray mallard, tied long
Wing: Two jungle cock eyes tied back to back. On each side of the jungle cock wings are two Amherst pheasant tippet feathers — one with a straight edge and one with a round edge. The straight-edged feather should be the longest, and is tied on first. On very small versions of this fly I use a cut out section from the Amherst tail feather (black and white), or sections from larger tippet feathers to build up the wing.
Sides: Jungle cock
Cheeks: Kingfisher
Topping: Crest feather from golden pheasant
Head: Black thread
Finish: Varnish
Hook: Kamasan treble size 6 B990 or Loop Designs MT hook, dressed with silver tinsel (acts as extension of body), a tiny Amherst pheasant wing, and a jungle cock on each side

Step 1: Fit the plastic tube in your vise. Attach thread, then tie and wind the silver wire. Tie in the floss and wind to complete the tag. Tie in the tail. Tie on and wind the ostrich herl butt.

Step 2: Tie the tinsel rib and palmer hackle feather right against each other. Make sure the rib end is tied under the entire body length, to ensure a smooth body base. Tie the thread in close turns to the front end of the fly to ensure the same.

Step 3: Tie on the flat tinsel at the front end of the body. Wind the tinsel back to the rear. Be sure you make a complete turn close to the butt, and then wind it forward to the front end of the tube.

Step 4: Wind the tinsel rib, then wind the hackle behind it as closely as you can. That way, the base of the hackle feather is protected by the much stronger rib over its entire length — fish teeth have a harder time tearing an oval silver rib than a hackle feather. To make this work, the rib and hackle feather can't have any distance between them when you start turning them around the body.

Step 5: Tie on the six wing feathers, jungle cocks first, then the bigger tippet feather and, on the outside of that, the smaller round tippet feather. Press your fingernail into the base of the tippet feathers — that makes them easier to position correctly. Make sure the jungle cock sticks out behind the biggest tippet feather, preferably in the middle.

Step 6: Tie on the throat. Then tie the jungle cocks and kingfisher on either side, and the topping over it all. Press your fingernail into the base of the crest feather to position correctly.

Step 7: Whip finish and varnish the head. In case you didn't use all the tube in the tying process, cut off excess tube.

Step 8: Dress the hook with a silver body, a wing made of tippet, jungle cocks on the sides and a little grey mallard as throat. Whip finish and glue/vanish the knot. Remember when tying this wing that part of the treble will be fitted into a silicone sleeve to hold the hook.

The Lady Amherst is a standard Atlantic salmon freshwater pattern. When the water is clear and low, very small versions tempt picky salmon. In muddy water, the bigger versions work well. White reflects all colors of light, so it can be used under all conditions, over all kinds of bottom — just adjust the size to the light and the water conditions. I fish this fly with a downstream swing on an intermediate fly line.

If you are using an HMH tube-fly tool and have trouble with the tube rotating, melt the end of the plastic tube to form a small collar. Cut off two small pieces of collar using sharp scissors to form a notch that matches the protrusion in the front of the tool. The matching notch will prevent rotation, and the sharp edge on the collar adds extra grip to hold the hook sleeve.

Crests don't always have the proper curve, making it impossible to tie a nice-looking topping. To shape topping and tail crest feathers, I put them in water for two or three minutes, press them onto the sides of small drinking glasses, and let them dry.

How to Tie a Floss Tag That Won't Slide Backwards on the Tube While Fishing

Step 1: Tie in the floss at the forward end of the tag, leaving an inch of floss sticking backwards.

Step 2: Wind the floss back over the loose end to the rear end of the tag, then turn it forward to the front. This gives you two layers of floss, which is less transparent than one. Tie off the end you have been winding, and trim.

Step 3: Finish the tag with the one-inch end, by folding it forward over the tag, tie off and trim excess.

How to Tie a Good-Looking, Flat Tinsel or Floss Body on a Tube

The most important thing is the body base! With a "bulky" base, you can't get a nice tinsel body.

Step 1: Use the thinnest thread you can find.

Step 2: When you finish the tag and tie on the tail, make sure you fasten the butts of the material with as few turns of thread as possible.

Step 3: Use the ostrich herl butt to cover the cut-off ends of tail and tag material, so you don't have a lump of material at the rear of the body.

Step 4: Tie on the rib and palmer hackle at the rear of the body, but make the butt ends of rib material extend to the front end of the body. Wind the thread closely over the extended ribbing — leave no gaps, and make sure you lay down one layer of thread.

Step 5: Cut off a double wrap length of flat tinsel and tie it in at the front end of body. Turn it tightly and closely all the way back to the butt, and then back to the front end.

Using two layers of tinsel, you avoid that irritating "triangle" with no material at the rear end of the body that comes from bending the tinsel forward before wrapping it. Another advantage is that when/if the upper layer of tinsel slides backwards due to hard casting or fishing, there's a layer beneath. Also, the first layer forms a perfectly smooth body base for the outer layer of tinsel.

STRAW SHRIMP

Tube: Plastic, from 1/8 to 1/12-inch (2 mm) O.D.
Body: Dubbing made from white Arctic fox tail, cut into
      1/2-inch pieces
Thread: White UNI-Thread 6/0 or 8/0
Antennae: Pearl Krystal Flash
Mouth parts: Section of gray mallard feather and soft underhair
      from a white Arctic fox tail
Eyes: Burned monofilament, transparent, red, or black
Rib: Uni-French oval silver, medium
Palmer hackle: Grizzly, long, soft
Back: A small juice-carton straw, with flexible section
Hook: Drennan single Carp hook size 6 Carbon Specimen; or
      Loop Designs double hook, black Nickel Double
      Salmon Tube Hooks LOOPMT

Step 1: Cut off the straw on either side of the flexible section, leaving about one inch of straight straw at each end. The front end of the back is cut a little narrower to allow a thicker body at that end. The cut shape of the straw-back of the shrimp determines the final shape of the shrimp body. The wider the back the narrower the body will be. If only the front end of the straw (front end of the shrimp) is cut narrow behind the eyes of the shrimp then the front end will appear much bigger as less body material will compressed by the straw. Don't cut the tail end of the straw narrow as it will give the straw shrimp a thick body at the tail end and it will look terrible. Flatten the straw and cut it in half along the seams you've made. Trim the head end into a torpedo or cigar shape with curved scissors. If you want the head end of the shrimp to be thicker, cut-out a section of straw on each side of the head to allow the hackle to spread out to the sides as well as under the fly.

Step 2: Place plastic tube in vise. Fasten thread and tie on tentacles: four strands of Krystal Flash, two about 2 inches long and two about 1 inch long. Tie on mouth parts: a small cut-out section of a gray mallard feather and over that a tuft of short under hairs from a white Arctic fox tail.

Step 3: Before tying the mono eyes on each side of the tube, build a tiny collar made of thread to force the eyes away from the tube. The eyes should stick out sideways and forward on the finished shrimp. Tie down the mono 1/2 inch back from the head end of the body to create a wider body base — this gives the shrimp a better silhouette seen from below. Eyes should stick out 1/2 inch.

Step 4: Tie on silver oval tinsel. Tie on the grizzly hackle by the wider stem end. The hackle fibers should angle back in the direction of the head.

Step 5: Tie a dubbing loop in the front end of the shrimp and turn the thread backwards to the rear end of the shrimp. Place the white dubbing in the loop, spin it, and wind it on the tube. The head end of the shrimp body should be a bit wider than the tail.

Step 6: Wind on the grizzly hackle.

A bright steelhead caught off a saltwater beach on Æro Island, Denmark.

Step 7: Before placing the straw back on top of the body, push the body and hackle fibers downward. Place the straw-section on top and fasten it on the tail end of the shrimp with thread, and whip finish. Wind the tinsel over the straw section to hold it into place. Finish with as few turns of thread as possible at the shrimp's tail.

Step 8: Cut off excess tube and cut straw in the shape wished — e.g. "split tail," single point, or simply cut it off.

Step 9: Preen out dubbing fibers on the body with a needle. Fit a hook sleeve in the front end of the tube.

If you need a faster sinking rate on the fly, you can add a thin layer of copper wire before winding the dubbed body.

The Straw Shrimp is a lightweight imitation designed for stillwater fishing or fishing on saltwater flats. It is meant for water depths of four or five feet. I use it for sea trout on a single-handed fly rod with a floating shooting head and a 15-foot leader with a 0.20 mm tip. I cast the fly, let it sink for five or ten seconds, then retrieve with five, 5-inch jerks of line, pause another five seconds to let it sink again, then resume the retrieve. Hooks for this fly can be single or double, but the points should ride downward. I use single carp hooks from Drennan — they can hold big fish. My double hooks are from Loop Tackle Design in sizes from 8 to 2 depending on the size of the fly.

TEN-ARMED STRAW SQUID

Tube: Plastic, 1/8-inch (3 mm) O. D., about 1 inch long, with silicone hook sleeve

Thread: Black UNI-Thread 6/0 or 8/0
Squid legs: Black and purple rubber legs
    Rib: UNI-French tinsel, medium oval silver
    Body: Mixed black and purple dubbing from Arctic foxtail
Sides of the body: A small juice-carton straw, with flexible section
    Hackle: Black with long, soft fibers
    Head: Black thread
    Hook: Sizes 8 to10 Kamasan B990 Salmon Tube Fly Treble
        for fresh water; in salt Gamakatsu treble 13B

Step 1: Flatten the straw, cut it to length as with the Straw Shrimp, then cut it in half length-wise. The front end of the back is cut a little narrower to allow a thicker body at that end. Don't trim the ends into cigar shape, just round the cut corners slightly at the ten-arm end.

Step 2: Place plastic tube in vise. Attach thread and tie on 10 rubber legs at the back end. Legs should be one to two times longer than the body.

Step 3: Tie in the black hackle and the tinsel. Be sure the tinsel is well secured — you have to pull on it hard! Wind on the hackle collar in front of the legs, secure, and trim excess.

Step 4: Make a dubbing loop in the thread at the leg-end of the squid. Place the mixed purple and black Arctic fox tail dub in the loop and spin it. Wind the dubbing body forward, secure it at front end of tube, and trim excess.

Step 5: Preen out the dubbing fibers along the sides of the body, flattening the fur on the top and bottom. You should end up with equally dense mats of fibers sticking out on the sides. Position two half-straw sections on the flattened top and bottom. Wind the tinsel around body and the straw sections hard enough to force the tinsel tightly into the straw's grooves. The tinsel holds the straw sections in position during fishing and casting. Secure tinsel at front of tube and trim excess. Preen the dubbing fibers out from under the tinsel to form wings on the sides of the body.

Step 6: Tie off with a few turns of thread in the front groove and whip finish.

Step 7: Trim the wings of the squid into shape. I prefer a cigar or eye-like shape. Glue or varnish the knot. If you need a faster sink rate, you can add weight by turning a thin layer of copper wire before winding the body, or you can add a black cone head.

The Straw Squid can be used for stillwater fishing, fishing in salt-water flats, or in freshwater streams. Because I fish it at night for salmon and bigger trout, I tie it in dark colors which improve visibility of the silhouette. I use floating lines or floating lines with an intermediate sinking tip, and cast over hunting fish. I fish the fly with a small treble or single hook.

EASY SILVER DOCTOR

Tube: Aluminium bottle tube, 1 inch long. Tie the fly before adding the plastic liner tube that protects your leader from wear and tear of the metal edges of the tube. If you add the liner tube before tying, the tube will rotate in the vise.

Thread: Red UNI-Thread 6/0
Hackle: Kingfisher blue
   Wing: A sparse bunch of yellow Arctic fox, 1 1/4 inch long, topped by equal-sized bunches of red, blue and brown Arctic fox. Each wing is tied 1/4 inch longer than the last.
   Hook: Loop Designs black nickel double tube hook

FLICKERING EMBER

Tube: Two plastic tubes, one thin enough to fit inside the other (See Chapter 19: Dag Midgård; Chapter 21: Bernd Nickoleit; Chapter 22: Hakan Norling). 1 to 1 1/2 inches of thick tube, and enough thin tube to stick out an inch, making a 2-inch total length. Epoxy the tubes together. Body is tied on thick tube; wings, front hackle/throat, and head are tied on the thin. The thin tube creates a small, neat head.
Thread: Black UNI-Thread 6/0 or 8/0
   Tag: Round gold wire, about 10 turns; red floss
   Tail: Gray mallard flank
   Butt: Red ostrich herl
   Body: UNI flat gold tinsel
   Rib: UNI-French oval gold
 Palmer: Light brown hen hackle
Wing 1: Sparse bunch of red Arctic fox, 2 1/4 inches long
Wing 2 (sides): Silver Arctic fox dyed fiery brown. One sparse bunch on each side of the red hair, and slightly longer. On the side of that, one strand of holographic gold Flashabou.
Wing 3: Bigger bunch of slightly longer silver fox hair dyed fiery brown. Leave the longer, stiffer hairs in this wing.
Cheeks: Jungle cock
 Throat: Gray mallard flank
  Head: Black thread
  Hook: Kamasan B990 Treble

The preferred hook for this fly is a loose-hanging treble fitted with a piece of silicone tubing to protect the knot and make sure the knot doesn't twist in the hook eye. A free-hanging hook is an advantage when fishing with tubes that have long wings. If a hair wing catches on a treble and is turned around one of the three points, a free-hanging hook will rotate in the current and eventually the wing will come free. A fixed treble will hold the wing in the twisted position and cause the tube fly to spin resulting in poor presentation and a twisted leader.

RED AND BLACK LODGE

Tube: Two plastic tubes, one thick/one thin, same lengths and procedure as for the Flickering Ember. The thin one must fit through the cone head.
Thread: UNI-Thread 6/0, color doesn't matter — you won't see the thread.
   Tag: Round silver wire and red floss

Tail: Fibers from red hen hackle

Butt: Black ostrich herl

Body: 1/3 flat UNI silver tinsel, 1/3 black floss and 1/3 flat UNI silver

Hackle: Red

Wing 1: Sparse bunch of red Arctic fox, 2 1/4 inches long

Wing 2 (sides): A slightly longer bunch of black Arctic fox tied on each side of Wing 1; red Angel Hair tied on each side of that.

Throat: Natural black hen hackle with fibers longer than the red hackle

Wing 3: Black Arctic fox tied forward and bent backwards by the cone head. Wing is double the length of the tube.

Cheeks: Jungle cock

Head: Small to medium black cone head

Hook: Kamasan Treble B990

THE GOLDEN FOX

Tube: Two plastic tubes, one thick/one thin, same lengths and procedure as for the Flickering Ember. The thin tube must fit through the cone head. The total length is between 1 and 2 inches.

Thread: UNI-Thread 6/0, color doesn't matter, you won't see the thread.

Tag: Thin gold round wire, about 10 turns

Tail: Soft underhair from red dyed Arctic fox, 3/4 inch long

Butt: Black ostrich herl

Body: Flat UNI gold tinsel

Rib: UNI-French gold, oval tinsel

Palmer: Natural black (not dyed) hen hackle with long soft fibers

Wing 1: Sparse bunch of hairs from a red Arctic fox, 2 inches long. They should just reach the butt. Tie 3 to 5 strands of red Angel Hair on each side of the hair wing.

Wing 2: Tie on a big bunch of black Arctic fox on each side of the first wing that reaches the end of the tail. Then tie two strands of gold Flashabou on each side.

Front hackle: A natural black hen hackle wound in front of the wings. The hackle helps lift the third wing and press it forward to meet the cone head.

Throat: Guinea fowl body feather wound as a hackle, next.

Wing 3: A large bunch of black Arctic fox reversed, so the hair tips point forward. This hair must be very long, about double the length of the tube, to stretch behind the hook when fishing. The longer top wing with built-up under wings give the tube a silhouette similar to a fish when wet. Pull all wing and throat materials to the rear, and — this is critical — tie the smallest possible head (three turns of thread, and varnish) on the tube in front of them. The cone head must be able to

slip over the wraps to force and hold the wings into final, correct position.

Head: Medium gold cone head, slipped on tube and pressed back hard. Cut off excess tube 2 mm in front of the cone, then melt the tube end into a collar to hold the cone in place.

Hook: Kamasan B990 tube treble or Loop double tube hook

This fly is used for large trout and salmon at night. The big dark fly is fished in a down-stream swing with a little movement of the rod tip. This fly has given me many a good fight with night-active sea trout. If you fish in shallow or slow-moving water, you can omit the cone head.

TOO EASY

Tube: Plastic 2 mm O. D., 1 1/2 inch long. Tube must fit through cone head.

Thread: UNI-Thread 6/0, color doesn't matter.

Tag: Ten turns of round silver wire and orange poly yarn or floss

Tail: A bunch of yellow Arctic fox, 3/4 inch long, with a bunch of orange on top

Butt: Black ostrich herl

Body: One-half yellow and half orange poly yarn or floss

Rib: UNI-French oval silver, medium.

Wing and throat 1: Sparse fluorescent yellow Arctic fox, 1 1/4 inch long

Wing and throat 2: Sparse hot orange Arctic fox

Wing and throat 3: Sparse red Arctic fox. All three wings are tied longer than the throats, and each wing is longer than the last.

Sides: Jungle cock reverse tied, tips pointing forward. Must be tied on before wing and Throat 4.

Wing 4: Black Arctic fox tied much longer than the other wings (3 inches long), tied pointing forward

Throat 4: Purple Arctic fox tied longer than the other throats, tied pointing forward. Whip finish with fewest possible wraps (same procedure as for Golden Fox) and varnish.

Head: Medium black or gold cone head. Hold Wing 4, Throat 4 and jungle cock backwards while pushing on the cone head. Cut off excess tube, leave 1 to 2 (5/64 inch) mm of tube to melt a collar.

Hook: Loop black nickel double tube fly hook

This brilliant tube fly works well in the currents. Fish it in a down-stream swing and it will catch trout and salmon. To get nice fluffy wings and throats when using Arctic fox tail, first brush the hair, pull out the longer stiff hairs and the short woolly hairs, and just use the midrange soft hairs for wings and throats. The rest of the hair can be used for dubbing.

CHAPTER 3

GRAYDON BELL

Cheshire, England

I was first attracted to fly-tying while watching my father tie at home. When he took a break, he would give me a turn at the vise. I was only three years old at the time, a fact taken into account when he offered his opinion of my work. Shortly thereafter, when he and I began fishing together, I took it upon myself to tie the flies for the next day on the water, although I suspect he never used these creations. After a few years of learning traditional patterns, people began to ask me to tie for them. By the age of ten, I was proficient at tying all manner of flies, including tubes, and I began to make a few pounds for my efforts.

Since then I have tied flies for almost every part of the world, from fully dressed, framed salmon flies, to billfish flies, down to the size 32s used on English chalk streams. During my service in the British Army I travelled widely, this allowed me to fish in many countries and to talk to other fly-fishers about their patterns and home waters. Over the years, I've sampled the fishing in Alaska (for trout, salmon, pike), Canada (trout, pike), Belize (permit), Norway (salmon), Russia (salmon), Bahamas (bonefish), Iceland (salmon), Czech Republic (grayling), and most of the major rivers in the UK and Europe (pike, salmon, trout, grayling).

More than 20 years ago, my interest in tube flies was rekindled on a fishing trip to Scotland for salmon. The hook-tied flies I was told to make and bring with me were not producing fish. I had noticed some tube flies back at the lodge, so I acquired them and they worked well. So well, in fact, that for a time after that I tied on tubes exclusively. For the types of fishing I was into —

salt water, salmon, and pike — they were ideal.

I began commercially tying tube flies about 15 years ago after a customer saw a tube fly I was fishing and asked if I would tie some for him. He showed the flies to a friend who then ordered some, and so it went. As more orders for tube flies came in, I began converting standard hook patterns onto tubes.

I tie flies on both hooks and tubes, but I rely on tubes when I know the fish will be large and aggressive. Tubes are much more durable than hook-tied flies because the fly moves up the leader away from a fish's teeth on the strike. I also like the fact that I can change the size and type of hook and still use the same fly. If I am fishing on a river or lake and I think the hook may snag on the weeds or the bottom, I tend to use a smaller size so I can protect it with the fly's body material. When fishing in the sea and no snags are likely, I will opt for a larger hook, keeping in mind the aesthetics of the match. I am not too concerned about the make of hook as long as it is strong and stays sharp, at the moment I am using Partridge hooks because I have had no problems with them so far.

As a professional tier, I have to give customers the best possible fly for their money, be it on a hook or tube, but when I have time to relax, I enjoy designing tubes. My primary considerations are as follows. Shape: Does the overall shape match the natural bait? Shine/silhouette: Does it attract the fish? Does it stand out from the background? Movement: Does it swim correctly? Color: Are the colors suitable for the fish I'm after and water visibility?

Weight: Is the weight correct for water conditions and the depth I want to fish? And is the fly castable?

The materials I use range from natural to synthetics, and I experiment with anything I can lay my hands on. I buy lengths of brass, aluminium, and plastic tubing in 2.5 mm to 3.5 mm diameters from model shops, then cut them to size myself. I line them with 1.4-mm stiff plastic tubing. The vise I use for tubes is a Dyna King.

THE LUDDINGTON

Tube: Aluminium 1/8-inch O. D., 45 mm long (1 3/4 inch), plastic lined, with silicone hook sleeve
Thread: Fluorescent yellow UTC, size 140
Butt: Fluorescent yellow thread and peacock herl
Rib: Silver holographic tinsel, medium
Body: Green Mylar tubing
Wing: Northern bucktail, dyed fluorescent pink, yellow, and fluorescent green
Throat: Northern bucktail, yellow
Cheeks: Jungle cock
Head: Black varnish or resin
Hook: Partridge X1 BR Outpoint Treble, sizes 8 to 14

Step 1: Place the plastic tube in your vise. Lay down an even bed of thread on the tube, stopping 5 mm from the end of the tube to allow room to slip on a silicone hook sleeve.

Step 2: Slide the green Mylar tubing over the tube. Tie it down and whip finish at the rear. Re-attach the thread at the front of the tube. With a few turns of thread tie down the Mylar at the head of the fly, trim and whip finish.

Step 3: Remove the tube from the vise and cover the body of the tube, including the front and rear whips, with epoxy and allow it to dry.

Step 4: Wind a 1/16-inch-wide section of fluorescent yellow thread at the rear of the tube. Tie in silver tinsel and peacock herl. Wind the herl butt, tie off and trim. Wind another 1/16-inch section of thread, then the tinsel rib. Trim excess. Apply a thin coat of varnish over the rib.

Step 5: At the head tie in a small bunch of fluorescent pink bucktail, barely longer than the back end of the tube. Tie in a small bunch of yellow bucktail, slightly longer than the pink, finally tie in a small bunch of fluorescent green bucktail, slightly longer than the yellow.

Step 6: Rotate the tube 180 degrees and tie in a sparse bunch of yellow bucktail, same length as the pink, as a throat. Tie in jungle cock feathers on either side.

Step 7: Make a prominent black head with either varnish or resin.

I use The Luddington in this size for salmon; for pike, I make a thirty percent longer, more heavily-dressed version.

LIZZY POP

Tube: Plastic 1/8-inch O. D., 45 mm long (1 3/4 inch) with hook sleeve
Thread: Fluorescent yellow UTC size 140
Tail: Light pink marabou; about 20 strands each of metallic gold Krystal Flash and fine metallic pink Flashabou; Roots of Canada red llama fibers
Hackle: Two dark orange saddles
Head: White deer hair, chartreuse deer hair
Eyes: Red 3-D eyes, 1/4 inch
Hook: Partridge X1 BR Outpoint Treble, sizes 8 to 14

Step 1: Place plastic tube in your vise. Attach thread halfway along the tube, wind thread to the head of tube and tie in pink marabou, about 40 mm in length, surrounding the tube evenly.

Step 2: Tie in strands of gold Krystal Flash and pink Flashabou. They should extend just past the ends of the marabou.

Step 3: Tie in red llama fibers to form a skirt over the marabou and flash tail.

Step 4: Tie in two orange saddles and wind a collar in front of the llama skirt, tie off, trim, whip, and varnish all the thread wraps.

Step 5: Spin on a collar of the white deer hair, leaving the tips untrimmed. As you proceed forward with more bunches of deer hair, trim the tips off. Spin in three bands of chartreuse deer hair on top of the head, then finish the nose of the fly with white hair. Whip finish and varnish the wraps.

Step 6: Remove the fly from the vise and trim to shape. The first cut should be along the bottom to make it flat. Trim the sides of the fly so it widens as it reaches the tail. Then trim the top of the head from the nose at a shallow angle, removing the hair until you reach the first stack of chartreuse hair. Trim the

Fly Plate: Clockwise from top: The Luddington; Blood Dog; Viper; Lizzy Pop.

chartreuse/white/chartreuse bands so they stick up in a quarter-inch-high, quarter-inch-wide (from front to back) block. Trim the remaining chartreuse and white hair on top of the head 1/4 inch longer in a rough collar that blends into the untrimmed deer hair and hackle/llama fiber.

Step 7: Burn a small socket into each side of the head with a hot point tool. Glue in 3-D eyes with Marine Goop.

Step 8: Apply head cement to the nose and head of the fly.

I spray the head of this bass fly with silicone before fishing it. A tube deer-hair bug tends to last longer than a hook-tied fly, which is why I like them.

VIPER

Tube: Plastic 1/8-inch O. D., 45 mm long (1 3/4 inch) with hook sleeve

Thread: Purple DK 8/0

Tag: Flat gold tinsel, which shows through the tail and gives a little flash

Wing: Ten claret saddle hackles, ten black saddle hackles, 90 mm long (3 1/2 inch). Four small, pink spade hen hackles

Skirt: Roots of Canada llama fibers in light blood leech, dark blood leech, and black

Eyes: Gold Mylar stick-on eyes, 1/4 inch

Head: Epoxy with dark rainbow glitter

Hook: Partridge X1 BR Outpoint Treble, sizes 8 to 14

Step 1: Place plastic tube in your vise. Attach thread halfway along tube, wind thread back until it's 5 mm from the end.

Step 2: Tie in a piece of flat gold tinsel. Wind the thread forward 10 mm, then follow the thread with the tinsel. Tie down to make a tag 10 mm long. Varnish the tag.

Step 3: In front of the tag, tie in ten claret saddles, with the curves facing inward, evenly around the tube. Trim, whip, varnish wraps. Tie in ten black saddles in front of the claret, spread evenly around the tube. Trim, whip, and varnish. Tie in four small pink spade hackles, evenly spread around the tube. Trim, whip, and varnish.

Step 4: Tie in skirt made from Light Blood Leech llama fibers half the length of the saddles. Over this tie a skirt of Dark Blood Leech llama, followed by black llama. Be sure the fibers are evenly spread around the tube. Tie off, trim, whip, and varnish.

Step 5: Build up a large head with thread, about 5/8 inch long, that tapers towards the nose of the tube.

Step 6: Mix 30-minute epoxy and add dark rainbow glitter. Mix well. Apply this evenly over the head of the fly.

Step 7: When the epoxy is almost dry, apply the Mylar eyes, pressing them into the sides of the head. When the head has completely dried, apply two or three coats of hard, clear varnish over the epoxy.

To vary the sink rate of this fly, I use aluminium or brass tubes. I fish this fly both from a boat and while wading, casting over and

retrieving through likely holding spots. For pike, I use a 10-weight rod, a floating line, and a leader between five and ten feet with a steel trace attached and no shock tippet.

BLOOD DOG

Tube: Brass 1/8-inch O. D., 40 mm long (1 5/8 inch), plastic lined, with hook sleeve

Thread: Black, size 8/0

Rib: Fine, gold holographic tinsel

Body: Fine red holographic tinsel

Collar: Peacock herl

Wing: Yellow bucktail

Hackle: Dark orange hen hackle fibers

Head: Black varnish

Hook: Partridge X1 BR Outpoint Treble, sizes 8 to 14

Step 1: Place the brass tube in your vise. Attach thread 10 mm from the front of the tube and wrap to the rear in closely touching turns, forming a smooth, even under-body. The underbody stops 5 mm from the back end of the tube. This allows room to slip on a silicone hook sleeve.

Step 2: Tie in two pieces of gold tinsel on opposite sides of the tube.

Step 3: Advance the thread in touching turns, making sure the body is flat, with no lumps or bumps. Stop 8 mm from the front of the tube.

Step 4: Tie in a long piece of red tinsel at the front. Wind the tinsel to the rear, then back to the front, in closely touching turns so the underbody does not show through. Trim excess.

Step 5: Take one of the gold ribs and wind it forward in six turns to the front of the body. Tie off. Repeat this in the opposite direction with the other gold rib, making a crosshatch design. Tie off and trim.

Step 6: At the front end of the body, tie in two strands of peacock herl. Wind forward to make a small collar. Tie off and trim excess.

Step 7: Apply three coats of clear varnish to the body of the fly. Allow time for each coat to dry completely between applications.

Step 8: Tie in the bucktail wing. It should extend 5 to 10 mm past the end of the tube and surround it evenly. Trim butts. Then apply the hen hackle fibers around the tube. They should extend half the length of the body. Trim butts.

Step 9: Build a small, neat head with thread. Whip finish.

Step 10: The head is finished with four coats of varnish. The first coat is clear, the second is black, followed by two more coats of clear. It is very important to let the varnish dry completely between coats.

The Blood Dog in this size is intended for steelhead; a half-sized version is excellent for trout. I fish it on a floating line for steelhead, casting upstream to pick off the fish at the tail end of a pool; that way I don't spook the fish in front. Pools are better than riffles because the tube is in the area of the fish longer. For trout, I cast up and across the stream and let the tube swing across holding fish.

CHAPTER 4

BILL BLACK

Roseburg, Oregon

RICH LIST

I started tying flies when I was 12 years old, and I began tying professionally at age 14, working under my brother, Dennis. When I was 18, he and I put together Umpqua Feather Merchants. I eventually set up and managed Umpqua's fly-tying factories in Sri Lanka, India, and Thailand. It's my guess that more than half the commercial flies manufactured in the world today are made by tiers I taught directly, or by tiers who learned their craft from the people I taught.

In 1990 I left Umpqua Feather Merchants to form Spirit River, Inc., a company specializing in unique fly patterns and materials, with an emphasis on synthetics, beads, and eyes.

My first experience in tying and fishing tube flies was in Baja in 1998. I found the larger patterns worked well, and I liked the fact that I could easily replace rusted hooks and keep fishing a productive fly. Because of that experience, I began adding a variety of tubes to my coastal salmon and winter steelhead fly boxes. I became even more interested in the potential of tube flies after meeting Bill Shelton, the inventor of the EZE Release hook, in a booth at a 2003 fishing show.

The eye on Shelton's ingenious hook is moved from the end of the shank to the start of the bend. This creates a rear pivot point that allows the hook to rotate 180 degrees. If the hook is barbless, it turns right out of a fish's jaw. Shelton increased the size of the now-blunt eye end of the hook by 25 percent. To hold the hook in normal, fish-catching position it is inserted into a release tube attached to a tag line connected to the main fishing line. When the tag line is pulled, the hook comes free of the tube and releases.

Using his EZE Release hook as a starting point, I developed a tube-within-a-tube system — the inner tube is soft, the outer tube is hard — for fly-tying. After the line is threaded through the doubled tube and tied to the hook eye, the blunt head of the hook and the leader are drawn up into the inner tubing, which locks the hook in position and prevents it from turning at the eye. To release a fish, all an angler has to do is reach down while maintaining tension on the line, and pull the tube fly up the tippet and off the hook head. The hook pivots, and bingo, a clean, no-hands release.

It's important to note that Shelton's catch-and-release hook was designed for floating bait fishing, where deep takes are common. He got the idea after unsuccessfully releasing a deeply hooked, 17 1/2-inch striper his son Billy had caught. The Coalition for Unified Recreation in the Eastern Sierra (CURES), representing government entities and local business people, secured a federal grant and matching private funds to study the effectiveness of the Shelton hook, as well as several others designed for catch and release. Dr. Tom Jenkins, a research biologist at the UC Santa Barbara's Sierra Nevada Aquatic Research Lab, conducted the study as a private consultant. He found that when fishing bait the Shelton hooks caught and released trout with nearly a 100 percent survival rate!

After I saw Shelton demonstrate his EZE Release hook, I couldn't get it out of my mind. Instinctively I knew there had to be a way to incorporate the EZE release system into fly-fishing. That night I went back to my hotel room and started playing with the samples he had given me. The next morning I was shocked to find I was the only one standing at his booth; he should have had a hundred people beating on his door!

When I returned to work, I hit the bench and tied up lots of prototypes, which I have tested on smallmouth bass and trout. Using EZE Release hook, I had great success with smallmouth on the main Umpqua, where it is not uncommon to hook and land

75 to 100 fish per day. When the river guides and lodge owners saw how easily I released my fish unharmed they all agreed the system was a winner. I have also caught and released fairly large lake trout on EZE Release tube-fly minnows.

Although the system lends itself to larger streamer patterns like minnows and Buggers, I have tied beetles and ants on the tubes that look and fish just fine. I have yet to try Shelton's new size 14 hook for really small tube flies.

Because the EZE Release tube fly is locked on the hook, the fly doesn't move up the leader on the strike, which means it absorbs as much punishment from fish teeth as a conventional fly. Because pliers aren't required to make a release, the fly escapes serrated steel jaws. I've caught and released up to 24 smallies before having to replace a worn-out fly.

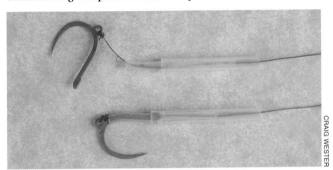

Top: The eye on EZE Release hook is at the bend of the shank.
Bottom: The EZE Release hook in fishing position.

To make an EZE Release tube fly, first tie your pattern on 1/8-inch O. D. hard-plastic tubing. After the fly is finished, super glue the soft tube into the rear of the hard tube. Be sure to leave some of the soft tube protruding so you can slip it over the hook head and shank. This method works well for larger flies like saltwater patterns, Buggers, and most streamers. Note: The beads and cones in some of the patterns shown have been drilled out slightly to accommodate an 1/8-inch tube.

A second option is to tie your fly directly onto the soft tube. This method is good for smaller flies and nymphs. Care must be taken to tie a somewhat loose fly, using lots of super glue because you don't want to crush the soft tube — if you do that, you won't be able to slip in the head of the hook. Nylon thread, which has a 15 to 20 percent stretch factor, can compress the soft tube after the fly is complete. I recommend using a polyester thread, available from UNI Products. Once the fly is tied, trim the tubing at the head of the fly, and you are ready to fish.

Spirit River offers a simple kit that contains tying instructions, hooks, and the hard and soft tubes. Consumers can call 541-440-6916 for the nearest fly shop dealer.

I make my own tube tying mandels from saltwater hooks. After cutting off the hook eyes, I find a size hook that fits snugly inside the tube and then wrap 6/0 thread to create a gradual bump on the shank. The bump is fine-tapered towards the cut off eye, and larger towards the bend. I glue the thread and let it dry, then slip the tube onto the shank and push it hard over the thread bump to keep it from turning. Because I work with various diameters of tube, I make these eyeless hooks in several sizes.

SRI MIGHTY MINNOW–SILVER SHINER

Tube: Plastic 1/8-inch O. D., 1 inch long; 1 inch of EZE Release clear soft tubing (sticks out of hard tube 3/8 inch)
Thread: Clear nylon
Body: Silver Holographic #194 Lite-Brite dubbing
Optional: Stripe three times with black marker as parr marks
Beard/Underbelly: One-half to 3/4 inch # 115 Pearl/Blue Lite-Brite tied in about the length of the tube body, twice the volume of the wing. Optional: stripe three times with black marker.
Wing: 1 inch of Pearl/Blue Flash Lite-Brite. This can be striped three times with black marker as well.
Eyes: Silver Real Eyes in size 5/32 inch or 3/16 inch, with silver Prismatic Tape stick-on eyes
Hook: EZE Release size 4

Step 1: Put hard plastic tube on your vise or mandrel. Attach tying thread. One-quarter inch from the front end of tube tie in Real Eyes with figure-eight wraps. Apply super glue to the thread. Rotate the tube 180 degrees so the eyes are on the bottom.

Step 2: Starting 1/8 inch from the rear end of tube, dub on a half inch long body of Lite-Brite that ends at the back of the eyes. Apply super glue.
Step 3: On the wraps that hold down the eyes, center tie in a sparse wing of Lite-Brite, then double the material back over itself, and lock it down with a few wraps of thread. Apply super glue. Rotate tube again, so eyes are on top.
Step 4: Just in front of the eyes, center tie in the beard, double it back, and lock it down with thread. Its base should cover the stem of the eyes. Apply super glue.
Step 5: Whip finish and super glue the head.

Fly Plate: Clockwise from top: Egg Sucking Leech; EZE Release Half 'N' Half; Black's Foam Ant; Conehead Rubber Leg Muddler; SRI Mighty Minnow – Silver Shiner; BC Minnow

Step 6: While holding the wing and beard material stretched out, stripe it with black marker. When you let the fibers go, they flare out and the marks look natural.

Step 7: Insert and super glue the inner tubing 5/8 inch into the tube fly. It should protrude 3/8 inch from the rear of the tube.

I've had good success on smallmouth with this pattern. The SRI Mighty Minnow can easily be adapted to imitate different types of fry. For a golden shiner I use gold #068 Lite Brite in the body and wing. I do a baby rainbow by coloring the back of the Silver Shiner with an olive green marker.

EGG SUCKING LEECH

Tube: Plastic 1/8-inch O. D., 1 inch long; 1 inch of EZE Release clear soft tubing (sticks out of hard tube 3/8 inch)
Thread: Black
Tail: Black rabbit fur strip, 2 1/2 inches long
Body: Black rabbit strip, wound as hackle
Flash: Three strands of pearl Crystal Splash the same length as tail, on each side
Legs: Three fluorescent orange rubber legs on each side, 1/2 inch shorter than tail
Head: Spirit River's Hot Beads in orange, size 1/4 . Melt end of tube to hold bead in place
Hook: EZE Release size 4

EZE RELEASE HALF 'N' HALF

Tube: Plastic 1/8-inch O. D., 1 inch long; 1 inch of EZE Release clear soft tubing (sticks out of hard tube 3/8 inch)
Thread: Clear nylon
Body: None
Tail: Four white saddle points, 1 1/2 inches long; six strands of pearl Crystal Splash, same length, on each side; topped by 3/4 inch of white bucktail, butts tied down the length of the underside of tube and over the eye stem
Wing: Gray bucktail, 1 3/4 inches long
Beard: White bucktail, 1 inch long
Eyes: Spirit River's I-Balz, chartreuse/nickel, 3/16 inch
Head: Gray thread
Hook: EZE Release size 4

This fly is an EZE Release conversion of the Clouser-Kreh original pattern.

BC MINNOW

Tube: Plastic 1/8-inch O. D., 1 inch long; 1 inch of EZE Release clear soft tubing (sticks out of hard tube 3/8 inch)
Thread: Clear nylon

Body: None
Tail: Sparse bunch of white bucktail, 1 inch long, butts tied down the length of the underside of tube, and over the eye stem
Wing: Chartreuse Crystal Splash, 2 inches long, under chartreuse bucktail, 1 3/4 inches long
Eyes: Spirit River's I-Balz, red/nickel, 3/16 inch
Hook: EZE Release size 4

This fly is an EZE Release conversion of Bob Clouser's classic pattern.

BLACK'S FOAM ANT

Tube: Plastic 1/8-inch O. D., 1/2 inch long; 5/8 inch of EZE Release black soft tubing (sticks out of hard tube 1/4 inch)
Thread: Black
Body/Head: Black, 2 mm or 3 mm Spirit River Fly Foam, tied down on top of the tube in two places to form three sections. The front section also has a small bit of white foam tied in as a indicator for easy visibility. Optional is to cover the back of the foam with a epoxy to give is a glossy coating.
Underbody: Either red or black Lite Brite
Legs: Spirit River's Round Rubber Leggs, three strands tied in to make six legs
Hook: EZE Release size 10

A red ant can easily be tied by simply switching from black thread and foam to red. I also do a nice Tube Beetle using 2 mm black foam, Flex Floss legs and a black Lite Brite body.

CONE HEAD RUBBER LEG MUDDLER

Tube: Plastic 1/8-inch O. D., 1 inch long; 1 inch of EZE Release clear soft tubing (sticks out of hard tube 3/8 inch)
Thread: 3/0 monocord or any strong thread to match the color of the deer hair
Body: Silver holographic #194 Lite-Brite dubbing
Wing: Black rabbit strip, 2 1/2 inches long, 1/8 inch wide, tied Matuka style (both front and rear)
Beard: 3/8 inch of Ruby Red #095 flash material kept short as bleeding gills
Collar: Spun natural deer hair, clipped in front to fit the inside of the cone head and forming a 360-degree collar at the rear
Head: Nickel cone head, 1/4-inch diameter. Melt end of tube to hold it in place
Hook: EZE Release size 4 or 10

Other effective color options are brown, olive, and white for a fry imitation.

CHAPTER 5

KEN BONDE LARSEN

Valby, Denmark

Tube flies are an important part of the Scandinavian fly-fishing heritage, and I enjoy tying both traditional and newer patterns for salmon and sea trout. Off-season, I tie every day. My own flies tend to be variations on existing patterns or are inspired by a new material or a color range. I have picked up ideas from anglers I have met by the water, from flies I have been shown, from magazines, books, and the Internet.

The layered wing and hackle technique is one of my favourites. I don't know its origin, but I have seen it used in a few other places by other tiers. Basically, you tie in three or more sections of wing, each an equal part of the final wing. The sections are separated by a hackle. If you want to put a cone head on the fly, the last hackle will be the front hackle; if not, you finish with a wing section. Varying the colors of the sections is typically done with lighter shades on the bottom and darker — often black — on the top. You can also vary the wing lengths, in which case the lower section should be shortest and the upper the longest. I often interlace the sections with a few strands of flash material to match the hues of the fly. Some discrete flash increases the effectiveness of flies meant for murky or peat-colored water.

The purpose of the layering technique is to get a wing with volume that does not collapse in the water. Wings made from Arctic fox and "temple dog" (also called Tempelhair) are very soft and mobile, but they compress into a narrow strip in heavy current. The hackles that separate the wing sections support them and keep the wing closer to its original, dry shape.

The fur from farmed Arctic foxes is very common in Scandinavia and somewhat more curled and thick than imported temple dog fur — which is probably not really from dog at all! Both types of hair are characterized by a dense and curly under fur covered by longer and straighter guard hairs. For tying, the guard hairs are usually removed, as are the shortest under fur fibers; this produces a dense, but supple wing. The quality of

MARTIN JOERGENSEN

these furs varies widely and you should always take the material out of the bag and sample it with your fingers before buying. Aim for soft, uniformly straight hair with a suitable length to the fly you are tying. Get fur with some volume, but not lamb's wool-like curls.

On Mörrum bottle tubes, I tie on both the thin inner plastic liner and the outer, machined metal tube. I add a hackle to the liner tube and pull it through the bottle so the base disappears into the rear of the metal. The hackle then becomes a skirt around the hook sleeve. I trim the plastic liner so it sticks out of the nose of the bottle about 2 mm, then melt it into a collar. I continue tying on the metal, adding wing, hackle, throat and cheeks — no body. I finish with a small, neat head tied on the plastic liner. Whether you use silver or anodized bottle tubes you will be very pleased at the way the metal shines slightly through the heavy turns of hackle.

Apart from these newer techniques I tie very traditional flies. In many of my patterns you will find traces of classic salmon flies and traditional hair winged flies. My flies are typically very Scandinavian in their appearance, and the majority of what comes from my vise has a hair wing. My preferred materials for hair wings are Arctic fox and temple dog. I live in Denmark so I have legal access to polar bear, jungle cock, and heron hackle. Because the perfect tool that holds all tubes doesn't exist, I shuffle between vises and adapters such as the Danish Fisker tube tool, a Danish product called the HC tube adapter made by Henning H. Christiansen, and a Renzetti tube vise.

BEIS FLY VARIATION

Tube: Black bottle tube
Inner tube: Plastic liner to fit inside bottle tube
Thread: Orange
Rear hackle: Orange saddle, wound and tied down on inner tube with hot orange thread
Wing: Three sections of golden brown temple dog (or dyed

Arctic fox hair) separated by turns of orange hackle
and a few strands of gold and black Krystal Flash

Cheeks: Jungle cock
Head: Black thread
Hook: Partridge or Owner trebles in sizes 6 to 10

Step 1: Put the thin plastic tube on your vise. Start the orange thread at the rear end of the tube, leaving enough space to accommodate the silicone hook sleeve (about 3 mm). Tie in the hackle and wind it three or four turns. Tie down the hackle, trim, whip finish, and cut the thread.

Step 2: Insert the front of the liner tube into the rear of the bottle tube and pull it through until the wrappings disappear inside the bottle. You can add some super glue for increased durability.

Trim the plastic so 2 to 3 mm sticks out the nose of the bottle, then melt and form a collar, leaving room to tie a small head behind it.

Step 3: Start the thread at the front of the metal tube leaving just enough space forward to complete the wing and head. Tie in a hackle and wind two or three turns. Tie down and trim excess.

Step 4: Tie in the first wing section and add a couple of strands of flash.

Step 5: Tie in a second hackle and wind two or three turns. Tie down and trim excess.

Step 6: Tie in the second wing section and add a couple of strands of flash.

Step 7: Tie in the last hackle and wind two or three turns. Tie down and trim excess.

Step 8: Tie in the last wing section and add jungle cock cheeks.

Step 9: Form a small head on the plastic tubing with thread, whip finish, and varnish.

This fly features the three-sectioned wing I have described. The method is the same in all the flies with this wing construction, and the number of sections, colors, and addition of flash material varies according to taste and need.

I fish my tube flies in the traditional Scandinavian manner: casting across and downstream with an underhand cast, often followed by one or more upstream mends to get the fly down in the water. Then I follow the fly with the rod tip, maybe adding some motion by gently tipping the rod up and down. I keep a small loop under the reel, to give a fish a bit of slack before the hook sets. The fly lines are mostly floating or sink-tip. I often use slow-sinking leaders to get the fly down in the current.

BLUE FLY

Tube: Blue bottle tube
Inner tube: Plastic liner to fit inside bottle tube (same procedure as with Beis Variation)
Rear hackle: Kingfisher blue, tied on inner tube as in Beis Fly
Wing: Blue Arctic fox tied in three sections as in Beis Fly. Blue hackle and sparse blue or black metallic Flashabou strands between each section.
Cheeks: Jungle cock
Head: Black thread tied on protruding plastic tube
Hook: Partridge or Owner trebles in sizes 6 to 10

BLACK KARUP MARABOU

Tube: Plastic, 1/8-inch O. D., 1 to 3 inches long
Tag: Flat silver tinsel
Tail: Red Antron yarn
Body: Black yarn or dubbed Lite Brite
Underwing: Red holographic Flashabou
Hackle: Black marabou
Head: Black thread
Hook: Partridge or Owner trebles in sizes 6 to 10

B/W

Tube: Aluminium, 1/8-inch O. D., 1 1/2 inch long, with hook sleeve
Rib: Fine oval silver tinsel
Body: Flat silver Mylar tinsel
Body hackle: Badger, turns start 1/2 inch from rear of tube
Wing: Three sections of Arctic fox—white/white/black—with fine black Flashabou strands between
Front/throat hackle: Guinea fowl
Head: Black thread
Hook: Partridge or Owner trebles in sizes 6 to 10

GREEN HIGHLANDER VARIATION

Tube: Plastic 1/8-inch O. D., 1 1/2 inch long
Inner tube: Plastic liner to fit inside body tube, which protrudes from the bottle nose to accommodate the small cone head
Butt: Yellow Lite Brite
Rib: Medium oval silver tinsel
Body: Mixed yellow and green Lite Brite
Palmer hackle: Lemon green
Wing: Four sections of temple dog (or Arctic fox) — yellow/hot orange/green/black — with yellow hackle and green Krystal Flash strands between last two sections
Front hackle: Yellow
Head: Black cone head, 3/16 inch, slipped over inner tube, which is melted to hold cone in place.
Hook: Partridge or Owner trebles in sizes 6 to 10

FIERY BROWN SPECIAL TURBO

Tube: Aluminium, 1/8-inch O. D., 1 1/4 inch long, lined, with hook sleeve
Tag: Fine oval silver tinsel
Butt: Orange Antron
Rib: Orange-brown Antron crochet yarn
Body: Orange-brown Antron crochet yarn
Wing: Three sections of temple dog (or Arctic fox)—hot orange/fiery brown/fiery brown—with fine gold or copper metallic Flashabou strands between
Throat hackle: Gold or fiery brown temple dog
Front hackle: Ring-necked pheasant rear saddle
Head: Black thread
Hook: Partridge or Owner trebles in sizes 6 to 10

Clockwise from top left: Fiery Brown Special Turbo; Blue Fly; Green Highlander Variation; Black Karup Marabou; Beis Fly Variation; B/W

CHAPTER
6

BART CHANDLER

Basalt, Colorado

BART CHANDLER

I'm a professional angler and outfitter, a guides' instructor, an instructor in fly casting, fly-tying, and guiding, and I give seminars and host bluewater and flats trips. I've been tying flies for more than 25 years. I stopped counting my years as a fishing guide after 20. My clients, some of them now fourth generation, have landed more than 100,000 trout.

About five years ago I was introduced to the world of tube flies after a client asked if I could tie him a few for a trip to Iceland for Atlantic salmon. I had already begun to wonder whether some of my favorite freshwater flies might work on the flats, but I hadn't experimented with them because their hooks weren't meant for salt water. After I started tying on tubes, and was able to switch hooks at will, that problem was solved.

On my next trip to the flats, I threaded my Basic Baitfish, a tube fly meant for trout, on a 15-foot leader, chose an appropriate saltwater hook, and caught several bones. As I cast other freshwater tubes, I noticed the fish were moving farther for my flies and that my cast-to-attacked ratio was much better than with the standard flats' offerings. On a clear day I saw an eight-pound bone swimming in a foot of water over a white bottom. It moved at least 30 feet to attack my Rhea Gunz, a 3 1/2-inch black Atlantic salmon fly, an all-rhea version of the Willie Gunn/Sunray Shadow. Bonefish canon says no way should that fly have worked.

From the Seychelles to Islamorada, from the Turks and Caicos to Belize, and from the Bahamas to Ascension Bay I've heard comments like, "We'll fish any color as long as it's tan." Or "The fish won't eat anything that shiny." Or "We don't use flies that big here." In fisheries where small flies are the rule I have found that tubes two or three times longer than the usual patterns catch more and bigger fish.

With over 25 years in the business, I know it's difficult for a guide to experiment with new patterns when he or she's working. I have given out dozens of tube flies to both guides and anglers only to hear later, "The fishing was pretty good so I didn't need to try anything new." Or, and this is my personal favorite, "The fishing was pretty tough so I didn't dare to experiment with anything new." Fortunately, not all anglers are so cautious. Bob Berger of Bonefish Bob's tackle shop in Islamorada, Florida, has fished one of my tube flies with success on the "Downtown Bones"of Islamorada, considered some of the toughest in the world. So far, Bob's landed four, eight- to ten-pounders and reports the fly is still in perfect shape. Fish the Shell Key Flea out there and see what he discovered. By the way, it's not tan.

For flats fishing with single hooks I like the Owner SSW, AKI Big Game, and Flyliner; Gamakatsu SC15's are useful when I need a light hook. I use the Loop Double Tube Fly hook for bonefish and for snook I rig it as a stinger behind a single "J" hook like an Owner size 2 SSW. I have found that double salmon hooks do less damage to bonefish. While long-nosed pliers are often required to remove single hooks, I have never had a double taken that deeply. In my experience, a double hook is about as effective

---

Clockwise from top: Shell Key Flea; Minimalist; Snapper Whacker; Gentle Surgeon;
Baby Lobster – Rhea; Light Gotcha; Bart's Basic Baitfish — Rhea; Rhea Gunz; Bart's Baitfish – Tarpon; Maad Max

BART CHANDLER

in a tube fly after it comes off the drying wheel. Instead of arming it with a bare hook, you can use a conventional fly. Switching your tube from a light SC 15 hook to a heavy-wire SSW turns your offering from a spooky-water bonefish fly to a permit fly. A hook-tied tarpon fly has to be discarded if it doesn't swim properly. With a different hook size or style, by rotating the hook in its sleeve, or by changing the length of the sleeve you can fine-tune a tarpon tube fly's performance on the water.

I use a lot of Zap-A-Gap super glue on my patterns, paying special attention to coating the body of the tube, the attachment wrappings for heavy eyes, under all wrapped hackles and bodies, and at the base of both hair and feather wings. I finish the heads of my saltwater flies with Zap-A-Gap even if I'm going to coat them with epoxy. Since a single tube has the potential of catching

as a single in the attacked-to-hooked ratio, but it really shines in the hooked-to-landed, and released-unharmed arenas. Although double hooks are not IGFA-legal for bonefish, their wider use may well be in the best interest of the fishery.

When fishing for bones, I use a 12- to 16-pound monofilament leader 15 feet long and add a 20-pound fluorocarbon bite-tippet for permit. For tarpon and snook, I rig 20-pound monofilament or fluorocarbon with a 60-pound fluorocarbon bite-tippet. I like fluorocarbon for butt-sections and heavy bite-tippets, but it's unnecessary for leaders. It's primary advantages are its longevity and its resistance to both water absorption and abrasion. Resistance to abrasion is an advantage because you can use lighter bite-tippets on big fish. Monofilament tippet absorbs water, which weakens it after a few hours use. Fluorocarbon's strength is the same in the afternoon as it was in the morning. If you don't replace your leaders or tippets each evening you might want to use a fluorocarbon leader. Invisibility doesn't promote more strikes from tarpon, bonefish, or permit but is an advantage when fishing for snappers or tunas.

Even though I tie and fish many small tube flies for bonefish, I often find myself using patterns that are larger and heavier than customary. If the fish are spooky I just cast farther in front of them. Large flies draw fish from great distances which gives the bigger ones a better chance to eat the fly before the "peanuts" do.

Most of my patterns are tied in several weights, sizes, and colors. The lightest bonefish flies are tied on 1/4-inch-long plastic tubes without eyes, while the heaviest fly, a 4-inch baitfish pattern, is tied on a 3/8-ounce titanium bullet sinker that I've drilled out and then glued a tube inside. I need a 13-weight rod and a hard hat to fish it, but it gets to the bottom of snapper holes even if when the current is running heavily. It caught the only grouper that I've ever taken on a fly rod. The Baby Lobsters and Snapper Whackers are tied on plastic tubes for shallow water and on heavy metal tubes for deepwater situations.

If I need a longer pattern, I'll stack two or three flies together. Component fly systems are even more useful if each segment is a simple, fishable fly in its own right. To make longer tails I carry an assortment of Minimalists tied on 1/4-inch tubes in different materials, colors, and lengths. For additional action, I slip 1/4-inch tubes tied with just rhea and Ultra-Violet Krystal Flash (U-V is a color that we can't see, but fish can) onto the front of the flies.

Adding a bead or cone head, a rhea feather or hair collar, or a long flowing tail aren't the only dramatic changes you can make

BART CHANDLER

literally hundreds of fish before it's ruined, it's worth the time and effort to maximize durability.

Although I tie on standard plastic and metal tubes, Loop Bottle Tubes are my first choice. Available in two weights and plated in either gold or silver, they concentrate weight at the head of the fly, which imparts great action. The Loop Bottle Tube is designed to work without a protective liner.

Because the lips of most metal tubes have sharp inside edges that can damage leaders, they come with a plastic liner installed. I remove this liner so I can use a larger mandrel, which makes the fly easier to tie. After the fly is completed, I re-insert a short length of liner into the front of the tube where chafing is most likely to occur. The rear sleeve prevents chafing at the back of the tube by stabilizing the hook. Some metal tubes can be chamfered with a Dremel tool to prevent chafing.

Whenever possible I tie with Rhea feathers, Arctic runner, Arctic fox, jungle cock, and Black Laced hen. These traditional, Atlantic salmon materials look alive in the water and move flats' fish better than chicken feathers, rabbit hair, calf tail, Kraft fur and most other synthetics. Rhea feathers, marketed for Spey flies, are surprisingly durable and easily dyed. They must be soaked in hot water for up to 30 minutes before each side of the feather can be stripped from the tip to the butt.

I really enjoy tying and fishing tubes flies. I haven't found a pattern that couldn't be adapted to a tube, or a situation where a tube couldn't be used effectively. Because tube flies allow me to use short-shanked hooks, I land more and bigger fish, especially when I'm fishing barbless. Normal-to-long-shanked, barbless hooks give the fish a leverage advantage that often results in a premature release. I tie some hooks with weedguards in advance; when I need a weedless fly, I just change hooks. Because I can slide the fly up the leader, out of the way, I remove hooks much more easily. I don't need as many flies because tubes last longer and cross over from species to species with just a hook change. I no longer have to tie and carry separate collections of saltwater and freshwater flies.

It's obvious that angling professionals have much to gain by switching from hook-tied flies to tubes. When they do, and their clients catch on to the real advantages, it won't be long before tube flies are the style of choice for saltwater anglers.

SHELL KEY FLEA

Tube: Loop Bottle tube for small flies; large flies on 1/8-inch O. D. hard plastic
Thread: White Danville flat-waxed nylon
Forward eyes: Silver/chartreuse I-Balz size 3/16 inch (for 2 1/4 inch bottle tube fly)
Stalk eyes: Forty-pound Envy Green Ande monofilament, melted, and coated with Zap-A-Gap
Body: Clear Antron
Inner wing: White Arctic runner
Top wing: White rhea
Belly-dividing strip: Four or five strands of UV Krystal Flash
Topping: Ten strands of UV Krystal Flash
Head: White thread
Finish: Zap-A-Gap and epoxy

Step 1: Put bottle tube in vise. Attach white Danville thread, coat tube with Zap-A-Gap, then form a solid thread base, stopping just short of the end of the tube.
Step 2: Tie in I-Balz at head of fly on top of tube. Zap-A-Gap the wraps.
Step 3: Rotate tube 180 degrees in vise. Tie in stalk eyes on top of tube, extending 5/8 inch from the end of the bottle. On top of stalk eyes tie in sparse bunch of white Arctic runner slightly longer than eyes. Zap-A-Gap the wraps.
Step 4: Tie in white rhea, twice as long as inner wing.
Step 5: Rotate tube 180 degrees and tie in a small bunch of 2 inch long strands of UV Krystal Flash for the belly strip.

Step 6: Coat the tube with Zap-A-Gap and dub in a body of clear Antron, wrapping to the head of the fly. Use a brush to pick out the body to the length of the inner wing.
Step 7: Rotate tube. Tie in ten strands of UV Krystal Flash over the Antron, the length of top wing.
Step 8: Rotate tube. Pull belly strip of Krystal Flash into a narrow seam and tie it down at the head. Whip finish and trim. Form small, neat head with thread.
Step 9: Zap-A-Gap and epoxy the head.

Meant for bonefish, this fly can be tied in tan, olive, and pink, and up to 4 inches long.

MINIMALIST

Tube: Loop small gold bottle tube; for shallow water use a 1/4-inch-long plastic tube
Thread: Red Danville flat-waxed nylon, just wide enough to hold down the wing base
Wing: 2 1/2 inches of tan rhea, Kraft fur, or Arctic runner, leaving as much of tube exposed as possible
Topping: Twelve strands of UV Krystal Flash (optional)
Beard: Eight strands of pearl Flashabou as long as the entire fly, and the last 10 percent curled with scissors like ribbon (optional)
Finish: Coat the head with Zap-A-Gap and epoxy

This fly can be tied from 1 1/4 to 3 1/2 inches long. Some variations: use Gotcha Pink thread, stick on red or gold Prismatic eyes, then coat head with epoxy. Add six black and clear Speckle Flake Legs, 3/4ths the length of wing, and dub a head with tan Antron.

When the wind is blowing hard, I use flies like the Minimalist to put an extra 10 to 15 feet on my casts. Because the head of this fly is aerodynamic and the wet rhea wing adds no drag, it cuts through the wind and completely turns over the leader.

SNAPPER WHACKER

Tube: Brass 1/8-inch O. D., 1 1/2 inch long; use plastic for a slow sinker
Thread: Orange Danville flat-waxed nylon
Tail: Tan Arctic runner
Mouth parts/antennae: Two strands of fine red and two of fine gold holographic Flashabou; 15 strands of UV Krystal Flash
Stalk eyes: Super eyes made with 60 to 80 pound shock tippet, red 3-D stick-on eyes, and epoxy (See Tying Instructions Step 5)
Legs: Six orange/black Speckle Flake Legs
Rear wing: Orange dyed guinea hen feather
Body hackle: Brown saddle
Body: Tan and brown Antron dubbing
Middle wing: Orange dyed guinea hen feather
Eyes: Gold/red I-Balz, 3/16 inch
Top wing: Orange dyed guinea hen feathers

Head: Orange thread
Finish: Zap-A-Gap and epoxy

Step 1: Put tube in vise. Attach thread, coat tube with Zap-A-Gap, then form a solid thread base, stopping just short of the end of the tube. Reverse thread.

Step 2: At rear of tube tie in tail of tan Arctic runner, 1 1/4 inch long. Zap-A-Gap the wraps.

Step 3: On each side of tail, tie in two red and two gold strands of holographic tinsel, the length of the tube. Top with 15 strands of UV Krystal Flash, same length, spread out.

Step 4: Attach legs, 1 1/2 inch long, on top of tail/antennae.

Step 5: To make Super eyes, melt ends of 60 to 80 pound shock tippet, then flatten them perpendicularly against a hard, smooth surface like glass. Apply 3-D stick-on eyes to the flattened ends. Coat eyes with a drop of epoxy. Tie in Super eyes, 1 1/4 inch long, on either side of tail and legs. Zap-A-Gap the wraps.

Step 6: Tie in guinea feather at rear of tube, over eyes, tail, and legs. Crush the stem butt to make it lie flat. Its tip should reach the end of the stalk eyes.

Step 7: At rear of tube tie in a long, brown saddle hackle by the butt.

Step 8: Coat the rear half of the tube with Zap-A-Gap and spin a loop of tan and brown Antron dubbing on the thread. To create bulk the Antron should be loose inside the loop. Wrap a tapered crustacean body, stopping half-way to the head of the fly. Brush out the dubbing fibers, then palmer the hackle forward to the middle of the tube, tie off, and trim hackle tip. Trim off hackle fibers even with the top of the body.

Step 9: At the stopping point, tie in another guinea feather. Crush the stem butt to make it lay flat over the back.

Step 10: Optional step. Rotate tube 180 degrees. Advance thread and tie in I-Balz at the front end of tube. Zap-A-Gap the wraps. Reverse thread.

Step 11: Coat the front half of tube with Zap-A-Gap, then finish winding the dubbed body to 1/8 inch from end of tube. Brush out Antron fibers.

Step 12: At the head of the fly tie in a third guinea feather. Crush the stem butt to make it lay flat over the back. Wrap a neat head with thread. Finish with Zap-A-Gap and epoxy.

This fly is meant for snappers and bonefish, but it might work for steelhead as well. It can be tied up to 2 1/2 inches long. Leave out the I-Balz and the fly will almost float.

GENTLE SURGEON

Tube: Brass 1/8-inch O. D., 1 inch long; use hard plastic for a slow sinker
Thread: Light pink Danville flat-waxed nylon
Tail: Tan Arctic fox 2/3 length of tube, topped by natural buck tail, the length of the tube
Mouth parts/antennae: One strand of red holographic Flashabou, the length of the tube, tied in above each of stalk eyes. Top with 15 strands of UV Krystal Flash, spread out.
Stalk eyes: Super eyes, 3/4 inch long

Legs: Two clear black/silver Speckle-Flake Legs over each eye, 1 3/4 times length of tube
Bottom wing: Three red Golden pheasant feathers, tied flat over tail and extending to eyes
Body hackle: Two brown saddles tied in by butts, wound Palmer style. Trim top fibers off flat.
Body: Light brown Antron dubbed and picked out to form a tapered crustacean shape
Top wing: Three, long, red Golden pheasant feathers tied in at head and flat over back of fly
Head: Pink thread
Finish: Zap-A-Gap and epoxy

For a variation, replace red Golden pheasant feathers with blue. This fly is intended for permit, tarpon, jacks, big snappers, Atlantic salmon, and steelhead.

BABY LOBSTER – RHEA

Tube: Brass 1/8-inch O. D., 1 1/2 inches long; use hard plastic for a slow sinker
Thread: Orange Danville flat-waxed nylon
Mouth parts/antennae: Two strands of red and two gold holographic Flashabou, the length of the tube, tied in on each side. Topped by 15 strands of UV Krystal Flash, spread out.
Legs: Six clear black/silver Speckle Flake Legs, the length of tube and tied on top
Tail: Sparse bunch of yellow Arctic runner, 2/3 length of tube, tied on top of legs
Stalk eyes: Super eyes, 5/8 inch long
Weighted eyes (optional): Attach I-Balz at head of fly before winding dubbed body
Body: Tan and brown Antron dubbed and picked out to form a tapered crustacean shape
Hackle: Two wraps of orange rhea, then four wraps of red-brown rhea at head of fly
Wing: Two orange Guinea feathers tied in at head and flat over back of fly
Head: Orange thread
Finish: Zap-A-Gap and epoxy

This fly is tied 3 to 4 inches long. As a variation, use large, orange Sparkle chenille for the body.

LIGHT GOTCHA

Tube: Plastic 1/8-inch O. D., 1 1/2 inch long
Thread: Pink Danville flat-waxed nylon
Body: Small to medium Pearl Sparkle chenille or Diamond Braid
Wing: Tan rhea, Kraft fur, or Arctic Runner, 3 inches long
Topping: Eight strands of UV Krystal Flash
Beard: Dozen strands of Pearl Flashabou, as long as fly, and the last 10 percent curled with scissors

Head: Pink thread
Finish: Zap-A-Gap and epoxy

Fly is tied up to 3 1/2 inches long. Variation: Use a Loop bottle tube, and instead of a body, tie in a large bunch of frayed Diamond Braid around the tube under the wing and trim at end of hook sleeve.

MAAD MAX

Tube: Loop bottle tube, large or small
Thread: Green Danville flat-waxed nylon
Tail: Two strands each of fine red and silver holographic Flashabou
Inner wing: Two badger saddles on each side
Topping: Small bunches of Highlander green Arctic runner
Beard/belly: Small bunches of white Arctic runner, same length and tied at same angle as topping
Outer wing: Two chartreuse, Black Laced hen feathers on each side
Cheeks: Two or three mallard or wood duck breast feathers, each side, coved, 1/3 length of finished fly
Veil: Eight strands of UV Krystal Flash
Eyes: Jungle cock
Head: Green thread
Finish: Zap-A-Gap and epoxy

Step 1: Put bottle tube in vise. Attach thread, coat tube with Zap-A-Gap, then form a thread base, stopping just short of the end.

Step 2: Tie in two red and two silver strands of holographic tinsel, cut them 3/4 length of finished fly.

Step 3: Tie in an inner wing of two badger saddles each side, coved. Apply Zap-A-Gap to wraps.

Step 4: On top of saddles tie in a topping of green Arctic runner, 1/3 length of finished fly Angle the hair tips slightly outward to give the fly broad shoulders. Apply Zap-A-Gap to wraps.

Step 5: Rotate tube 180 degrees on vise. Tie in a beard/belly of small bunches of white Arctic runner, same length and tied at same angle as topping. Zap-A-Gap wraps.

Step 6: Rotate tube 180 degrees on vise. Tie in two chartreuse Black Laced hen feathers on each side, coved. The bottom feather should be 3/8 inch longer than the top. Crush the butts with pliers to make them lay flat. Apply Zap-A-Gap to wraps.

Step 7: Tie in cheeks of two or three mallard or wood duck breast featherson each side, coved, 1/3 length of finished fly. Crush the butts with pliers to make them lay flat. Zap-A-Gap wraps.

Step 8: As a veil, tie in eight strands of UV Krystal Flash, doubled and spaced evenly around the tube.

Step 9: Tie in jungle cock eyes, and wrap a neat head. Finish with Zap-A-Gap and epoxy.

Variations: red (or blue, or yellow) thread, red (or blue, or yellow) Black Laced hen, and red (or blue, or yellow) Arctic runner topping. The fly is tied 3 to 4 inches long. It's a great pattern for snook and small-to-medium sized tarpon. It can also be used for reef fish, salmonids, and dorado.

BART'S BASIC BAITFISH - RHEA

Tube: Small Loop bottle tube
Thread: Black Danville flat-waxed nylon
Wing: Pair of 1 1/2 inch long badger saddles, each side, coved
Topping: Half a dozen strands of UV Krystal Flash, 3/4ths the length of badger
Cheeks: Two mallard or wood duck breast feathers, each side, 1/3 length of finished fly
Eyes: Jungle cock
Hackle: Two wraps of tan rhea, same length as Krystal Flash
Head: Black thread
Finish: Zap-A-Gap and epoxy

BART'S BAITFISH – TARPON

Tube: Small Loop bottle tube
Thread: White Danville flat-waxed nylon
Tail: Two red and two silver strands of holographic tinsel, doubled over and cut 3/4 length of finished fly
Inner wing: Pair of 4 inch long badger saddles, each side, coved
Topping and beard: White Arctic runner, angled as for Maad Max to create broad shoulders
Outer wing: Three white saddles on each side, coved, slightly shorter than badger
Cheeks: Two or three large mallard or wood duck breast feathers, 1/3 length of finished fly
Veil: Fifteen strands of UV Krystal Flash, doubled over, and 3/4 the length of badger
Eyes: Jungle cock
Head: White thread
Finish: Zap-A-Gap and epoxy

Use a large Loop Bottle tube or heavy brass for ocean-side fish, deep channels, or big snappers. Tied on a plastic tube with a light hook, this fly will float in mangroves. I fish this pattern in 2 to 6 inch lengths.

RHEA GUNZ

Tube: Loop bottle, large or small
Thread: Black Danville flat-waxed nylon
Flash: Two red and two silver strands of holographic tinsel, doubled over and cut 3/4 length of finished fly
Hackle: Two wraps of yellow rhea, under two wraps of orange rhea, under two of purple, under four of royal blue, under eight of black. Zap-A-Gap between hackles.
Eyes: Jungle cock
Veil: Purple Krystal Flash, sparse, spread evenly around the tube
Head: Black thread
Finish: Zap-A-Gap and epoxy

Variations: Two wraps of white rhea, then four of kingfisher blue, four of royal blue. Two of white, four of yellow, six of orange. Two of yellow, eight of bubble gun, two of white. I tie this pattern from 2 to 4 inches.

CHAPTER
7

ABRAHAM CONCEPCION
Golfito, Costa Rica/ Florida Keys

BETSY BULLARD

When I was a year old, in the early 1960s, my father quit his job at the Chiquita Banana company in Golfito, and we moved about 15 miles south along the Pacific coast to Pavones. I have been fishing the waters around Costa Rica's Golfo Dulce, one of the world's largest and deepest bays, since the age of five when my brothers took me with them on a commercial trip. I grew up surfing and fishing around my home, and never left the area until I got married.

I began commercial fishing by myself in 1984. Eight years later I took a job at Roy's Lodge in Zancudo as a cook and soon became a sportfishing captain. On my first day as a captain for Roy's, my American customer caught an 800 pound black marlin on conventional gear. In 1995 I started captaining for Golfito Sailfish Rancho, the first four-star rated hotel in Central America. My first clients at the rancho were also Americans, Betsy Bullard and her son Jesse. Betsy and I married that same year. She and I opened Pez Volador, a small sportfishing operation in Zancudo in 1996. Two years later we purchased the Golfito Sailfish Rancho.

Our first visitors were Mark Mandell, Peter Hylander, and John Ockerman. Mark had come to Golfito to write an article for *Flyfishing in Salt Waters* magazine. Fishing with Markito, I landed my first-ever fish on a fly rod, a bonito. As a parting gift, the boys left us a Biscayne rod, a Pate reel, and flies. Since 1998, with the help and advice of many kind friends, including Kevin Kurtz, Stu Apte, Flip Pallot, and Jose Wejibe, I've been working on my salt water fly-fishing and fly-tying.

In the last two seasons I have fly caught 137 sailfish, and four marlin: one black (170 pounds) landed in 22 minutes, and three blues (150, 175, 350-400 pounds). The largest marlin was hooked on one of my 1 inch diameter, green and pink, 80 Percent Sailfish poppers while Flip Pallot was in the boat filming his television show; I fought the fish for seven hours. It was one of the largest marlin Flip had ever seen hooked on a fly, and the butt of the 12 foot leader was inside the tip top several times before the fish finally came off, well after dark.

Because customers always come first at the rancho, I don't get to fish that much in high season, December through April. I do get to observe fly-fishers on the water, casting over fish on an almost daily basis. I video-record them in action, which helps to identify mistakes and improve the next day's success.

As a captain and a fly-fishing instructor, I have tried and seen tried all the commercially tied billfish poppers. Customers using these flies routinely miss fish after fish. Sometimes the combined weight of hooks and feathers cause the back of the popper to sink, thereby ruining the pop. In my experience, the noise a popper makes is more important than color. Some popper heads soak up water like a sponge, don't pop, and cast like coconuts. Often a raised billfish will give a fly-fisher the chance for a second, or even a third cast, so it is important to be able to quickly and easily pick the popper off the water.

In trying to design a fly that produced better results for our customers, I looked for popper foam that was very light, high floating, and that wouldn't absorb water. Edgewater foam meets

---

From top: Abraham's 80 Percent Sailfish Fly (1/2 inch - red); Ballyhoo; Abraham's 80 Percent Sailfish Fly (1/4 inch - blue); Abraham's 80 Percent Sailfish Fly (1 inch pink); Abraham's 80 Percent Sailfish Fly (1 inch - chartreuse); Abraham's 80 Percent Sailfish Fly (1/4 inch - pink)

all those requirements. I am using WTC-inc. adhesive-backed Mylar skirt tape because it is very light, non-absorbent, and there is no additional thread or glue to weigh down the fly. The self-adhesive is very strong, and if it comes off, the tape is easily replaced. It is also very slick. Unlike some of the thinner, textured synthetic materials, it will not tangle and catch on a fish's bill, giving the impression that the fish is hooked when it isn't. I dress the popper heads with as few feathers as possible to keep the wet weight down and the correct balance for maximum pop.

My goal was to create a fly that produced consistent success: 80 percent of raised billfish hooked and landed.

Fishing these poppers in the 2005 Quepos Harry Gray International Tournament I landed and released 11 sails out of 13 raised, and took third place. Also in 2005, in the Golfito Banana Bay Tournament, I landed nine sails out of 11 raised (and a blue marlin) and took first place. The year before in Harry Gray International Tournament, it was a different story, and a learning experience. I landed 13 sails and lost ten hooked fish in four days. Fishing the same flies and hook rigs, my tournament partner, Danny Chemelko, was also 13 for 23. We examined the 4/0 and 5/0 hooks and they appeared undamaged. Too late to correct the situation, I figured out what was going wrong: the hook wire was too thin. Under the pressure of a sailfish run against heavy fly gear the hook gape was actually opening up, allowing the fish to come off, then the wire sprang back! Because of all the lost fish, Danny and I took fourth place.

Except for light-tackle fly-fishing, I now use double, 8/0 heavy wire hooks. My shortest fight on a sail to date is one minute and 22 seconds. My average time is four minutes, from hook-up to landing. Stu Apte has called me "the fastest billfisherman on the fly."

ABRAHAM'S 80 PERCENT SAILFISH FLY

Tube: Edgewater white foam popper blanks (the popper head is the "tube" — the hollow, dressed portion of this fly) in sizes 1-inch diameter x 1 1/2 inch long; 3/4 x 1 inch; 1/2 inch x 1 inch; and 1/4 inch x 1 inch. The 1-inch, 3/4-inch, and 1/2-inch blanks come predrilled with six holes around the perimeter on the backside and a cupped face on the front.

Thread: None

Tail: Five, 6- to 7-inch marabou plumes or schlappen, in dark green, red, white, or pink for the 1-inch, 3/4-inch, and 1/2-inch poppers. The 1/4-inch poppers are not dressed with feathers, just the Mylar skirt.

Body: None

Skirt: Stick on, Mylar skirt material from WTC-inc.com in 2-inch x 8-inch, with 1/16-inch-wide skirt strands for 1-inch, 3/4-inch, and 1/2-inch popper heads; for 1/4-inch heads, use 1 1/2-inch x 6-inch, 1/16-inch-wide strands. The skirt on the 1/4 inch popper is cut to make the fly 4 inches in overall length; the others are all 8 inches. Colors: chartreuse, dark blue, red, and hot pink

Abraham Concepcion (left) and Roiner Sanchez with a sailfish caught on his 80 Percent Fly.

BETSY BULLARD

Head: Stick on, WTC-inc. head tape, 1 1/4 inch wide, to match skirt color

Eyes: Silver Prismatic stick-on, 3/4-inch diameter for 1-inch, 3/4-inch, and 1/2-inch popper heads; 7/16-inch diameter for 1/4-inch heads

Hook: Size 8/0, Gamakatsu Octopus, 4X strong, double-hook, wire rig for 1-inch poppers (see rigging instructions below). Double, wire-rigged 6/0 or 5/0s for 3/4 inch and 1/2 inch; and single, unwired Owner SSW 3/0s or 2/0s for 1/4-inch poppers

Step 1: If your popper blank isn't predrilled, bore six, 1/16-inch diameter holes, around the circumference, equal distance apart. Drill five of the holes 3/8 inch deep, 1/16 inch from the edge of the popper head; drill one hole 1/8 inch from the edge and all the way through — this is the hole for the shock tippet. On the side of the head opposite the drilled holes, grind out a cup face to increase the pop.

Step 2: Select five, 6- to 7-inch long marabou plumes with thick, stiff stems. Apply 5-minute epoxy to the ends of the stems, then with the feathers' curves facing outward, stick the stems into the five, 3/8-inch-deep holes. Let the epoxy cure.

Step 3: Cut a 4-inch piece of skirt tape and tightly wrap it around the side of the head, aligning the front edge of the skirt bridge (the unfringed portion of the skirt tape) with the front edge of the popper. The end of the wrap should overlap the start of the tape by 1/2 inch.

Step 4: Cut a 4 1/4 inch piece of 1 1/4-inch-wide tape. Aligning the edge with the front of the popper, tightly wrap it around the head, covering the skirt bridge and the beginning of the fringe. The end of the wrap should overlap the tape's start by 3/4 inch.

Step 5: Turn the hole for the shock tippet to the bottom, then apply stick on eyes to the sides of the popper.

Double-Hook Wire Rig

Step 1: Bend 10 inches of single-strand, 50- to 70-pound titanium wire in the middle to make a 5-inch double length with a loop at one end.

Step 2: Push the loop through the eye of an 8/0 hook. Pass the loop over the hook point, then pull on the tag ends, drawing the wire through the eye, snugging the loop under the shank. This is the rear hook.

Step 3: Position the rear hook point down. With pliers, pinch the doubled wire 1 inch from the tip of the tag ends, and bend it back over the top (not the bottom!) to make a tight second loop.

Step 4: Turn the rear hook point up. Slip the tag ends of the wire through the eye of a second 8/0 hook, and slide the eye up to the end of the 1-inch loop. The doubled wire from the point-up rear hook should run along the top of the front hook's shank, and through the eye, leaving about 2 inches of doubled wire between the hooks. The tag ends should run under the shank and stop before the start of the front hook's bend.

Step 5: Tie down the wire on the front hook with tight wraps of thread, canting the rear hook off the perpendicular by about 45 degrees.

Step 6: Coat the thread with 5-minute epoxy.

After the shock tippet is slipped through the popper head and tied to the eye of the front hook, the knot is then drawn back into the head, holding the hook rig in place. If the hooks aren't fixed, and hang down under the popper, they will foul the fly on the cast.

My standard billfishing outfit is a 12- to15-weight rod, matched to an intermediate sink-tip line. If the water is choppy and a smaller head won't pop correctly, I go up to a 1-inch size. For areas where the water is often rough, like Venezuela, the 1 inch popper is ideal.

To fish a 1/2-inch or 1/4-inch popper, I use a 9- or 10-weight rod. With six-pound and under tippets, the 1/4-inch popper puts very little pressure on the line. I had a sailfish on the 1/4-inch fly for five minutes on two-pound test before it broke off. I have landed one sailfish on six-pound, six on 12-pound, and four on 16-pound tippet.

My light tackle sailfish rig for less than 12-pound tippet is 30 feet of 12- or 13-weight running line (thin shooting line behind the head) for less drag in the water. For marlin, I use 35 to 45 feet of the same running line. I back the running line with 550 yards of 60-pound Spiderwire.

For information on finished Abraham's 80 Percent Sailfish Flies and kits, contact Golfito Sailfish Rancho at 1-877-726-2468 or info@golfitosailfishrancho.com.

BALLYHOO

Tube: Plastic HMH 1/8-inch O. D., 2 1/2 inches long, with a 2-inch-long silicone hook sleeve. The tubing fits inside the hook sleeve 1 inch. This makes a 4-inch baitfish.

Thread: Clear nylon

Body: Large Spirit River E-Z Body, natural pearl, 5 inches long

Pectoral fins: Two flattened sections of pearl Krystal Flash, 1 1/4 inch long, 1/4 inch wide

Eyes: Mylar stick-on, yellow, 1/4-inch diameter

Body, beak tip, and fin color: Black permanent marker

Glue: 5-minute epoxy and waterproof super glue

Hook: Owner SSW 4/0

Step 1: Melt a collar on one end of the plastic tube. Slide the collar end of the tube inside the hook sleeve 1 inch. Slip the EZ-Body over the tube.

Step 2: Securely tie down the end of the EZ-Body at the front of tube with clear thread, 1/8 inch from the tip. Pull back on the EZ Body to compress it around the tube, and wrap back with clear thread for 1 inch. This forms the ballyhoo's beak. Whip finish and trim thread.

Baby Sailfish dipped from the Pacific Ocean off the Osa Peninsula in Costa Rica.

Step 3: Push the EZ Body forward, toward the beak, expanding the mesh to make the baitfish body and head shape. The body depth behind the head should be approximately 1/2 inch. Holding the shape with the fingers of one hand, securely tie down the material 1/8 inch from the end of the silicone hook sleeve. Whip finish and trim thread.

Step 4: With scissor points, open but do not cut the EZ Body mesh, 3/4 inch from the back end of the beak and the start of the head, on both sides of the fly.

Step 5: Cut a section of pearl Krystal Flash, 1 1/4 inch long x 1/4 inch wide. Keeping the strands together and as flat as possible, compress and push one end of the section through the opening in the EZ-Body and 1/4 inch inside. Super glue the insertion point and fin base to hold the fin in place. Let dry.

Step 6: Repeat Step 5 with a second section on the other side of the fly.

Step 7: Trim the fins with scissors, cutting across the ends at a 30-degree angle with the long point on top.

Step 8: Apply the stick-on eyes.

Step 9: Trim the excess EZ-Body sticking out past the rear tie-down point to 3/4 inch and divide it into upper and lower tail fins.

Step 10: Mark the fly's back, the tips of tail, and the tip of beak with black marker.

Step 11: Apply a thin coat of 5-minute epoxy to the beak, head, eyes, insertion point of pectoral fins, and to the pectoral and tail fins. Let dry.

Ballyhoo are the prime baitfish in the Golfito area. At night, schools of ballyhoo rise to boat and dock lights. Bonito, jacks, and snapper come up after them. I fish this fly near the surface on a 12-foot, fluorocarbon leader with a 9-weight rod and a floating line. If I want to get down a little, I use the unweighted fly and a 555 Cortland Ghost Tip.

DAVID CROFT

Chipping, near Preston, England

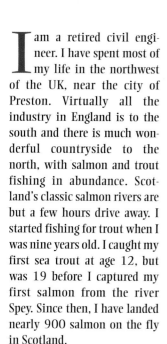

I am a retired civil engineer. I have spent most of my life in the northwest of the UK, near the city of Preston. Virtually all the industry in England is to the south and there is much wonderful countryside to the north, with salmon and trout fishing in abundance. Scotland's classic salmon rivers are but a few hours drive away. I started fishing for trout when I was nine years old. I caught my first sea trout at age 12, but was 19 before I captured my first salmon from the river Spey. Since then, I have landed nearly 900 salmon on the fly in Scotland.

I recall tying trout flies as a child, having been shown the half hitch knot by my father — I was fortunate indeed to have had a father whose great loves were fishing and shooting. This was at the end of the Second World War and as there was little available in the way of materials, I relied on feathers plucked from my pillow. Soon after becoming a salmon fisher, I took up salmon-fly tying in earnest. Richard Waddington, the prolific author and inventor of the Waddington shank, was a great influence in my early years. During the Sixties, the tube fly became popular in the UK, not only in large sizes but also in tiny wisps of flies that accounted for many summer salmon that had been in the rivers for weeks. All my spring fishing and virtually all my autumn fishing is carried out with tubes. Only my summer fishing is a mixture of double hooked salmon flies and tube flies, the small tubes sometimes being too light for the fast current and more liable to skate.

On rare occasions in very high and colored water I use a spinning outfit. I avoid spinning because it offers much less control over the lure than a fly rod and fly line. Apart from the skill and joy of fly casting, the ability to adjust the speed of the fly by mending the line both upstream and down is not an option with a spun bait. In the UK, we fly enthusiasts often mimic our spinning colleagues with a variety of fly lines and tube flies, succeeding in nearly all water conditions and temperatures, albeit with more effort when using large flies and fast sinking lines.

A few years ago I became interested in creating a fly alternative for the "floating Devon," a popular and productive British spinning lure. A Devon is a small wooden plug drilled end to end

From top clockwise: Croft's Original gold head/body with alternating black; yellow; and orange bucktail; red head/body with red bucktail; chartreuse head/body with alternating black; green; and chartreuse bucktail; small red head/body with red bucktail; silver head/chartreuse body with alternating black and light blue bucktail; yellow head/body with alternating yellow and orange bucktail; orange head/body with alternating orange and black bucktail.

so it can be threaded up the line; angled plastic fins near the head cause it to flutter and spin in the current. I have had great success with 1- to 1 1/2-inch floating Devons fished in normal spinning fashion, with a small weight three feet up the line sufficient to bump on the pool bottom. Thus rigged, the lure swims a few inches above the river bed, yet rarely becomes snagged. When all other methods fail, salmon resting in pools for some days are often taken by small floating Devons.

A floating Devon style fly would fish at a constant height of three to six inches from the bottom, following its contours and depressions without being caught up — an impossible feat with sinking fly and a conventional full-sinking line. Clearly, the replacement fly had to be very buoyant, and the leader end of the fly line had to reach bottom quickly after the fly hit the water, and once there, it had to remain in contact with the stream bed. This called for a fast-sinking tip with a fine, floating running line behind to reduce drag. The superb Teeny T-Series lines fit the bill admirably, offering sink rates from four to nine inches per second. The Wet Cel 2 lines sink at about three inches per second.

Not only did the fly body material have to float, it also had to be strong enough to withstand hours of casting. I experimented with all manner of foams, wood, balsa, spun deer hair and cork, sometimes combined, with varying degrees of success. I tested the prototypes in the stream at the bottom of my garden for float and flutter. The final and most satisfactory version was a cork body with a beech wood head. The search for a floating Devon alternative pushed my fly-tying in a new direction — my tying bench now includes a drill press, grinding wheels, and a painting section.

Croft's Originals were first used in March 2000 on the North Esk, a small river on Scotland's East coast which still enjoys a good run of early salmon. I have fished the North Esk in March with the same colleagues for the last ten years, and I return to the same beat again for a fortnight in September. Not surprisingly, my friends' first reaction to the new fly was mild amusement, accompanied by some shaking of the head.

Finding conditions nearly perfect, with a good stock of fish, it was a fair trial for the fly. In the event, the Original accounted for five fish landed, with eight hooked. Several more pulled it. The five other fishers landed five salmon between them on conventional lines and flies and on spinning gear. All the Original-caught salmon were hooked in the front of the mouth, as if they had nipped at the fly as it passed by in front of them. This made for a quick and easy release. The takes were distinctly sharp pulls, and tightening the line quickly with the left hand is suggested. The fly never caught on the bottom, nor were any flies lost. The leader was about three feet long; a longer leader would allow the fly to ride higher in the water.

To maximize the river bottom contact with the end of the line, it is usually necessary to cast a very square line or even an slightly upstream line to give the fly time to get down and fish round covering the most amount of river possible. Holding the fly line between finger and thumb, you should be able to feel the slight vibrations caused by the line sliding over the river stones, and if you cannot, you should use the next heavier line or cast more upstream. Throughout the cast, the fly is, of course, helping to pull the line over the streambed.

The next trip was in May to the river Spey, known as the Queen of Scottish rivers. The beat was renowned for its classical floating-line fishing and we were catching slowly but steadily. One of the most normally prolific pools on the beat was yielding no fish at all, nor did we see any splashes. With the ghillie assuring us there were indeed resident fish in the pool, it seemed a perfect challenge for the "Original" fly. Only six casts later, I was playing such a lively resident fish, which was landed and weighed 8 pounds. It was my eight-hundredth salmon.

My return to the North Esk in September illustrated the ability of the fly to interest resting salmon. My guest, an excellent and respected fly-fisherman, fished one of the better holding pools without a pull. I followed him down with the "Original" and hooked fish on the second, fourth, eighth, and twelfth casts!

A visit to a lower beat on the Spey in August 2001 was also very revealing. Again, beautiful floating-line/small-fly water, with a plentiful supply of fish, but almost all had been in the river for a week or longer. The team of seven rods was landing only three or four fish a day, and we were surprised that more salmon were not taking. Under these conditions, fishing about a half an hour a day for four days, the Original accounted for salmon of 13, 14, and 16 pounds. Of the six fish caught during the week over 12 pounds, the other six rods fishing conventional flies accounted for three salmon of 15, 17, and 19 pounds.

On our March trip in 2002 more rods fished the Original. Of the 20 fish landed, 11 fell to it. Some of the success may be put down to the fact that the resting fish had seen many flies near the surface, usually quite small, or larger flies at mid height. We all know how soon they turn off. Could it be, that when suddenly in front of their noses appears a lively, different looking bright fly, they nip it?

CROFT'S ORIGINAL BUOYANT FLIES

Tube: 2-inch-long piece of the polypropylene tube used for "cotton buds" ear cleaners for babies (substitute 3/32-inch O. D. hard plastic)

Thread: Black Kevlar

Wing: Bucktail 2 to 2 1/2 inch, alternating with sparse Krystal Flash

Body: 1/4-inch diameter by 1/2-inch-long corklets used in "coarse" fishing in the UK

Head: Beech wood dowel, the same or slightly larger diameter as the corklets. Finished head length is 3/8 inch.

Head/body/wing color combinations:
- Silver head/chartreuse body, alternating black/light blue bucktail
- Red head/body, red bucktail, red/pearl Krystal Flash
- Orange head/body, alternating orange/black bucktail, orange Krystal Flash
- Chartreuse head/body, alternating black, green, chartreuse bucktail
- Yellow head/body, alternating yellow, orange bucktail, orange Krystal Flash
- Gold head/body, alternating black, yellow, orange bucktail, chartreuse Krystal Flash

Finish: Glue, sealing primer, and paints

Hook: Kamasan B990 size 10 treble and a 3/16-inch gold bead as a bearing between hook eye and fly

Step 1: The fly body consists of two or three cylindrical-corklets, depending on desired length. These are drilled through the center with a hole to fit snugly on the plastic tube through which the nylon leader will be threaded.

Step 2: The head is made from a beechwood dowel similarly drilled, with the front end rounded off on a grinding wheel and cut to length. The wooden head gives the fly strength and the plastic tube adds rigidity.

Step 3: Glue the corks and head onto the tube. When the glue dries, file down the cork behind the head a little. Wind on a few tight turns of Kevlar thread to compress the filed-down cork and form a bed for the hair wing. Whip finish. Seal the body with a primer and then paint with the color of choice.

Step 4: Tie on the wing in-the-round, spreading the bucktail around the body. Top with Krystal Flash, form a neat collar and whip finish.

Step 5: Apply a final coat of paint to the head, followed by a varnish coat. Trim excess plastic tube.

The overall length of the body, including the head, is about 1 1/2 inch but of course, this may be increased or decreased. The length of the flies from the head to the extent of the longest wing hairs is 2 to 3 inch.

MIKE CROFT

Tacoma, Washington

I am a graphic artist who spends his spare time fishing local waters, both salt and fresh for trout and salmon. Salmon are my favorite. In recent years, my state's salmon populations have so tragically diminished that I have taken to fishing Baja California.

I started fly-tying in 1963 in North Bend, Oregon under the tutelage of Harold Grey, owner of the local fly shop. I had a knack for it and soon I was tying commercially for local shops as well as shops in the Willamette Valley. I began tying flies on tubes around 1989. Much of the winter food for salmon includes small transparent critters such as newly hatched candlefish and euphausids. The small, milky-colored tubes found on spray cans like WD-40 worked fine. Gradually I moved up to larger tube flies for adult candlefish and herring. In Mexico, I fish tube flies almost exclusively. These flies last forever unless left out in the sun where they can get hot enough to curl the Mylar.

TUMS (TRIPLE UNBRAIDED MYLAR STRANDS)

Tube: Plastic 1/8-inch O. D., with heat shrink tubing as a hook sleeve. Joined tubes are 2 1/4 inches long. Finished fly is 3 inches long.

Thread: Clear monofilament

Wing: Top wing is one, doubled-over strand of 1/4-inch, black-dyed braided Mylar. Cut your Mylar about 1/2 inch short because it will get longer as it unravels. Bottom wing is two strands of doubled-over, 1/4 -inch braided pearl Mylar. Use one doubled strand on each side of the tube.

Gills: Red floss, trimmed short

Eyes: Silver stick-on Mylar, 1/4-inch diameter

Head: 5-minute Z-poxy

Hook: Mustad 34007 size 4 or 2

Clockwise from top right: TUMS; Croft's Italian Glass Minnow; Croft's Slider; Croft's Sardina; Croft's Marabou Candlefish pink/white; olive/white; chartreuse/white; purple/pink/white; brown/white

After you have the wing tied on and the epoxy head finished, unravel the Mylar with your bodkin needle. Don't unravel before you get the head epoxied or it turns into a different pattern I call "Gob of GOO." You can make the pattern fuller or longer to match the silhouette of your own baitfish.

The strands of unraveled Mylar act like a Slinky toy when drawn through the water. They stretch and stretch until they reach a critical point, then they snap back, giving the fly great action and flash.

The idea for this fly fell into my lap while I was fishing Zonker flies for sea-run cutthroat with a friend and beginning fly tier, Chuck Springer. As Chuck hadn't quite mastered the knot holding down the Mylar body and the rear section of the rabbit fur wing, his fly started to unravel. Up to that point we were catching and releasing fish pretty evenly and on this day there were a lot to catch. As Chuck's fly gradually came apart he began to out-fish me. A little at first, then he was taking two fish to my one, and finally four to one.

Of course, fish are not always turned on by flash. But when they want it, this is one sweet and easy fly to tie. Variations of the unraveled Mylar can be added to other patterns for action and flash. If you can't find the black-dyed Mylar braid for the back of the wing you can dye it yourself. Use a good black dye that uses an acid mordant but don't let the temperature get over 140 degrees. Higher temperatures cause the Mylar to curl.

CROFT'S MARABOU CANDLEFISH

Tube: Plastic 1/8-inch O. D., with heat shrink tube as hook sleeve. Finished fly is 2 3/4 inches long.

Thread: Clear monofilament
  Wing: Top half (back of fly), the color of marabou is your choice (See list below). Bottom half (belly) marabou is white, veiled with pearl Flashabou.
  Gills: Red floss, trimmed short
  Eyes: Silver stick-on Mylar, 3/8-inch diameter
  Head: I like to wrap the head with the butts of the Flashabou to give it the sparkle you would see in the gill cover of a baitfish.
  Finish: Coat the head with 5-minute epoxy
  Hook: Mustad 34007 sizes 8 to 2

This is my favorite casting fly for coho salmon while they are still feeding. It is fast and inexpensive to tie. It looks ugly when dry but when wet it is very close to the natural.

Olive over white

This is the match-the-hatch coloration, but be aware that when the bait is thickly schooled you don't want to match the hatch. Since candlefish accept this fly as a real bait they don't scatter when it is stripped through the school. This means the salmon working the outside can't see it, and you won't get many hits. I fish these colors when there are only a few candlefish showing, and in the water separating schools of bait. I use 12-inch hops on the retrieve with occasional three-foot darts.

Chartreuse over white

The first two hours after dawn and last two hours of the evening are the best times for these colors. It is also a good color scheme when schools of bait are thick. If you pull this combination through the school, it will open a yard-wide circle around the fly. In deep shadows you can follow the fly even if you can't see the fish. Set the hook when you see the fly dart off faster than you are retrieving it. Many fish will hit the fly from behind while swimming towards the boat. If they don't turn, they will spit the fly before you even feel them. Keep your eyes peeled and you will be surprised at how many hits you are getting.

Pink over white

This is a great summer color when crab spawn is on the surface. Crab spawn looks brown to my eyes, but pink is crab spawn color for silver salmon. To tell if fish are feeding on crab spawn, check their stomach contents. Spawn is gritty like sandpaper from the tiny, developing crab shells.

Purple, pink, over white (The Mrs. Nelson)

This is the only Marabou Candlefish color combination with a name. It was developed by Bill Nelson, one of the original founders of the Federation of Fly Fishers and a high-scoring guide at April Point Lodge on Vancouver Island, British Columbia. The Mrs. Nelson is my favorite fly on dark overcast days. The addition of the pink along the sides is an old trick to make the fly more appealing to king salmon, should one wander by.

Brown over white

Captain Tom Wolf (See Chapter 36: Tom Wolf), the only licensed saltwater fly guide in South Puget Sound, popularized this color scheme. In strong midday sunlight, the backs of many baitfish show a distinct brown color. This can be a dynamite combination for sea-run trout when tied in flies less than 1 1/2 inch long.

CROFT'S ITALIAN GLASS MINNOW

Tube: Copper 3/32-inch O. D., 1 1/2 inch long, with heat-shrink tube as hook sleeve and Moretti Italian Glass Head. After the head is made, annealed, and cooled I line the tube with a very small diameter Teflon tube.

Thread: Clear monofilament

Body: Bottom half (belly) is white Arctic fox. I think it's the best material to form the body of a minnow because it keeps its shape when wet. I use about one-half of a good-sized pinch. Top half (back) is natural dark Arctic fox, about the same amount as the lower body. I work in a little pearl Krystal Flash or Flashabou over the white belly.

Gills: Red floss, trimmed short

Hook: Mustad 34007, size 6 or 4

For years, I have fantasized about stepping onstage at a fly-tying demonstration wearing a welding mask and carrying a torch. Imagine the audience's curiosity as I drop the shield and light up the torch! With the Italian Glass Minnow, fantasy has become reality.

First I melt and spin white glass onto an end of the copper tube. I add dots of color for the eyes and the back of the head, then re-melt and shape it. The Italian Glass Minnow is much heavier than a regular tube fly but lighter than a weighted Clouser Minnow. The problem I find with a Clouser is that the up-point hook often catches small fish in the eye; the Italian Glass Minnow's hook rides point down. The black-and-white model was designed for black rockfish and is tied in male spawning colors.

CROFT'S SLIDER

Tube: Clear or white 1/16-inch plastic, 1 inch long, with white electrical shrink tube over the entire length and formed into a hook sleeve. Joined tubes are 1 1/2 inches long.

Thread: Clear monofilament

Body: White closed-cell foam, 2 inch long. Cut mirror images of body halves. Glue halves to the shrink tube with a thick super glue. Hook sleeve keyhole should

In 2000, Mike Croft caught and released this Cannibus sativa *88-pounder (estimated street value: $186,000 U. S. D.) in East Cape, Baja on a 3 1/2-inch blue-and-white* sardina *tube fly, 3/0 hook, and 20-pound tippet. The fight lasted three minutes. Photo shows scale sampling prior to release.*

Joe Uhlman shows off a British Columbia coho caught on an Italian Glass Minnow.

be parallel to the sides of the body. Color just the back with black permanent marker. Cover the body with a white craft glue that will dry clear and sprinkle it with medium gold glitter. Note: Gold glitter is not really gold but pearl.

Tail: A small pinch of white marabou tied on the hook shank, not the tube
Eyes: Silver stick-on Mylar, 1/4-inch diameter
Finish: Three coats of Softex
Hook: Mustad 34007 size 8

When a salmon or cutthroat rakes through a school of bait, the cripples show up on the surface on their sides, swimming in erratic death throes. I have noticed they don't swim on the surface very long before something takes them.

CROFT'S SARDINA

Tube: Plastic 1/8-inch O. D., about 2 1/2 inches long for a 4-inch fly. Hook sleeve is heat-shrink tube slightly longer than the plastic tube.
Thread: Clear monofilament
Top wing: Blue blood quill marabou, stripped from the feather stems and tied with mixed metallic blue, green, and copper Flashabou
Bottom wing: White blood quill marabou, stripped from the feather stems and mixed with pearl Flashabou
Eyes: Silver stick-on Mylar, 5/16-inch diameter
Head: 5-minute Z-poxy
Hook: Mustad 34007 sizes 2 to 3/0

My marabou candlefish was so successful that I decided to try a more full-bodied fly. Marabou has magical fish-catching ability but it compresses so much in the water that a deep-bodied baitfish like a herring is a real challenge. I fussed around for eight years until I finally figured out a way to get a large epoxy head and deep silhouette on a marabou fly.

Step 1: This fly is tied with marabou stripped from the feather quills. Be sure you use blood quills, as their marabou is longer. Strip all the marabou from a one side of a blue feather, then tie the clump on top of the tube near the hook holder, like a big tail. Strip off the other half and tie the fibers on top of the first clump. Do the same with a white feather on the underside of the tube. Note that the total length of the finished fly will be the length of the tube plus the length of the marabou. Keep this in mind and you can adjust your fly to whatever small, deep-bodied baitfish you are trying to imitate. Whatever you do, don't spare the marabou!

Step 2: Between the feathers, layer in a few strands of Flashabou for added sparkle.

Step 3: After you have the fibers from six or so feathers on top and six on the bottom, carefully tie half of a stripped blue feather facing forward on top and half of a white one facing forward on the bottom. When these forward facing fibers are pulled to the rear with a little saliva they will give you a tear-drop silhouette. This shape is not possible with the marabou tied in the normal butts-forward fashion. Holding the feathers out of the way, whip finish the thread at the front of the tube.

Step 4: To give the fly a fish shape instead of a feather-duster shape, work up some saliva, stick the fly in your mouth and pull it through a couple of times. Try not to think about those feathers dragging around the chicken coop a few months back. And don't breathe in unless it is through your nose as you will get small pieces of marabou stuck in the back of your throat. The fly should come out of your mouth damp but in the shape of a fish. Fine-tune any rogue feather strands that don't lay right with your bodkin. There won't be very many of these.

Step 5: When you have the perfect deep-bodied shape take an eye dropper add enough Zip Kicker (an accelerant for super glue) to soak the head. Pinch the head a little to make it flatter on the sides and shape the forehead if needed again with your bodkin. When you are happy with the shape carefully add a couple of drops of super glue to the head. Super glue without accelerant will penetrate the whole feather and ruin the fly. With accelerant on the feathers the super glue only spreads a little way before it stops and sets up. It might take a couple of tries on different flies to get this right. You only get one chance per fly and if it isn't quite perfect you can tweak the shape just a bit with the epoxy. After the super glue hardens, which will only be seconds, the fly will keep the fish shape, deep-sided and narrow backed.

Step 6: Add the eyes, and epoxy the whole head. Don't fluff out the wet feathers before the glue dries, as they will blow onto and stick in the epoxy. Let it dry overnight then tie it on a leader and watch it swim in a bath tub. After I finally figured out how to tie this fly I was able to toss out my rubber duck.

CHAPTER
10

RUDI HEGER

Siegsdorf, Germany

RUDI HEGER

In 1979, I started a small, fly-fishing mail-order business that has grown into the largest fly-fishing catalogue in German-speaking countries. We are the distributor for Sage rods in middle Europe and represent many other American companies as well. My formal education is in hotel administration/culinary arts — I was once recognized as Bavaria's best pastry chef!

When my parents closed their hotel and restaurant on the River Traun in 1985 our fly-fishing business moved onto the premises, and there we remain. I own the fly-fishing rights to five miles of the Bavarian Traun and I have leased another 15 miles of excellent trout waters in Bavaria and Austria, including the world-famous, Austrian Gmundner Traun.

I have been fly-tying for 35 years, and I tie 40 percent of my big-fish flies on tubes. I fly-fish on average about 85 days a year, of which at least 25 to 30 days are spent in the Florida Keys — in my opinion if you want to learn fly-fishing tactics and presentations, that is the place to go. A good friend of mine, Captain Ray Fetcher deserves credit for many of the new approaches I am using. Most of these techniques can be adapted to other fisheries.

The rest of my fishing days are usually spent in British Columbia, Austria, Spain, and throughout Europe. I fish for steelhead, pike, catfish, carp, huchen, grayling, trout, and other species. Over the last seven years I've spent considerable in fly-fishing for giant European catfish.

The Big Meal flies are an improvement over my huchen and pike and steelhead tube flies that first appeared in *Tube Flies* (Frank Amato Publications, 1995). Over the last ten years I have altered materials to give these flies better action in the water, and I have increased their overall size and bulk to appeal to the biggest predators. I switched from bucktail to Tempelhair because it is softer and therefore has more movement. Polar bear hair would also work, but I don't tie flies with it; I have too much admiration for those magnificent creatures. Although I have used Big Meals on tarpon, I don't make a habit of it. The Keys' hot tarpon flies seem to get smaller and smaller, not larger.

I fish Big Meals with fairly heavy sinking lines, such as Mastery Streamer Express or Mastery Wet Tip Express, on five-foot leaders. The lightest rod I use for sparsely dressed Big Meal flies (for steelhead in colored water) would be an 8-weight like the Sage 890-4 xi2. I prefer a Sage 9-weight for pike and sometimes for huchen. Heavily dressed huchen flies demand a 10-weight. For European catfish I like 11- and 12-weight rods.

In 2004, using a black Big Meal fly I caught a world-record European catfish on Spain's Rio Ebro. The fish was 198 cm (6 feet 6 inches) long and weighed 104 pounds. I hooked it from a pontoon boat and it took me about 45 minutes to land on an 11-weight rod. The fish towed me around quite a bit, but I have

RUDI HEGE

materials and keeps them from slipping off.

Step 2: Tie a bunch of black Tempelhair on the tube and top it with a single strand of Krystal Flash, 5 inches long. Rotate the tube on the vise 90 degrees.

Step 3: Tie a bunch of gray bucktail on the tube and top it with a single strand of Krystal Flash, 5 inches long. Rotate the tube on the vise 90 degrees.

Step 4: Tie a second bunch of black Tempelhair on the tube and top it with a single strand of Krystal Flash, 5 inches long. Rotate the tube on the vise 90 degrees.

Step 5: Tie a second bunch of gray bucktail on the tube and top it with a single strand of Krystal Flash, 5 inches long.

Step 6: Wrap a body of Pearl Spectraflash chenille, covering about 2/3 of the tube. Tie down the chenille and trim excess.

Step 7: Repeat Steps 2 through 5, again tying in two bunches of Tempelhair, alternating with two of bucktail. The Tempelhair should be about four times the volume of the bucktail. Top with a few 8-inch strands of pearl and black Krystal Flash.

Step 8: Between the four bunches of Tempelhair tie in one bunch of Light & Bright and two or three grizzly Zonker strips.

Step 9: Tie in four strands of 10-inch-long Spectraflash Hair, evenly spaced around fly.

Step 10: Form a nice head and lacquer it. Cut the Zonker strips to length: 3-inch, 5-inch, and 8-inch lenghs. Cut Spectraflash Hair to a 10-inch length.

developed effective tactics of fighting big fish. Some of these tactics are adapted from the Keys' tarpon fishery.

BIG MEAL STREAMER

Tube: Copper, 1/8-inch O. D., 1 1/2 inches long
Thread: Black
Tail: Bunches of black Tempelhair alternating with gray bucktail, both 4 inches long
Tail topping: Pearl Krystal Flash, 5 inches long
Body: Spectraflash Chenille Pearl/Gray or Pearl/Pink
Wing: Bunches of black Tempelhair alternating with gray bucktail, both 4 inches long
Wing topping: A few strands of pearl and black Krystal Flash, 8 inches long, tied around fly, and four strands of Spectraflash Hair, 10 inches long, spaced evenly around the fly. The color of the Spectraflash Hair should complement the color of the Zonker strips.
Cheeks: Grizzly Zonker strips, 8 inches and 3 inches. Depending on how bulky I want the fly to be, I use two or three of these strips.
Hook: Tiemco 600 SP, 2/0

Step 1: Put the tube on your vise. Tie in the thread and wind a little bump at the rear of the tube. This acts to spread out the

BIG MEAL VARIATION

Tube: Copper, 1/8-inch O. D., 1 1/2 inches long
Thread: Black
Tail: Gray Tempelhair, 4 inches long, tied in four bunches, 360 degrees around tube
Tail topping: Strand of Pearl Krystal Flash, 5 inches long, over each bunch of Tempelhair
Body: Pearl Spectraflash Chenille
Wing: Gray Tempelhair, 5 1/2 inches long, tied in four bunches, 360 degrees around tube
Wing topping: A few 9-inch strands of pearl Krystal Flash and metallic silver and metallic blue Flashabou, tied 360 degrees around head
Hook: Tiemco 600 SP, 2/0

Top: Big Meal Streamer; Bottom: Big Meal Variation

PETER HYLANDER

Seattle, Washington

MAUREEN HYLANDER

I've been fly-fishing and fly-tying for more than 30 years. I learned to fish on the Jersey shore and in Vermont's fresh water. For a decade, off and on, I fly-guided in Colorado on the Gunnison/East Fork, the Taylor, and the Eagle rivers. I've worked in fly shops in Madison, New Jersey and Vail, and I taught fly-fishing, casting, and tying in Seattle at the Swallow's Nest for seven years.

In addition to my home waters of Puget Sound, I've fished the Sea of Cortez for 16 years, from Loreto to East Cape; the Atlantic coast for bluefish, stripers, redfish, cobia, and weakfish; Costa Rica's Pacific coast for billfish, tuna, and roosters; and the Yucatán for bonefish, permit, and snook. I am currently hosting an annual Baja Loreto trip for 25 fly-fishers, a nice mix of seasoned vets and neophytes, in mid-July-early August, through FISHABOUT 1-888-409-2008, www.fishabout.com.

I tied my first flies on tubes 15 years ago for a trip to Baja. I was trying to make some poppers for billfish and couldn't find hooks long enough or with a big enough gape, so I dressed the popper tails on tubes and slipped them into backs of foam heads. The switch to dressing all my flies on tubes came easily: tube flies are no harder to tie, they offer a much more versatile tying platform than hooks, and they last a lot longer on the water.

In 1996 I started my own company, Seattle Saltwater, because no one was making the materials/gear I needed. I tie flies with standard, hardware store tubing, and there was no vise available that would accept and firmly hold the sizes I was using. At that time, foam popper heads had to be colored with spray paint, and they chipped and blistered almost immediately. Seattle Saltwater manufactures a tube-fly vise with a stairstep mandrel that holds all the basic, hardware store tube stock; kits and materials for tube flies; and permanently multicolored, foam popper heads. For information, contact me at Seattle Saltwater, P.O. Box 3727, Crested Butte, CO 81224; phone: 970-349-6715; email: seattlesaltwater@msn.com.

I developed the Squishy Fish before the annual Baja trip in 1996. Mark Mandell had sent everyone who was going a copy of a snapshot he'd taken the previous year of the area's prime baitfish, the flat iron herring. He proposed a contest (with no prize but glory) for the best imitations, the winners to be decided at the end of the trip. Experimenting with materials from hardware and marine stores, I came up with a highly-adaptable, basic pattern. I was interested not only in making a fly that worked, but in creating the simplest, most accurate imitation. In my opinion, simple is best when it comes to fly-fishing and fly-tying. That includes

From top: Squishy Fish 1; Squishy Fish 2; Squishy Fish 3; Squishy Fish Threadfin Herring; Squishy Fish Rooster; Seattle Saltwater popper

shopping at hardware and marine stores for supplies whenever possible.

The Squishy proved itself on its first outing. Big dorado and sailfish would sometimes just hang beside the panga, mouthing this fly. It provoked — and survived! — the most vicious attacks imaginable from solo billfish and wolfpacks of 30- to 40-pound dorado.

The Squishy's Flexo Chrome Mylar body is porous. Before casting, hold it underwater and squeeze it like a turkey baster. It will fill up with water. That, and the concealed nose weight give the fly an almost neutral buoyancy; when tied to a leader, it swims like a live bait. Fished on a sinking line, it can be cast and retrieved in normal fashion. It is excellent fly for "chunking," drifting through a chum line. It can also be dead drifted over submerged pinnacles, or behind a wind or current-driven boat. Under dead drift conditions, it is important to keep the line tight at all times. Strikes are quick, savage, and often come when the angler is wool-gathering.

The Squishy Fish design has a couple of other distinct advantages. The double layers of Flexo cushion the rod tip from the impact of the 7/16-inch nickel cone head on a blown cast. The Softex permanently bonds the layers of Flexo and makes an excellent foundation for top paints. The doubled Flexo and the Softex finish create a rough (scale-like), compressible body that has the feel of a real bait. Gamefish take Squishies deeper, and hold on to them longer.

SQUISHY FISH SARDINA

Tube: A three-part assembly: 2 inches of (Nylaflow) 1/8-inch O. D. hard plastic; 3/8 inch of 1/8-inch I. D. / 3/16-inch O. D. soft vinyl; and 3 1/4 inch of 1/4-inch O. D. polyethylene for a 3 3/4-inch baitfish. The length of polyethylene determines the length of the finished fly.

Thread: UNI-mono thread, medium/clear

Nose weight: 7/16-inch diameter cone head

Body: Flexo Chrome Mylar, 1/2 inch wide, 10 inches long

Eyes: Yellow or silver Spirit River 3-D Prismatic size 6.0 (3/8 inch)

Glue: 30-minute epoxy

Finish: Softex

Spray paint: OMC Johnson 1957-59, Outboard Green

Hook: Owner AKI 6/0

Step 1: Cut the three kinds of tubing to length. Slip the hard plastic 1/4 inch into the soft vinyl, and the soft vinyl into the polyethylene, leaving about 1/8 inch of soft vinyl protruding from the end of the polyethylene. Apply epoxy to junction of hard plastic, soft vinyl, and polyethylene.

Step 2: Slide the cone head over the hard plastic tube. It will stop at the soft vinyl. Jam the hard plastic into a piece of foam so

JOHN THOMPSON

MARK MANDELL

epoxy flows down and fills the concave backside of the cone head, including the front of the polyethylene. Let epoxy cure.

Step 3: Carefully heat up and melt the tail end of the polyethylene. Mash the softened tube against a hard, flat surface to create a permanent lip and slip it onto the vise while it is still warm. The lip keeps wraps and materials from slipping off the back of the tube.

Step 4: Slide the assembled tubing onto a vise, fastening it securely. Seattle Saltwater's tube-fly vises and adapters have a stair-step mandrel that is specifically designed to accommodate the multiple diameters of the Squishy body, and other saltwater tube flies.

Step 5: Cut a 10-inch piece of Flexo (for a 3 3/4-inch fly) and slip it over the front end of the tubing. Position the Flexo so its center (5 inch) is directly in front of the cone head, and the natural crease in the material is in line with backbone and belly. Tie down the Flexo, making the wraps as close as possible to the front of the nose weight. If these wraps are not tight and secure, the finished fly will not retain its shape. Translation: it will fall apart. Use several half hitches to finish the wraps, apply a few drops of Softex to saturate them, and trim the mono.

Step 6: Take hold of the forward section of Flexo and push it back, inverting the material over itself (turning it inside out). You are making a body of two layers of Flexo. Be sure to press the front (with the small-diameter Nylaflow tubing) back firmly and evenly to create a tight, neat nose on the fly.

Step 7: Grasp the doubled Flexo at the tail end of the fly, and push it forward until you get the desired profile, fat or skinny, of your baitfish imitation. By feel, locate the lip melted into the aft end of the tubing, and tie down the Flexo just forward of it. Use firm wraps and several half hitches to secure the body at the rear. Again, coat the wraps with Softex, and trim the thread.

Step 8: Remove the fly from the vise, and trim the Nylaflow tubing 1/8 inch from the nose of the fly. Do not trim the tail yet.

Get some paper towels out before the next step!

Step 9: Holding the fly by its tail, dip the whole body into a jar of Softex. Remove the fly and let the Softex drain back into the jar. With a paper towel squeeze as much excess Softex out of the fly as you can. Latex gloves help here. Once the Softex dries, the fly can't be reshaped. Let the fly dry a few minutes. Be sure and cover the jar of Softex. It evaporates quickly.

Step 10: Using the tail as a handle, spray paint a dark black on the fly. I use touch-up paint from OMC. It is actually Johnson outboard green that I get from my local OMC parts house. Gloves help here, too. Trim the tail to size, and flare it out all the way around the tubing.

Step 11: After the paint dries, put a dab of Softex where you want the stick-on eyes to go, and apply them over the wet Softex. Put a large dollop of Softex over the eyes, covering them completely. Allow the finished eyes to dry.

The main reason I use the 1957-59 Johnson outboard paint is the color, which I think is perfect to imitate this baitfish. But there are other advantages to marine or engine paints. They are fast-drying, have good abrasion resistance, and they dry hard so you don't have to worry about your flies sticking together in the box.

Almost any saltwater baitfish can be successfully imitated using the Squishy's basic structure and materials, as is evidenced by the Squishy Fish Rooster.

SQUISHY FISH ROOSTER

Tube: A three-part assembly: 2 inches of (Nylaflow) 1/8-inch O. D. hard plastic; 3/8 inch of 1/8-inch I. D. / 3/16-inch O. D. soft vinyl; and 3 1/4 inch of 1/4-inch O. D. polyethylene for a 4 1/4-inch baitfish. The length of polyethylene determines the length of the finished fly.

Thread: UNI-mono thread, medium/clear

Nose weight: 7/16-inch diameter cone head

Body: Flexo Chrome Mylar, 1/2 inch wide, 10 inches long

Comb: Seven 4-inch lengths of 30-pound braided nylon loop material, marked with black permanent marker

Eyes: Yellow or silver Spirit River 3-D Prismatic size 5.0 (5/16 inch)

Glue: 30-minute epoxy; Zap-A-Gap; Hard as Nails

Spray paint: OMC Johnson 1957-59, Outboard Green; and Hammerite Rust Cap, Hammered Light Blue

Finish: Softex

Back flash: Diamond Dust gold-ultra fine Glitter

Hook: Owner AKI 6/0

Step 1: After putting the assembled tube body with cone on your vise, build a thread base 1 inch long on the polyethylene starting right behind the cone head. Apply Zap-A-Gap.

Step 2: On top of the tube, tie down the butt of the first comb close to the back of the cone head, with the tip pointing towards the nose of the fly, and the braid's curve facing down. Tie the butt of the second comb on top of the first, so the two combs stand side by side. Repeat with the other five combs. Whip finish and Zap-A-Gap.

Step 3: Continue through Step 5 of the basic Squishy Fish instructions. Poke the tips of fine-jawed, curved forceps through mesh along the back seam 1 inch from the nose of the cone head (for a 3 1/2-inch fly). Take hold of the tail end of the fly, and push the single layer of Flexo forward a little, expanding the mesh. Use the forceps to pull the first comb through the mesh. Follow it with the other combs along a 3/4-inch length of back seam.

Step 4: Take hold of the forward section of Flexo and push it back, inverting the material over itself (turning it inside out). You are making a body of two layers of Flexo. Be sure to press the front (with the small-diameter Nylaflow tubing) back firmly and evenly to create a tight, neat nose on the fly.

Step 5: Grasp the doubled Flexo at the tail end of the fly, and push it forward until you get the desired profile, fat or skinny, of your baitfish imitation. By feel, locate the lip melted into the aft end of the tubing, and tie down the Flexo just forward of it. Use firm wraps and several half hitches to secure the body at the rear. Coat the wraps with Softex, and trim the thread.

Step 6: Use your forceps to reach through the second layer of Flexo and draw the combs out through the top layer of mesh. The first comb should come through 1 inch from the nose of the fly; the last should come out about 3/4 inch from the first.

Step 7: Remove the fly from your vise. Trim the Nylaflow tubing at the nose of the fly. Trim combs to about 2 inches long.

Step 8: Mask off the comb with tape before you dip the fly in Softex. Wipe off any Softex that gets on it. Drain and blot the Softex, same as for the Squishy Fish.

Step 9: Leave the masking tape on the comb, mask the sides and belly, and spray on the light blue back color. If you're going to spray paint the dark stripes, first cut out a template. There are four stripes on each side, as shown.

BETSY BULLARD

Fishing with Golfito Sailfish Rancho Captains Maudiel Quiros (left) and Geovanny Concepcion (right), Mark Mandell (center) caught this estimated 45-pound roosterfish on a Seattle Saltwater popper at Punta Burica, Costa Rica in July 2001.

Step 10: When the stripes are dry, remove all tape and trim the combs to length. Apply a tiny drop of Zap-A-Gap to the ends of the braid to keep them from unraveling. Use a black permanent marker to color the combs. Immature roosters have random white stripes on their combs.

Step 11: Brush the fly's back (but not the comb) with a light coat of Hard as Nails and while it is still wet carefully sprinkle on a little bit of Glitter. Hard as Nails reacts unfavorably with black permanent marker ink, turning it a mottled reddish brown.

Mark Mandell and I collaborated on this variation on the basic Squishy Fish design. The pull-through-the mesh technique we developed can be used to create realistic and mobile fins for a variety of baitfish imitations.

Dorado inhale Squishies.

The Squishy Fish Threadfin uses the same pull-through technique as the Rooster. A natural threadfin herring's body is very narrow from side to side, and deep from back to belly. To get this effect with Flexo, use your thumbnail to flatten the material's natural crease, top and bottom. To get a deeper, faster sink with this somewhat bulkier fly, use two or more cone heads. The natural curve of the 1/4-inch polyethylene coupled with this fly's extra-wide body makes it spin and flutter erratically on a fast retrieve like a stunned bait. To prevent line twist put a small, black swivel between the leader and the class tippet.

SQUISHY THREAD FIN HERRING

Tube: A three-part assembly: 2 inches of (Nylaflow) 1/8-inch O. D. hard plastic; 3/8 inch of 1/8-inch I. D. / 3/16-inch O. D. soft vinyl; and 4 1/4 inch of 1/4-inch O. D. polyethylene for a 5 1/2-inch baitfish. The length of polyethylene determines the length of the finished fly.
Thread: UNI-mono thread, medium/clear
Nose weight: 7/16-inch diameter cone head (1 or more)
Body: Flexo Chrome Mylar, 1/2 inch wide, 15 inches long
Comb: Seven 5-inch lengths of 30-pound braided nylon loop material, marked with olive permanent marker
Eyes: Yellow or silver Spirit River 3D Prismatic stick-on size 6.0 (3/8 inch)
Glue: 30-minute epoxy; Zap-A-Gap; Hard as Nails
Spray paint: OMC Johnson 1957-59, Outboard Green; Zynolyte Super Metal, Super Brass
Finish: Softex
Back flash: Diamond Dust gold ultra fine Glitter
Hook: Owner AKI 6/0

SEATTLE SALTWATER POPPER: BLUE AND WHITE

Tube: HMH 1/8-inch O. D., 1 1/4 inch long; 1 inch of silicone tubing as a hook sleeve
Thread: UNI-mono thread, medium/clear
Flash tail: Pearl Flashabou and fine silver holographic tinsel
Wing: All tied in cove style: 5 or 6 long white saddle hackles to a side; topped by 2 kingfisher blue saddles; topped by a blue-dyed grizzly saddle.
Collar: White bucktail, 3 layers, each veiled with pearl Flashabou
Back: Light blue Krystal Flash
Glue: Zap-A-Gap
Finish: 30-minute epoxy
Popper head: Seattle Saltwater blue and white foam, 3/4 inch
Eyes: Yellow doll's eyes, 5/16 inch

This fly, sample in the plate tied by Mark Mandell, has caught many Costa Rican roosterfish, including an estimated 45-pounder in 2001 at Golfito Sailfish Rancho. Mark learned to tie poppers by looking over the shoulder of one of the all-time tube-fly masters, Joe Butorac.

MARTIN JOERGENSEN

Copenhagen, Denmark

In Scandinavia, tube flies are more common than most places, but beyond the Danish sea-trout streams and Norwegian and Swedish salmon rivers the concept is not as widely accepted as you might think. My day-to-day — and favorite — fishing primarily targets sea trout in the ocean around my country. Wade-fishing from the beach, I cannot recall having seen tubes on tippets other than my own in the pursuit of these beauties.

I have been fly-fishing for about 20 years now and have tied my own flies almost from the beginning. My daytime job has been in computers and computer journalism for a couple of decades, too, so it was very natural for me to combine my interests: fly-fishing, writing, photography, and computers. I have contributed to fly-fishing and fly-tying magazines in Europe and the U. S., and about 10 years ago I put together my first web page on fly-fishing. This has since developed into The Global FlyFisher.com, one of the largest and most popular web sites on the subject. Together with three American friends I continue to develop and expand the site.

Tube flies have always fascinated me. I like to experiment, and tubes are a perfect platform for experimentation because they eliminate the creative restrictions of hook length and shank

diameter. My very favorite pattern is the Muddler with its spun deer hair head, and some of my best tubes have been voluminous flies tied with Muddler heads.

Although most of my tube patterns are traditional in appearance and tying methods, some of the unique tube flies seen on salmon rivers like the Mörrum in Sweden inspired me to try something different. The original Mörrum flies tubes were made from aluminium or copper stock lathed or machined down to a bottle-like shape. This concentrates weight at the head of the fly and improves action, and a conical front end makes for a nice wing shape and angle, and a small, neat head.

The original Mörrum bottles were interesting, but they lacked front collars; a collar facilitates close, secure tying at the head. And the rear ends of the tubes were too large in diameter to accept silicone hook sleeves. I thought I could improve on the basic design. In 1999, I started a joint venture with André Fournier Bidoz, the French manufacturer of beads and cone heads, to produce a short, bottle-shaped tube with a front collar and a small-diameter rear end to fit a hook sleeve. In 2000, André started manufacturing these tubes in two lengths, 15 mm and 22 mm, and two weights, brass and

Clockwise from top right: SHCZCDNTM; CZCDNTM; The Inkspot (orange); Dustball Tube; The Plipper; The Inkspot (green); The Inkspot (purple); Tube Louse

Captains Jeremias Cerdas and Maudiel Quiros with a red and white Plipper-caught blue trevally off Coiba Island, Panama

MARK MANDELL

no vise. Now, I even leave out the glue, using pliers to tighten the straps, and I insert the hook directly into the plastic tube instead using a piece of silicone for a hook sleeve. Why do I call this fly "The Plipper"? Take a popper, give it a lip, and what do you get? One of my most successful sea-trout patterns is a foam diver based on this pike fly, but scaled down to fit a smaller mouth.

SHCZCDNTM (SHORT HEAVY CHICAGO-ZÜRICH-COPENHAGEN DELAYED NUTRIA TUBE MUDDLER)

Tube: Bidoz 15 mm brass bottle tube
Liner tube: Thin plastic
Thread: Brown
Wing: Nutria, mink or similar fur cut as a zonker strip
Thorax: Red or copper Lite Brite (optional)
Collar: Stacked natural deer hair
Head: Spun and trimmed deer hair
Hook: Single, double, or treble, size 4 or 6

Step 1: Before you start tying you must line the metal tube with plastic. Failing to do so will cost you your fly within the first few casts because the metal tube will cut your tippet. Thread the inner plastic tube through the metal tube, and heat it with a lighter or candle to form a small collar. Pull the liner snug as it cools off and trim the opposite end to about 2 mm outside the metal tube. Heat this end to form a second collar, effectively holding the inner tube tight. Be careful not to overheat the plastic. That will narrow or fully close its thin hole, which the tippet is supposed to pass through.

Step 2: After having secured the tube in your vise, attach the thread on the rear edge of the sloping front part of the bottle tube.

Step 3: Prepare a zonker strip from nutria or mink skin two to 3 mm wide and 1 1/2 times the tube length.

Step 4: Tie down the strip with the hairs sloping to the rear of the fly. You might want to add some varnish or super glue to secure it.

Step 5: Add a small ring of red or copper flash dubbing over the base of the strip. This step is optional, but adds a nice touch to the fly.

Step 6: Prepare a bunch of natural deer hair. Select hair with natural light and dark striped tips and a length of no more than 3 cm or a little more than an inch.

Step 7: Remove any under fur and stack the hair in a hair stacker to even the tips. Trim the butts to a length a bit longer than the tube. Position the hair on the middle of the sloping part of the tube with the thread passing over the bunch one-third from the butts. Pass the thread lightly around the hair in the same spot three times. On the third pass tighten the thread and let go of the hair to flare and spin it. Ideally it forms an even collar around the tube.

Step 8: Prepare an additional two or three bunches of hair. Trim the tips before tying them in and press them hard to the rear of the fly to form a Muddler head.

aluminium. Since then I have tied many patterns on these tubes and I am happy to say the Bidoz product has been well received, and that André has added different colors and extension tubes. The product line is still in development, and André and I regularly correspond to play around with new ideas.

My fly boxes for sea trout seem to accumulate small aluminium bottle tubes, like the Dustball and Inkspot, which are easy to cast on a light rod and still have some remarkable capabilities for penetrating the surface and getting to a fishing depth in an instant without snagging up.

The Plipper is a result of my obsession to create an inexpensive, easy to tie, and durable fly for pike. My first attempts were dressed on large hooks, but on the first strike the foam shredded to bits and the flies were trashed. I switched to tying on tubes because ruined flies could be discarded without losing the hook. I wound up punching and folding a strip of foam to form a lip, a forehead, and a body in one step. Early models had a rabbit-strip tail, but it turned out that omitting the tail made no difference to the pike. Prototypes were tied with tying thread, but whip finishing and varnishing was more effort than I wanted to put into this fly, so I started attaching the foam on the tubes with plastic tie straps used for binding together electrical wiring. A couple of drops of super glue, two plastic ties and I was done — no thread,

Step 9: Whip finish in front of the last bunch behind the front collar on the tube. Varnish or glue liberally and let dry.

Step 10: Trim the head using a pair of serrated scissors. If you can trim away the deer-hair collar under the fly to reveal the flash dubbing and leave room for a single or double hook.

Step 11: Attach a small piece of silicone tubing to the rear of the fly and insert a hook of your choice.

This fly is very simple in its construction and quite easy to tie. It builds on the CZCDNTM (Chicago-Zurich-Copenhagen Delayed Nutria Tube Muddler) below, which in turn builds on a pattern I did many years ago called the Full Metal Jacket Nutria Muddler, or FMJNM for short. Nutria Muddlers have over the years become an obsession with me — I have made a large number of variations — and in a weak moment I might be tempted to call them my signature pattern. Nutria Muddlers are close to perfect sculpin imitations with lots of mobility and profile. I fish this fly on a floating or intermediate line and let the fly do the sinking. I use downstream, quartering casts followed by upstream mends to get the fly down, or straight casts and steady strips in still water.

CZCDNTM
(CHICAGO-ZÜRICH-COPENHAGEN DELAYED NUTRIA TUBE MUDDLER)

Tube: Plastic 1/8-inch O. D., 2 inches long, with silicone hook sleeve
Thread: Brown
   Rib: Medium oval silver tinsel
   Body: Flat silver Mylar tinsel
   Wing: Nutria, mink, or similar fur cut as a zonker strip, 2 1/4 inches long
   Collar: Stacked natural deer hair
   Head: Spun and trimmed deer hair

This large fly is well suited for hunting big trout or sea trout at night. Fish it on the surface with a floating line. I sometimes grease my Muddlers to keep them floating high. I haven't tried the fly with a sinking line, but others have. Floating fly, sinking line can be a killer combination.

TUBE LOUSE

Tube: Bidoz 15 mm aluminium bottle tube
Liner tube: Thin plastic
   Thread: Black
Rear hackle: Brown mottled hen
   Body: Black tying thread
   Wing: Black Arctic fox
   Throat: Hot orange Arctic fox
Front hackle: Brown mottled hen
   Head: Black tying thread

This is a generic, dark-colored salmon pattern for light-line, deep fishing.

DUSTBALL TUBE

Tube: Bidoz 15 mm aluminum bottle tube
Liner tube: Thin plastic
   Thread: Tan
   Body: Tan dubbing
Front hackle: Tan hen, short
   Head: Tan thread

This is one of my tube patterns for sea-run sea trout. Small and neutral as it may seem, the trout love flies like this.

THE INKSPOT

Tube: Bidoz 15 mm aluminium bottle tube
Liner tube: Thin plastic
   Thread: Black
   Wing: Arctic fox, color of choice
Front hackle: Grizzly hen
   Head: Black thread

This universal small pattern can be used on anything that swims, and must be fished deep. With variations in wing color (yellow, orange, chartreuse, etc.), it can be adapted to most situations calling for a small, heavy fly.

THE PLIPPER

Tube: Plastic 1/8-inch O. D., 1 1/2 to 2 inches long, with silicone hook sleeve if necessary
Foam: Colorful closed-cell foam, 1.5 mm (about 1/16 inch) thick, cut into 5/8-inch-wide, 5 1/2-inch-long strips
Glue: Super glue (optional)
Plastic electrical (cable) ties: The self-locking kind, used to bundle wiring, as small as you can find.

The Plipper is a fly meant for pike, and the choice of hook and hook style should reflect this. This sheet-foam popper fly was designed with two things in mind: easy-use-and-throw-away-construction, and large pike!

All my flies can be armed with treble, double or single hooks, according to personal taste. I prefer the Partridge tube-fly trebles size 4, 6 or 8 depending on the size and dressing of the fly, but the Loop double is a worthy alternative. For single hooks I find that many short-shank carp or saltwater hooks work well. I almost always use soft plastic or silicone tubing, clear or colored (see page 111) to hold the hook eye unless it fits into the rear of the tube itself.

TIM JOHNSON
Sheboygan, Wisconsin

I fly-fish many of the tributaries of Lake Michigan which have good fall runs of king and silver salmon, brown trout, seeforellen, the occasional lake trout, and lake run, brook trout of three to four pounds. In summer I fish local rivers and lakes for bass, bluegill, northern pike and muskellunge, and the spring creeks of western Wisconsin for trout. I do a little salmon guiding in the fall, and I hunt deer, black bear, turkeys, and small game. I use the collected skins and feathers to augment my supply of tying materials.

I was introduced to fly-tying by a friend, Tom Weber, in 1981, and I've been at it ever since. I started with streamers, bucktails, and trout flies. I got into steelhead flies in the early 1980's because we have excellent runs of these fish in the spring. I began tying salmon flies about nine years ago.

I became interested in tube flies because they save money. I tie an awful lot of flies, and at almost a dollar apiece for large hooks that really adds up. Because I'm not buying all those extra hooks, I'm able to put away a little extra cash for fly-tying materials, shotguns and shells, and on rare occasions, a night out with my lovely wife, Penny.

I started to include tube flies in my vest in the mid-1980's when I began tying for trolling trips on Lake Michigan with friends and family. I now tie traditional, full-dress salmon patterns on tubes, as well as many of my own creations, and Rangley (Carrie Stevens style) streamers — about a third of all my flies. If you can tie it on a hook, you can tie it on a tube!

I adjust the sink rate of my flies by using different tube materials. I get aluminum, copper, and brass tubing from the local hardware store and cut it with an inexpensive tubing cutter. Then I finish the tubes by flaring them with a reamer, small jewelers' files, and sandpaper. I don't line my metal tubes with plastic. When properly smoothed and polished the edges won't cut a leader. All of equipment that I use for my tubes is of the hardware and hobby store variety — nothing fancy.

My favorite tube flies? That's like asking a parent to choose his favorite child! I love them all, but if I'm pressed, I do have a few patterns that I'm partial to: Undertaker, Orange Heron, Grey Ghost, and Spey flies such as the Deep Purple Spey, Purple King, and Claret Spey are the meat and potatoes of my arsenal. Colors that I've found to be really good on Lake Michigan are champagne and watermelon, root beer, purple, black, blues, whites, and greens. I use these colors in a number of combinations. My favorite fly is the one that works!

In local streams, the best colors seem to vary from year to year. One year the color may be purple, and another it may be black, or black and blue, or orange. One of my friends fishes a variation of a Polar Shrimp almost exclusively. Other effective patterns are Coal Cars, Freight Trains, Undertakers, Hairy Marys, and Green Butt Skunks. I tie all of these on tubes, and vary the

Clockwise from top left: Fish Me Spey; Steinberg; Eye Candy; First Edition; Black Ice; Penny's Pride; Mixed Feelings

size and type of hook according to the size and type of species, and local regulations. I vary the size of the tube, too. Sometimes smaller is better.

To fish for the king and silver salmon in the fall I use 14- and 15-foot, two-handed Spey rods in 10- and 11-weight. Big Spey rods handle heavy tube flies with ease. I also use 8-, 9-, and 10-weight, single-handed fly rods of nine to ten feet for steelhead and large lake-run brown trout in the spring and fall. I've found a mini-lead-head to be effective when used with a floating line and a nine- to ten-foot leader in rivers. Braided leaders work well and in my experience they last a lot longer than tapered monofilament leaders. I also like weight-forward lines, shooting heads, and Spey lines.

I fish tube flies in streams as you would any wet fly: quartering down and across, stripping at various rates, depending on current and the depth of the water. When necessary, I modify the fly depth with sink tips, lead-heads, or split shot.

When fish are near the surface on Lake Michigan, I use sink tips made of sections of lead-core from 6 to 12 feet long. This allows me to fine tune my depth and get to where the fish are. If you're concerned about line-twist, use a swivel and take the silicone sleeve off of the tube fly. Problem solved. When we fish tube flies with conventional spinning and casting gear, we use downriggers, dodgers, and planer boards.

In the summer months on Lake Michigan I switch over to heavy saltwater casting, or "boat" rods with large trolling reels loaded with three or four hundred feet of 17- to 25-pound-test line, either braided or mono. Using this gear I troll tubes on downriggers, dodgers, and planer boards. Browns, lake trout, and landlocked salmon provide plenty of excitement and really keep you busy when they take the tube fly of the day!

I owe much to the input of Ed Strzelczyk, George Close, Jack Bauman, and Royce Dam for the success of my patterns and improvements in my fly-tying.

BLACK ICE

Tube: Brass 1/8-inch O. D., 3 inches long, with silicone hook sleeve
Thread: Black
Tag: Fine gold oval tinsel
Body: Black floss
Ribbing: Flat gold tinsel and fine gold oval tinsel, tied in a diamond pattern
Throat: Black bucktail or black bear
Underwing: Black bucktail
Wing: Four black neck hackles
Sides: Blue peacock body feathers, two to a side
Cheeks: Jungle cock
Head: Black thread
Finish: Hard as Nails, two or three coats

Step 1: Select tubing appropriate to your quarry and the type of water you'll be fishing, i.e. heavy tubing for deep trolling or heavy current.

Step 2: Install a 3-inch-long tube on your tube-fly tool. Tie on a tag of gold oval tinsel, make four to five wraps, tie off, but do not trim. Leave at least 4 inches of tinsel at the tag end. This is used for the diamond wrap later.

Step 3: Tie in a 4-inch piece of flat gold tinsel for the rib and let it hang.

Step 4: Tie in four-strand black floss at the front of the fly. Wind it back to the tag, then wrap forward to the front of the fly, leaving 1/4 to 3/8 inch for the head. Tie off floss and trim excess.

Step 5: Wrap the flat gold tinsel rib in equally spaced increments toward the front of the fly. Tie off and trim.

Step 6: Reverse-wind the oval tinsel over the first rib in equal segments to create a diamond pattern. This reinforces the ribbing so it doesn't unwind after a big fish takes it. Tie it off at the point where the first rib is tied in and trim.

Step 7: Tie in a black bucktail throat on the underside of the tube. The throat should be about 3/4 inch longer than the tube. This is a rough measurement, nothing is cast in stone. I tend to vary things according to the pattern I'm tying.

Step 8: On top of the tube, tie in an under wing of black bucktail, about the same length as the throat. The bucktail supports the wing and gives it a nice silhouette. I apply a little super glue on the tie-in point, and it doesn't hurt to add a whip finish or two half hitches, either.

Step 9: For the wing, tie in four long black neck or saddle hackles, the same length as the under wing. Strip the barbs off at the tie-in point of each feather and place two per side, with the "good" (shiny) side facing out.

Step 10: Add two 1-inch-long blue peacock body feathers to each side for shoulders. Locate the feathers with two or three loose wraps and manipulate them so that they lie in an upright position. A little trick you can use here is to squish the quill. Use a hemostat or similar tool to flatten the quill so that it will not roll on the tube.

Step 11: Next add two jungle cock eyes, one per side, for the cheeks. A length of about 3/4 inch should be about right.

Step 12: Finally, tie a small neat head and whip finish. My head cement choice for these flies is Sally Hansen's Hard as Nails nail polish. Give the head of the fly two or three coats for a nice shiny, smooth finish.

I tie this fly and the others that follow in sizes equivalent to a Partridge Carrie Stevens 10XL H/W Streamer Hook. I use heavier tubes in high water, lighter tubes in slack water. I downsize the flies if I am fishing for stream trout, smallmouth bass, and pan fish. I increase the size of the tube fly for muskies and pike.

On my tubes, I like beak hooks (short shank 0X) in sizes 2, 4, 6, etc. from Tiemco, Daichi, Partridge, Mustad, VMC, Eagle Claw, and Gamakatsu. I experimented with making my own hooks, but didn't do too well with that. Now I just stick with the manufactured variety. I vary the size of the hook according to the size of my quarry. I use micro aquarium hose (1/8-inch O.D.) for all my hook sleeves.

FIRST EDITION

Tube: Copper 1/8-inch O. D., 2 inches long, with silicone hook sleeve
Thread: Black
Tag: Silver oval tinsel and orange floss, equal lengths
Tail: Golden pheasant crest and two small guinea fowl feathers
Butt: Black ostrich herl
Body: Dark green floss 2/3 of body, bright green dubbing 1/3 of body
Rib: Medium oval silver tinsel and fine oval silver tinsel, wrapped in diamond pattern
Palmer: Soft black hackle over body's bright green dubbing section
Throat: Silver doctor blue over black hackle
Wing: Two teal feathers over two guinea feathers
Topping: Golden pheasant crest
Cheeks: Jungle cock
Head: Black thread
Finish: Hard as Nails, two or three coats

FISH ME SPEY

Tube: Brass 3/32-inch O. D., 1 3/4 inch long, with silicone hook sleeve
Thread: Black
Body: Fine oval gold tinsel 2/3 body; orange dubbing 1/3 of body
Palmer: Orange hackle wound through dubbing only
Rib: Fine oval gold tinsel wound through dubbing
Throat: Blue ear pheasant hackle under teal or gadwall
Wing: Four orange hackles
Cheeks: White tipped wood duck
Head: Black thread
Finish: Hard as Nails, two or three coats

MIXED FEELINGS SPEY

Tube: Brass 3/32-inch O. D., 2 1/4 inches long, with silicone hook sleeve
Thread: Black
Tag: 1/3 fine oval gold tinsel, 2/3 orange floss
Body: Black floss
Rib: Flat gold tinsel and fine gold oval tinsel, in diamond braid pattern
Throat: Gadwall over blue ear pheasant hackle or gray heron
Wing: Peacock wing quill or turkey quill

Cheeks: Jungle cock
Head: Black thread
Finish: Hard as Nails, two or three coats

STEINBERG

Tube: Aluminum 1/8-inch O. D., 3 inches long, with silicone hook sleeve
Thread: Black
Tag: Fine gold oval tinsel
Body: Black floss
Rib: Flat gold tinsel and fine gold oval tinsel, in diamond braid pattern
Throat: Black bucktail or black bear
Underwing: Black bucktail or black bear
Wing: Four black neck hackles
Sides: Red golden pheasant feather tied over a ring-necked pheasant rump feather, each side
Cheeks: Jungle cock
Head: Black thread
Finish: Hard as Nails, two or three coats

EYE CANDY

Tube: Aluminum 1/8-inch O. D., 3 inches long, with silicone hook sleeve
Thread: Black
Tag: Fine oval gold tinsel
Body: 2/3 yellow floss, 1/3 magenta floss
Rib: Flat gold tinsel
Throat: Light orange bucktail
Underwing: Yellow bucktail
Wing: Four chartreuse saddle hackles
Sides: Lemon woodduck feathers
Cheeks: Teal breast feathers
Head: Black thread
Finish: Hard as Nails, two or three coats

PENNY'S PRIDE

Tube: Aluminum 1/8-inch O. D., 3 inches long, with silicone hook sleeve
Thread: Black
Tag: Fine gold oval tinsel
Body: Peacock green floss
Rib: Flat gold tinsel and fine oval gold tinsel, in diamond braid pattern
Throat: Yellow bucktail
Underwing: Yellow bucktail
Wing: Four yellow neck hackles
Sides: Two per side blue peacock body feathers
Cheeks: Jungle cock
Head: Black thread
Finish: Hard as Nails, two or three coats

BOB KENLY

Table Rock Lake, Missouri

LINDA NEWLAND

I was born in Brooklyn, New York, in 1935, but moved with my family to northeastern New Jersey in 1940. Back then, New Jersey was a vastly different place. There were clear streams and wide forests that afforded plenty of opportunities for a kid to fish and hunt. My parents bought me a fly-tying kit when I was still in grammar school, this to go along with the $15 (an enormous sum in that day) cane rod I had up saved for from my paper route. After that first introduction to fly-tying I was forever hooked. My tying materials came from a local farmer who generously supplied me with chicken, turkey, and goose feathers.

After high school graduation, and a stint in the Army, I went to technical school and became an airline mechanic. Career and family ended my fly-fishing and tying for many years, but I never lost interest. In June of 1995 my wife and I retired to southwestern Missouri's Ozark Mountains on Table Rock Lake, where she could pursue her watercolor art and I could tie flies and fish.

The tube patterns I design are commercially produced to my specifications on a custom basis by another tier. Although we specialize in flies for Alaska and eastern Russia (Kamchatka), we also develop patterns to fill clients' special needs. Our customers want something better design and construction than can be found through the usual sources, and we spend considerable time talking to the client to ascertain what he/she wants and expects.

After a client returns from a trip we do a follow-up to see if we can improve our products and services.

My interest in tube flies started in 1992 after reading *Salmon Flies and How to Tie Them* by Poul Joergensen. One of the chapters mentioned their popularity in Scandinavia and made me want to tie up a few, just to see what they were like. Without a clue how they were constructed or fished I bought some tubes from Kennebec River (HMH) Fly and Tackle and started tying. In 1995, Mark Mandell and Les Johnson's book, *Tube Flies*, as published and it answered a lot of my lingering questions. For more than ten years I've tied flies exclusively on tubes. My number one reason for using them is that I don't have to carry bulky fly boxes. I do just fine with a few baggies of flies and a small box of hooks in assorted sizes.

For my heaviest tubes, I use HMH 1/8-inch O. D. copper. My medium-weight tubes are tied on Gordon Griffiths 1/8-inch O. D. lined brass, which I cut to length as needed. For a lighter brass tube, I use Rooney (See Chapter 25: Tanya Rooney) Tube Works 3/32-inch O. D. These are unlined metal, with flared and polished ends to eliminate wear on the leader. The Rooney 1 inch tube is a joy to tie on and fish. HMH makes an even lighter 3/32-inch O. D. aluminum tube that I'm fond of as well. This tube is produced in 1/4-inch increments so I don't have to remanufacture the tube to get the length I want.

Clockwise from top left: Go-Go Girl; The Belly Gunner Shrimp; Linda's Shrimp;
The Homer Roach (fresh water); The Homer Roach (salt water); The Purple Hays

I buy HMH's 3/32-inch O. D. Freshwater tubes by the gross, and I tie hundreds of flies on them. Their fine diameter and 5-inch length is great for all sorts of applications. I generally leave the tube a little longer than required, which allows me room to make a perfect fly each time without crowding at the end. When I'm done I simply cut off the excess tube at the nose of the fly. Mark Mandell started me tying on tiny 1/16-inch O. D. Teflon tubing, and together we worked out some of the bugs in its application. Teflon can be difficult to tie on because of its flexibility and susceptibility to crushing, but it does make a very nice, very small tube fly.

Until Ashima stopped manufacturing them, I used their C-887 hooks on all my tubes. Now I've switched over to the Daiichi X510, which I find a viable substitute. Peter Thornley of Preston, England, introduced me to double 180-degree hooks made from standard Mustad 3551 trebles. The third hook (the separate one) is broken off, and the remaining two are bent until they are 180 degrees apart, in the same plane as the hook eye. For Alaska fishing I've found them a big improvement over single hooks which have a tendency to snag instead of fair hooking tightly packed salmon.

All of my tube flies are tied with epoxy to add longevity. I've developed several coloring techniques for this adhesive. After I form the fly head with 5-minute epoxy and allow it to dry, I lightly sand the head with fine sandpaper and paint it with white acrylic artist's paint, or the color I intend the head to be. For the second coat I mix 2-Ton epoxy with a small amount of denatured alcohol to thin the mixture. Alcohol also slows down the drying a bit to give me time to work. I then add a small amount of artist's acrylic color to the epoxy and mix well. Should the epoxy/paint mixture become too stiff I add more alcohol. I apply this mixture to the head. To make a variegated effect, I take a small amount of artists acrylic paint (that includes glow-in-the-dark colors if desired) on a toothpick and apply small amounts to the wet epoxy in a random pattern, and put it on a drying wheel. I cover the

completed head with a final coat of clear 2-Ton epoxy to protect the head and give it a nice finish.

Although I'm certainly not the first to tie on tubes using sequins I have invented several fly-rod patterns using this technique. I remanufacture Gordon Griffiths "Bottle Tubes" to make them more like the Swedish Mörrum style tubes. Although the lip on the improved bottles keeps materials from sliding off, I didn't like tying on a sloped platform, and the lip tended to crowd materials. Once I mastered the Mörrum style I found it much easier to get the results I wanted. I redrill the machined tube to accept a 3/32-inch liner made from a plastic HMH Freshwater tube, I then chuck the tube in my drill press and file off the lip to make a smooth transition to the inserted plastic tube.

I tie for all species of Pacific salmon, and for steelhead and Dolly Varden. Several Alaskan friends test my latest designs and offer their opinions before the patterns are offered for sale. Depending on water flow and clarity, my colors range from the very bright pinks, oranges, greens, white, and purples to the dark shades, particularly black. Pacific salmon can be moody beasts, often requiring a fly in the face to trigger a strike so flies must be carefully weighted to match the prevailing conditions. As a general rule I follow "bright flies for bright days, dark flies for overcast days," but since salmon don't read rules a good color selection is always wise. My Alaska flies are usually fished with an intermediate sinking line, a three-foot leader, and stripped according to the water conditions.

My flies can be purchased through my web site: http://go.to/nordicway

THE PURPLE HAYS

Tube: Brass 1/8-inch O. D., lined, 1 1/4 inches long, with silicone hook sleeve

Thread: Clear nylon sewing thread and purple 8/0

Tail: Eight strands of pearl Krystal Flash, 2 1/2 inches long; two purple rabbit strips, 2 inches long

Body: Purple Body Glitter (metallic braid from Gordon Griffiths)

Ribbing: Fine silver holographic tinsel

Collar: Two purple schlappen hackles, folded and wound together

Egg: Small, hot pink chenille, two wraps

Epoxy: Devcon 2-Ton 30-minute

Hook: Size 4 to 1/0 single, or 180-degree double (See Tying Instructions)

Step 1: Place lined brass tube on your tube tool with a hook sleeve installed. Attach purple thread.

Step 2: Tie in four strands of Krystal Flash 180 degrees apart on either side of the hook sleeve.

Step 3: Tie the rabbit strips directly over the Krystal Flash, skin sides facing inward. Whip finish and trim thread.

Step 4: Attach clear nylon thread and tie in the ribbing and Body Glitter. Advance the thread. Wind on the Body Glitter, leaving enough space forward for the collar and egg. Tie off and trim excess Body Glitter.

Step 5: Wind the ribbing forward and tie it down. Cut off excess ribbing and whip finish.

Step 6: Cover the body and the thread wraps on the hook sleeve with epoxy. Place on a drying wheel and cure overnight.

Step 7: Attach purple thread and tie in the two schlappen hackles by the tips, fold them together and wind to achieve a dense, swept back collar. Tie down stems, trim excess feather, and put a thin coat of epoxy on the thread wraps.

Kamchatka char caught on a Kenly tube fly.

Step 8: After the wraps are dry, tie in a piece of pink chenille and make two wraps forward, tie off, trim excess, and cover the remaining exposed tube with thread. Whip finish. Trim thread. Epoxy the wraps and let dry.

The Purple Hays is the one fly I wouldn't think of going to Alaska without; in fact it's probably one of the most effective flies I've ever tied. It started out as a shrimp pattern but when I showed it to an Alaskan friend he said it would be better if I made it into something more like an Egg Sucking Leech. Since his name is Hays, I named the fly after him. Purple isn't the only color I tie it in. but among my clients it's the most popular. Being tied with liberal amounts of epoxy and without a traditionally wound hackle, the Hays is almost "bomb proof." Some of my customers have been using the same fly for three years!

Where such hooks are allowed, such as the Kenai River, double opposed hooks are a very effective alternative to trebles. They are easily fabricated from standard trebles. Simply cut off the welded tang, removing one of the three hooks, then bend the other two to form a 180-degree double. This is a common practice in the UK. Besides better lip-hooking characteristics, the horizontally set points snag fewer salmon when they are tightly packed in rivers.

GO-GO GIRL

Tube: Plastic clear HMH 3/32-inch O. D. (fresh water), 2 1/2 inches long, with silicone hook sleeve. Excess tube is cut off after the fly is finished.

Thread: Hot pink 8/0 or 6/0

Tail: Hot pink marabou

Rear body: Hot pink thread, tied over 1/4 inch of the tube end of hook sleeve, covered with 2-Ton epoxy

Sequins: Silver, three to a side, covered with 2-Ton epoxy

Bead: Faceted 4 mm in hot pink, drilled to 3/32 inch and covered with 2-Ton epoxy

Wing: Hot pink marabou

Topping: Pearl Krystal Flash

Beard: Hot pink marabou

Eyes: Doll's eyes, 1/4-inch diameter, attached first with Goop to hold them in place, then I use 5-minute epoxy to fill the gaps between the eyes. I paint the filled gaps with artist's acrylic paint and cover the area and the eyes with 2-Ton epoxy to protect them.

Cone head: Black 3/16-inch diameter, hole drilled out to 3/32 inch (if necessary). Melt the end of the tube into a collar to hold on the cone.

Epoxy: Devcon 5-minute and Devcon 2 Ton

Hook: Size 6 or 4

I use 5-minute epoxy for shaping and initial gluing steps, but because it lacks strength and tends to yellow and lose clarity, I re-coat with 2-Ton epoxy. I always wrap thread on my hook sleeves where the sleeve and main tube overlap and cover the thread with epoxy during the construction process. Unlike many tiers who use the hook connector merely to hold the hook, I incorporate the connector into the design, a decision driven by aesthetics.

A lot of fishermen who travel to Alaska seem to shun fishing for chum or pink salmon, but these fish can provide great action when other salmon species are absent or have a case of lockjaw. I first saw a hook-tied version of the Go-Go Girl in 1995 while fishing silver salmon on Alaska's Kuskokwim River. My guide had one ragged specimen he said came from a client residing in Washington State. The idea of using sequins on a fly was new to me. It took a long time to work out a procedure to convert the Go-Go Girl to a tube, but as an Alaskan friend told me, "Silly fish break their necks to hit this fly."

LINDA'S SHRIMP

Tube: Plastic HMH clear 3/32-inch O. D. (fresh water), 2 inches long, with silicone hook sleeve. Excess tube is cut off after the fly is finished.

Thread: Bright orange

Tail/feelers: Light orange marabou or dyed yak hair, 1 1/2 inches long

Antennae: Few strands of orange Pearly, a Gordon Griffiths product (Krystal Flash may be substituted), 2 1/4 inches long

Body: Lead wire covered with flat silver tinsel, covered with bright orange thread, ribbed with metallic thread or tinsel of choice, covered with 2-Ton epoxy

Eyes: Painted on with tiny dots of black acrylic paint. The whole body is then recoated with 2-Ton epoxy, to which a small amount of glitter has been added.

Beard: Bright orange Chinese cock

Wing: White yak hair, 1 inch long

Cone head: Brass 5/32-inch diameter, hole drilled out to
fit the 3/32-inch tube (if necessary). Melt protruding
end of tube to hold cone in place.
Hook: Size 6 or 4

*In 2001, an Alaskan customer asked for a small shrimp pattern she
could use on Dolly Varden in the lower Kenai Peninsula's Anchor
River. She wanted the fly to be small in size, bright in color and as
translucent as possible. My pattern is modeled on the Polar Shrimp,
but with a solid epoxy body wound with lead wire. The lead wire is
covered with silver tinsel and then overwrapped with bright thread.
The gaps in the thread allow the tinsel to show through; when covered in epoxy, this gives the body a translucent look. This is a very
effective tube fly for all Alaskan species. Other good colors are hot
pink, chartreuse, purple, black and a light shrimp pink.*

THE BELLY GUNNER SHRIMP

Tube: Teflon 1/16-inch O. D. for small flies, at least 2 inches
long; plastic HMH clear 3/32-inch O. D.
(fresh water) with silicone hook sleeve for larger
flies, same length
Thread: Bright green 6/0 and clear nylon sewing thread
Rear body: 3/8 inches of hook sleeve is covered with green
thread and epoxied.
Tail/feelers: Hairsprayed and brushed chartreuse marabou,
1 1/2 inches long, and chartreuse Krystal Flash or
Pearly, slightly longer
Eyes: Small black beads strung on clear leader material and
covered with epoxy
Legs: 1-inch-long clump of hairsprayed and brushed chartreuse marabou tied on bottom side of tube, in front
of epoxied thread rear body. Tie an additional clump
between each of the brass cones, and in front of the
last cone. Starting at the nose of the fly, trim the first
three of the five sets of legs at an angle to keep the
fly swimming upright. The first set should be about
1/4 inch long; the third set about 3/8 inch long. Last
two sets of legs remain full length.
Cone heads: Three 5/32-inch brass for the Teflon tube version;
three 3/16-inch brass drilled to fit for the Kennebec
River fresh water tube version
Shellback: Green Swiss straw covered with epoxy mixed with
sparse glitter
Hook: Size 6 or 4

*I developed the Belly Gunner Shrimp after being tutored in the art of
tying Russian Bullets by Jurij (Yuri) Shumakov (See Chapter 29:
Jurij Shumakov). I wanted to make a fly that looked like a shrimp,
swam like a shrimp, was very mobile in the water, and sank deep to
get in a salmon's face. The three-cone body concept pioneered by
Shumakov perfectly added both weight and shape. To strengthen
fragile marabou without reducing its mobility, I coat the flues with
hairspray, then brush them out on a flat surface with a toothbrush
until they are dry.*

*The name Belly Gunner Shrimp was chosen to honor Yuri's
father, a WWII Russian air crewman who survived the conflict from
the first day to the last.*

THE HOMER ROACH
(FRESHWATER VERSION)

Tube: Plastic HMH clear 3/32-inch O. D. (Freshwater),
2 1/2 inches long, with silicone hook sleeve. Excess
tube is cut off after the fly is finished.
Thread: Clear nylon sewing thread
Rear body: Hot pink thread covering 1/4 of hook sleeve.
Front of the body is undressed, clear tube.
Wing: Silver Flashabou tied 360 degrees around tube
Collar: Webby red hackle
Head: Lead wire covered with 5-minute epoxy, topcoated
with a layer of 2-Ton epoxy mixed with red acrylic
artist's paint
Eyes: Silver 3-D stick-on, 1/8-inch diameter. The head and
eyes are covered in clear 2-Ton epoxy.
Hook: Size 4 or 2

*This flash fly has great longevity because it's tied on a tube and all
the thread windings are hidden under the epoxy head. Purple, pink,
chartreuse, and black are also very effective color combinations.*

THE HOMER ROACH
(SALTWATER VERSION)

Tube: Plastic HMH clear 3/32-inch O. D. (fresh water)
5 inches long, with silicone hook sleeve. Hook on this
fly extends beyond the end of the wing. Excess tube
is cut off after the fly is finished
Thread: Clear nylon sewing thread
Wing: Silver Flashabou topped by green Flashabou, 50-50
proportion, tied on top of the tube
Collar: Two red Chinese cock hackles folded to give a swept-
back appearance
Head: Lead wire covered with 5-minute epoxy, covered with
2-Ton epoxy mixed with light green acrylic paint
Eyes: Silver 3-D stick-on, 1/4-inch diameter. Recoat the
head with clear 2-Ton epoxy mixed with glitter.
Hook: Size 4 for silvers; Size 2 for kings, either single hooks
or the preferred 180 degree double opposed hook

*I designed this fly for Kachemak Bay in Homer, Alaska. On an
incoming tide, salmon crowd the shoreline waiting for enough water
to enter the Homer Spit Lagoon. Stiff winds off the bay make fly
casting difficult, and depending on the height of the tide, currents
can be very strong. The Roach's 6-inch overall length and heavy
head help get it out to the fish. The fly has lots of movement in the
water thanks to all the Flashabou, and it resembles a small baitfish, which incoming salmon seem very aggressive toward. I refined
the pattern by moving the hook points slightly beyond the wing to
catch salmon that snap at the tails of baitfish as they swim past.*

NICK KINGSTON

Dublin, Ireland/Australia

NICK KINGSTON

I was born in Bristol, England, and my family moved to Invercargill, New Zealand when I was seven months old. I was five when we moved to Brisbane, Australia where I lived until June 2001 when I relocated to Dublin, Ireland, to work as a claims officer for an insurance company. Now back in Australia for a year, I am the salmon-fly advisor for www.aussiefly.com and the fly-tying editor for www.powerfibers.com.

I started fishing at age 14 and began fly-fishing three years later when a friend gave me an old fly rod he no longer used. I took up fly-tying when I was 18 after my parents bought me a starter kit for Christmas; before that I used the flies that my friend had tied.

Most of my Australian fishing was "bread and butter," the American equivalent would be blue gills or crappie, except this was in salt water. The target species were bream, whiting, flathead, and tailor (similar to bluefish), with the odd freshwater trip for snub-nosed garfish, spangled perch, tilapia, trout, and Australian bass — not the same species as largemouth or smallmouth, but they look a little similar and are found in the same type of habitats. I either waded or fished from my one-man canoe in rivers and bays.

While on holiday in Ireland in 1999 I bought some commercially dressed salmon flies to decorate a tweed hat. Because I wasn't impressed with the quality of the flies, when I got back to Australia I picked up a few books on salmon flies and taught myself to tie them. *Tying the Classic Salmon Fly* by Radencich, *Atlantic Salmon* by Bates, and *Waddington on Salmon* by Waddington introduced me to the concept of tube flies, and I found more references on the Internet.

I started tying Dahlberg-style divers on tubes for Australian bass when it dawned on me that a plastic tube with a small hook was a lot lighter than the same fly tied on a 2/0 stinger hook! A hair bug on a tube floats longer and higher than a conventional version, and it hooks fish in the mouth rather than in the throat. This one reason why I tie hair bugs on tubes. Another is that they survive more strikes than hook tied flies, this because the fly slides up the line, away from fish teeth. I tie my deer-hair flies a la Ed Haas, with plenty of cement on the wraps.

It turns out that hair bugs are no more difficult to tie on a tube than a hook. The only difference is you are spinning deer hair on a relatively wide-diameter tube rather than a thin hook shank. I take my time and use loose initial wraps. To aid the spinning process I twist with my fingers as I pull the wraps tight.

I tie my flies on tubes from cotton tips. (Try getting tube-fly supplies in Australia!) The boxes I buy contain one-half pink and one-half blue tubes. I use the blue ones for cleaning and the pink ones for flies. When I put hook sleeves on my tubes, I make them from the clear silicone tubing used in fish-tank air lines. If I am using a glow-in-the-dark bead as a bearing between the tube and hook eye, I eliminate the hook sleeve.

I tie my hair bugs in a variety of sizes from 1 1/2 inch to 7 or 8 inches. Hook size depends on the length of the fly — as long as most of the hook is hidden and the point is cleanly exposed, any brand of hook will do. I often snell the hook onto the leader so the

shank lies in line with it. I prefer this to silicone sleeves because I feel they hold the hook too rigidly and interfere with hooking performance.

Since moving to Ireland I have done a lot more fly-fishing, mainly for trout, and I am planning to experiment with pike this winter using some new tube flies of my own design. The frog pattern works well when stalking pike in flooded pastures in the Dublin Mountains.

TUBE ENCEPHALO-SQUID

Tube: Plastic tube from Q-tip ("cotton bud"), 2 1/2 inches long with a silicone hook sleeve or a glow-in-the-dark bead as bearing between tube and hook eye

Tentacles: Small emu body feathers, natural or dyed red, pink, or orange

Skirt: Talon Finnish raccoon hair in salmon, brown, or gold color

Eyes: Talon True Eyes, pale green. These are glass eyes with a metal stem

Body: Large emu body feathers and large hen grizzly feathers, natural or dyed red, pink or orange

Thread: White, flat-waxed nylon and white 8/0

Finish: Varnish

Hook: Any large single hook

Step 1: Put the tube on your vise and attach the flat, waxed nylon thread. Build a small ball of thread at the butt of the tube. Whip finish and cut off the thread.

Step 2: Attach the 8/0 thread in front of the ball. Tie in four small emu feathers about 3 inches long evenly spaced around the tube, flaring them out against the ball.

Step 3: Tie the metal stems of the Talon True Eyes against opposite sides of the tube, so the eyes extend about 3/8 inch from the tube's end. This creates flat sections on the top and bottom of the tube.

Step 4: Apply a bunch of raccoon hair on both top and bottom flat sections. The tips of the raccoon should extend past the eyes and at least half the length of the emu feather tentacles. Make sure the butts are covered with a thin, even layer of thread; it should be about 1/2 inch long.

Step 5: Tie in a large emu feather, butt first, with the barbs pointing towards the rear. Wind the feather in tight, side by side turns. Tie down and trim excess. Tie in a large hen grizzly feather and wind it the same way. Alternate emu and hen feathers to the front of the tube. The last feather should be a grizzly hen. The palmered section is 1 1/4 inches long.

Step 6: Make a very small head with thread, whip finish, and varnish.

In Australia we fished for snapper on the flats after dark with small live squid, which were not easy to come by. I discovered that a fly approximately the same size and shape would do just as well, if not better. *At about the same time I received a big bag of emu feathers, which made excellent tentacles. I tie this fly with natural colored feathers, or with feathers tinted light red or pink, or with a mixture of colored and natural feathers.*

NICK KINGSTON

Australian whiting caught on a Tube Encephalo-Squid.

The Encephalo-Squid has been fished in Australia since the beginning of 2000, and it has caught snapper, bream, flathead, and tailor. Depending on the target species, I fish it on an intermediate to fast-sinking line. My best results have come from casting against the tide and fishing the fly on the swing. On nights where there is no moon, I use a glow-in-the-dark bead between the tube and the hook. I don't use any particular hook. Any suitably-sized single or treble is fine.

TUBE DAHLBERG DIVER

Tube: Plastic tube from Q-tip ("cotton bud"), 2 inches long for a 3-inch fly, with a silicone hook sleeve or a glow-in-the-dark bead as bearing between tube and hook eye

Thread: 6/0 or 8/0. Heavy thread isn't required to spin hair if care is taken.

Tail: Marabou, olive over orange, over black, 2 inches long

Skirt: Moose body hair, gray, 2 inches long

Head: Green, brown, and white deer hair, tied in alternating bands, spun and clipped to shape

Finish: Varnish

Hook: Any large single hook

I tie this bug as small as 2 inches overall length. The small version I fish on a 6-weight; the larger version on an 8-weight.

TUBE FROG

Tube: Plastic tube from Q-tip ("cotton bud"), 2 inches long, with a silicone hook sleeve or a glow-in-the-dark bead as bearing between tube and hook eye

Thread: 6/0 or 8/0

Legs: Green saddle hackles and emu feathers knotted together

Body: Green deer hair, spun and clipped to shape

Finish: Varnish

Hook: Any large single hook

From top: Tube Frog; Tube Encephalo-Squid (pink); Tube Encephalo-Squid (gold); Tube Encephalo-Squid (brown); Tube Dahlberg Diver

CHAPTER
16

SKULI KRISTINSSON
Reykjavik, Iceland

I live in the countryside about an hour's drive east of Iceland's capital city, Reykjavik. I started fly-tying and fly-fishing in 1979; until 1988 most of my fishing was in lakes for trout, with a few days of salmon fishing each season. In 1988 I began working as a river keeper in the Ellidaar River that runs through the center of Reykjavik. Since 1990, I have been tying salmon flies and streamers professionally. I started guiding on the West Ranga River in 1994, and since 1998 I have been a camp manager for the Lax-a Angling Club, the largest salmon and trout outfitter in Iceland.

In the beginning, most of my salmon-fly tying was on small double and treble hooks, but because tubes are very popular in Iceland I started to tie tube flies as well. Tube flies first arrived in Iceland about the same time they came into use in the UK, probably in the fly boxes of angling tourists. A lot of people from the UK fish Iceland every year. In the early days, when fly lines weren't as good as they are today, fast sinking tubes helped anglers get their flies down to the fish. Flies tied on tubes also swim differently than hook-tied flies. Today two-thirds of the flies I tie are on tubes.

In Iceland, tube flies are used in all types of water and at all water levels, from the beginning of the season to the end. In the small rivers, tubes are usually fished with floating lines, but in the larger streams like the East Ranga, sink-tip lines are used. Until the arrival of Loop's brass bottle tubes, most Icelandic tube flies were conversions of standard Atlantic salmon patterns like the Black Sheep and Frances. With a bottle tube, you can tie a heavily-dressed fly that is easy to cast, and that has good action in the water because of the long, soft wing. The Pool Fly originated on a bottle tube. We generally don't dress our bottles as heavily as the Scandinavians. As to color and size of fly, there are no hard and fast rules here. We sometimes use big tubes with good success in low-water conditions.

In addition to Atlantic salmon, our rivers also hold sea trout. Although flies for sea trout in Iceland are usually hook-tied streamers, tubes are being used more and more, and particularly in autumn in the bigger glacier-fed rivers when anglers want to get flies down to the fish.

Clockwise from top left: Black Boss; Red Frances; F-Boss; Somerset Pink; Small Black Sheep; Black Sheep; Pool Fly; Ranga Shrimp

RANGA SHRIMP

Tube: Slipstream aluminum, 1/8-inch O. D., 1 to 1 1/2 inches long with silicone hook sleeve
Thread: White
Body: 1/3 medium Lagartun oval silver tinsel and 2/3 blue Arctic fox dubbing
Rear wing: Four jungle cock eyes evenly spaced around tube
Rear hackle: Gray heron, long
Rib: Oval silver tinsel over the blue Arctic fox dubbing
Front hackle: Vulturin guinea speckled hackle
Finish: Varnish, three or four coats
Hook: Partridge Salar Treble

Step 1: Slide the hook sleeve about 3/16 inch over the end of tube, then put the tube on your tying tool.
Step 2: Tie in the oval silver tinsel and wind it in tight turns over one third of the tube. Tie down tinsel but do not trim excess, which will be used for the ribbing.
Step 3: One at a time, tie the four jungle cock feathers around the tube. Because jungle cock feathers are expensive I use the bigger feathers and repair any splits with vinyl cement.
Step 4: In front of the jungle cock, tie in and then wind a gray heron hackle. Tie down and trim excess. I tie the heron long to get as much movement as possible. Blue ear pheasant is good substitute for heron, which is illegal in the USA.

Step 5: For the front two-thirds of the body, dub blue Arctic fox tail under fur on the thread and wind it forward. Then wind the tinsel over it in an even rib. Tie down and trim excess tinsel.
Step 6: Tie in the guinea hackle. I use the Vulturin guinea speckled hackle, but it is not a common feather and normal guinea hackle will substitute. Wind the front hackle, tie down, and trim. Form a small head with black thread. Whip finish.
Step 7: Varnish the head with three or four coats.

BLACK SHEEP

Tube: Slipstream brass, 1/8-inch O. D., 1/2 to 1 1/2 inches long with silicone hook sleeve
Tag: Oval silver tinsel
Body: Black wool
Hackle: Silver Doctor blue
Wing: Yellow over black Arctic fox tail
Cheeks: Jungle cock
Head: Red thread
Finish: Varnish, three or four coats
Hook: Loop double hook

SMALL BLACK SHEEP

Tube: Brass 1/8-inch O.D., 1/2 to 2/3 inch long, or silver bottle tube varnished black, with silicone hook sleeve

While Mosi the Labrador looks on, Skuli nets an Atlantic salmon for Richard Stacey on the Djúpós Pool of the West Rangá, about an hour's drive from Reykjavík, Iceland.

Body: Black wool (omit if using black bottle tube)
Hackle: Silver Doctor blue
Wing: Yellow over black Arctic fox tail
Cheeks: Jungle cock
Head: Red thread
Finish: Varnish, three or four coats
Hook: Loop double hook

POOL FLY

Tube: Gold brass bottle tube, 1/2 to 2/3 inch long with silicone hook sleeve
Beard: Orange polar bear
Wing: Orange, yellow and black Arctic runner (Icelandic pony) hair. Between the layers of yellow and black hair are a few strands of Sunburst Flashabou.
Head: Black thread
Finish: Varnish, three or four coats
Hook: Loop double hook

RED FRANCES

Tube: Slipstream brass tube, 1/8-inch O. D., 1/2 to 1 1/2 inches long with silicone hook sleeve

Tail: Three red and three white, stripped cock hackle stems; natural red and white and brown calf hair
Body: Red wool wound in a carrot shape
Rib: Oval gold tinsel
Hackle: Natural red cock hackle
Head: Red thread
Finish: Varnish, three or four coats
Hook: Partridge Salar Treble

This is the most popular fly in Iceland, whether dressed on tube or a hook. It is also tied in black with a yellow head.

BLACK BOSS

Tube: Slipstream brass tube, 1/8-inch O. D, 1 to 2 inches long with silicone hook sleeve
Tail: Black Arctic fox tail with pearl Krystal Flash strands along both sides
Body: Black wool
Rib: Oval silver tinsel
Hackle: Black cock or hen hackle
Finish: Varnish, three or four coats
Hook: Partridge Salar Treble

This is a variation on the Snelda, a popular fly in Iceland.

F- BOSS

Tube: Slipstream brass tube, 1/8-inch O. D., 1 to 2 inches long with silicone hook sleeve
Tail: Yellow, orange and black Arctic fox tail
Body: Black wool
Rib: Oval silver tinsel
Hackle: Black cock or hen hackle
Finish: Varnish, three or four coats
Hook: Partridge Salar Treble

This is another variation on the Snelda.

SOMERSET PINK

Tube: Silver brass bottle tube 1/2 to 3/4 inches long with silicone hook sleeve
Hackle: Fluorescent pink hen
Wing: White over fluorescent pink Arctic runner hair with little purple pearl Angel Hair between the layers
Cheeks: Jungle cock
Head: Fluorescent pink thread
Finish: Varnish, three or four coats
Hook: Loop double hook

MARK MANDELL

Port Townsend, Washington

BETSY BULLARD

I have been tying flies exclusively on tubes for more than a decade now. The reason I shifted from flies tied on hooks is very simple: I have a limited attention span. After I get a fly's proportions right, I want to tie a handful of fair copies, and move on to something new. Tube flies give me this option because they survive the rigors of fishing so well. A dozen tubes of one pattern, color, and size will usually last me an entire season. Because there are no integral hooks to rust away, a fly is lost only if the leader breaks, and it takes many dozens of fish landed to render a tube fly unusable. This is true even of flies tied with fragile materials like marabou and deer hair. Any pattern that takes a lot of time and materials to tie, like a big saltwater streamer or a deer-hair bug, is well worth putting on a tube.

Inspired by the flies submitted for this book by Graydon Bell and Nick Kingston, I only recently began tying Dahlberg diver-type hair bugs. As Nick said in his chapter, tying hair bugs on tubes means you can use a small, light hook, which allows a higher float and makes divers pop back to the surface with authority; and the flies don't shred or get fish slimed because they slide up the leader on the strike. As with most flies, hair bugs are no more difficult to tie on a tube than a hook.

There are also patterns that can only be tied on tubes because no hook shank is long enough, or if it is, the gape and weight would destroy the swim balance and make the flies impossible to cast. The Don Gallo and MegaDon patterns that follow are prime examples of only-on-a-tube.

From top: MegaDon dorado; Don Gallo; Tube conversion of Clouser Minnow; MegaDon striped mullet; MiniDon sardina; MiniDon Pacific herring; MegaDon squid; Tube conversion of Lefty's Deceiver

DON GALLO

Tube: Plastic HMH 1/8-inch O. D., 1 1/2 inches long, and 3/4 inch of silicone tube as a hook sleeve

Thread: Clear nylon

Tail: 10 or 12 white saddles

Tail flash: Two strips of 1/32-inch-wide gold holographic tinsel on each side

Body: White bucktail, two collars, 3 inches long, veiled with pearl Flashabou

Eyes: Two 7/16-inch nickel cone heads slid on a 5/8-inch-long stem of 1/8-inch O. D. brass tubing with Spirit River 6.0, 3-D silver Prismatic eyes epoxied inside the cones

Belly: Stacked white bucktail, in three layers, veiled with pearl Flashabou

Back: Natural brown bucktail

Topping: Pearl Flashabou and yellow Krystal Flash

Cement: Zap-A-Gap

Head finish: 30-minute epoxy

Hook: Owner AKI size 4/0 to 6/0

Step 1: Assemble the eye components in advance. After cutting the brass eye stem to size with a K&S tubing cutter, slide on the cone heads nose first, and use a nail point and hammer to flare the ends of the tube so the cones won't fall off. With thread wraps put 1/4 inch of space on the stem between the cones, then partially fill the insides with epoxy and let it cure. Seat the 3D eyes on a bed of fresh epoxy, and cover them with a little more epoxy. I generally do a dozen or more sets of eyes at a time, first one side, then the other.

Step 2: Join the hard tubing and hook sleeve with a 3/8-inch overlap, put it on your tube tool, and overwrap the join area with clear monofilament thread.

Step 3: Tie in five or six white saddles on either side of the tube, cove style. Leave the marabou fluff on. Apply Zap-A-Gap to the wraps. Add two strands of gold holographic Mylar tinsel, same length as saddles, to each shoulder. Trim hackle stem butts even with the face of the tube join.

Step 4: Encircle join with a 3-inch-long collar of white bucktail. Veil with pearl Flashabou. Zap-A-Gap the wraps.

Step 5: Advancing the thread forward, tie a second, slightly shorter bucktail collar on the join. Trim hair even with face of join. Veil with pearl Flashabou.

Step 6: Rotate the fly 180 degrees so it is belly up. On top of the 1/8-inch O. D. tube tie in eyes 1/4 inch forward of join with figure-eights. Apply Zap-A-Gap to the wraps.

Step 7: Lay down a slightly shorter, tapering bunch of bucktail on top of the tube, over the center of the eye stem, with butts facing the nose of the fly. The tips should blend in with the tips

In 2004, 16-year-old Robin Blanco-Concepcion landed a world-record roosterfish of 47 pounds at Golfito Sailfish Rancho, Costa Rica, on an unweighted, 3 1/2-inch, gray-and-white Lefty's Deceiver tube fly tied by Mark Mandell.

BRIAN HORSLEY

BETSY BULLARD

on the second collar. Use figure-eight loops to hold the material in place. Add matching bunches of bucktail on either side of it. Use minimum turns of thread and drops of Zap-A-Gap to hold. Repeat this twice more with successively shorter bunches of hair, moving the tie-down point forward each time, until you are tying down just in front of the eye stem. As you tighten down on the thread, the angle of the hair will steepen, forming the prominent belly. Zap-A-Gap the wraps. As the glue is setting up, cut away the excess bucktail, forming an evenly tapered nose. Overwrap the bucktail with nylon thread, compressing it into a narrower shape. Zap-A-Gap the wraps.

Step 8: Veil the throat and belly with more pearl Flashabou, small length as bucktail. Rotate the tube 180 degrees.

Step 9: If the space between the face of the tubing join and the nose of the fly is too deep, the wing will not lay flat along the back. To fill in the void, tie down a short bunch of white bucktail just in front of the eyes, trim the butts flush with the join face, and Zap-A-Gap. Trim away excess bucktail at the nose.

Step 10: Tie in brown bucktail at the nose, figure-eighting the wraps behind the eyes. Tie in a second bunch of brown hair, shorter than the first. If voids remain along the sides, add smaller bunches of brown bucktail to fill them in. Zap-A-Gap. Top with five strands of yellow Krystal Flash, longer than the brown bucktail. Trim hair at nose, whip finish, and Zap-A-Gap.

Step 11: Apply a thin coat of 30-minute epoxy to the nose and head, working it in behind the eyes to fill any voids. Dry on

wheel. Trim excess tube at nose. Apply a second coat of 30-minute epoxy. Dry on wheel.

This Lefty's Deceiver (saddle hackle tail, bucktail collar) variant came about after many days of frustrating inshore fishing in southwestern Costa Rica. Golfito Sailfish Rancho boat crews had raised dozens of roosterfish into casting range with skipped, live threadfin herring, 7 to 9 inches long, but after the baits were jerked away we couldn't get the roosters to break the surface and strike a popper. Roosterfish are highly selective — if not highly intelligent — with exceptionally keen vision; they will follow inches behind a retrieved fly, all the way to the rod tip without striking. Once their killer instinct is roused by a tease bait it rarely lasts more than a few seconds.

I decided to devise a big (overall length and bulk), castable fly to match the threadfin that would sink rapidly, nosefalling at more than a foot a second. To get that sink rate, I used two of the biggest cones made to form its dumb bell eyes. The idea was that if a rapidly sinking fly was dropped very close to an attacking rooster it would trigger an immediate, instinctive take. That proved to be the case, time and again. This fly, with its dense body and big, nickel cone head flash, dives away and down the instant it hits the water, practically shouting, "Eat me before I escape!"

The biggest rooster taken on the Don Gallo was 35 pounds. The fish was visible in the back of a breaking wave, three feet below the surface. With a 60-foot cast, I dropped the fly in front of its nose as the tease bait was jerked away. Its gills flared, mouth opened, and it sucked down the fly without hesitation. On the same trip, Betsy Bullard, owner of the Golfito Sailfish Rancho, caught her first fly-rod rooster, a 25-pounder, on the Don Gallo.

This fly is not safe to cast with less than a 13-weight rod. With a 13-weight or better, the Don Gallo sails like a bullet, or to be more exact, a pair of bullets. It rides with hook point up, like an oversized Clouser.

If I am tying at top speed, a Don Gallo takes me 30 minutes to complete, not counting the time on the drying wheel. One fly uses about a third of a normal-sized bucktail. If it was tied on a hook, getting the hook point clear of the collar would require the length and gape of a 10/0, instead of a 4/0 or 6/0. It's the perfect candidate for a tube fly.

I have scaled this pattern down to create a MiniDon version, using 3/8-inch nickel cone heads, Spirit River 5.0, 3D Prismatic eyes, and 3/16-inch brass tubing for the eye stems. This fly's overall length is 4 1/2 inches instead of 7, can be armed with a 2/0 hook, and is castable with an 8- or 10-weight rod. With its deep-bodied silhouette, mobile tail, and eye flash, it makes an excellent imitation of the flat iron herring — called sardina in Baja — and the Pacific herring found further north. Like the original, it sinks quickly to fishing depth.

MEGADON

TAIL ASSEMBLY

Tube: Brass 5/32-inch O. D., lined, 5/8 inch long

Thread: Clear nylon

Tail: Five or six, 4 1/2-inch-long saddles to a side, same color as body

Body: Two bucktail collars, 2/3 length of saddles, in staggered layers

Veil: Pearl Flashabou

Cement: Zap-A-Gap

Head finish: 30-minute epoxy

BODY ASSEMBLY

Tube: Brass 5/32-inch O. D., lined, 2 inches long

Connector: 100-pound monofilament, 3 1/4 inches long, with a surgeon's knot tied in one end. Slip the mono through the tail assembly tube, then with heavy thread securely tie the 100-pound down on the body tube leaving about 3/4 inch of bare tube at the front, and 1 1/4 inch of 100-pound between the nose of the tail assembly and the back of the body tube. Whip finish and trim. Apply Zap-A-Gap.

Hook sleeve: Vinyl tubing 3/16-inch I. D. (5/16-inch O. D.), 1 3/4 inches long. Heat the sleeve in very hot water to soften it, then push it over the front end of the body tube until it extends about 1/2 inch past the back end. The front 1 inch of the tube should remain exposed.

Tail: First layer is eight long saddles or schlappen to each side, tips blending into tail assembly feathers; second layer is a repeat of the first, tied in about an inch forward.

Tail flash: Two strips of 1/32-inch-wide holographic tinsel on each side

Betsy Bullard caught her first fly-rod roosterfish on a Don Gallo tube fly at Punta Burica, Costa Rica.

Fishing with Maudiel Quiros (center) and Robin Blanco-Concepcion (right) in May 2005, Mark Mandell (left) landed and released a 24-pound Pacific jack crevalle at Playa Zancudo, Costa Rica. It took a cone-head, 3 1/2-inch, gray-and-white Lefty's Deceiver tube fly.

Body: Three bucktail collars, 3 inches long, each veiled with pearl Flashabou
Eyes: Two nickel cone heads, 7/16-inch diameter, on a 5/8-inch-long, 1/8-inch O. D. brass tube stem, epoxy-filled with 3/8 inch 3D Prismatic eyes (Spirit River 6). See Don Gallo Tying Instructions, Step 1.
Belly: Stacked bucktail, same procedure as Don Gallo, veiled with pearl Flashabou
Back: Contrasting color of bucktail, same procedure as Don Gallo
Topping: Pearl Flashabou and Krystal Flash, color to match bucktail
Cement: Zap-A-Gap
Head finish: 30-minute epoxy
Hook: Owner 8/0 or 10/0

The MegaDon has the same advantages as the Don Gallo: a big, meaty silhouette combined with a super-fast sink. The hookless tube rear extension brings the overall length to close to ten inches. Though it's larger, this fly isn't much heavier than the Don Gallo; obviously, the same rod weight warnings apply. Again, it's intended for teased up saltwater fish that won't break the surface to take a popper. The hook point on the MegaDon can be adjusted to ride at any angle, straight up or offset. I tie it in hot pink, striped mullet, and dorado.

TUBE CONVERSION OF CLOUSER MINNOW

Tube: Plastic HMH clear 3/32-inch O.D., 5/8 inch long, with a 1/2-inch-long silicone hook sleeve. I always melt a little collar on the back end of a plastic tube

before I slide on the hook sleeve. This gives the sleeve something to grip onto when it is wrapped down with thread.
Thread: Clear nylon
Wing: White bucktail or white marabou under fluorescent pink or chartreuse
Topping: Pearl Krystal Flash or pearl blue peacock Angel Hair
Eyes: Silver dumb bell, various weights, mini to large
Head finish: 30-minute epoxy, worked behind and around the eyes and dried on wheel
Hook: Size 4 or 6

All innovation credit goes to Bob Clouser, the originator of this classic hook-tied pattern. If I had to choose one fly for all my saltwater fishing for coho salmon, it would be a Tube Clouser, tied in pink and white, or chartreuse and white with a little veil of pearl Krystal Flash or Angel Hair for sparkle. I reduced the number of tying steps from the original to facilitate the conversion and speed production. Winged with either bucktail or marabou, and finished with an epoxy head, this fly is almost indestructible. I have caught and released more than 50 four- to eight-pound salmon on a single fly.

I fish 2 1/2- to 3 1/2-inch Tube Clousers from a boat in offshore rips with high-speed sink-tips, and along the kelp beds inshore with intermediate, clear sink-tips. I've used the same colors and sizes on Florida's east coast and taken bluefish, jacks, cero mackerel, and speckled trout in the Atlantic surf and in estuaries and rivers.

TUBE CONVERSION OF LEFTY'S DECEIVER

Tube: Plastic HMH clear 3/32-inch O.D., 5/8 inch long, with a 1/2-inch-long silicone hook sleeve
Thread: Clear nylon
Wing: Three or four white length saddles tied cove style
Collar: White bucktail
Back: Gray bucktail, sparse
Sides: Krystal Flash Rainbow, a few fibers per side
Gills: Red saddle hackle fibers
Head: Black thread or Spirit River Cross-Eyed cone head, black nickel, 3/8-inch diameter
Eyes: Silver or yellow stick-on 3-D, size 3.0
Head finish: 30-minute epoxy
Hook: Size 1/0 or 2/0

Lefty Kreh's Deceiver is without a doubt the most well-known and widely used saltwater pattern in the world. Lefty's blending of hair and feathers is impossible to improve upon, but when put on a tube a Deceiver's lifespan is extended three- or four-fold. I chose to include this particular size (3 1/2 inch overall) and color combination because it is one of my all-time favorites. I tie it either unweighted on a plastic tube, or with a Spirit River tungsten cone head, or on 1/2-inch of 1/8-inch O.D. copper tubing. I started using the cone head after Anil Srivastava sent me samples of his Shock & Awe tube fly (See Chapter 33: Anil Srivastava). Fish it with floating, sink-tip, and full-sinking lines.

SERGIO EDUARDO MARCHIONI

São Paulo, Brazil

I was born in Brazil in 1963. I work as an Internet programmer and web master of the Brazilian fly-fishing sites Pesca com Mosca (translation: Flyfishing), Fly Cast, and several others. My own web site, Pesca com Mosca, tries in some small measure to introduce fly-fishing and fly-tying to my country. Brazil is still new at fly-fishing but because of its diverse aquatic environments and species the potential is very great. Fly-fishers are able to pursue their sport at any time of the year here, in either fresh or salt water.

I have been fly-tying for eight years, now, and I tie at least a few hours every day. I started tying tube flies initially out of curiosity. I just wanted to tie something practical and different on something other than a hook. I soon realized how efficient the method was, and saw its advantages over hook-tied flies. Although my tying studies continue on traditional hooks, I admit I have more affection for tying on tubes. Bob Kenly, Martin Joergensen, and Ken Bonde-Larsen, among others, helped foster my love of tube flies.

Although my Tube Matuka was designed for fish in the *Tucunarés* family (peacock bass), it works well on other predatory freshwater fish such as black bass and trout (tied in smaller sizes), and local river species: *apaiari* (Oscar, a large cichlid), *matrinxãs* (Brycon cephalus), and *tabaranas* (Salminus hilarii).

In salt water, I use lead-weighted versions of the Tube Matuka and Tube Ghost, and the Tube Lula-Squid, with and without cone-head weight, for near-shore reef species, *badejos* (grouper), *enchovas* (jacks), *carapaus* (mackerel), *xaréus*, and *olhetes* (the yellowtail "king of kingfish").

Among my other projects is a new tying bench I have developed. Instructions for its construction are at: http://www.pesca commosca.com.br/ english/bench.htm. I also sell completed benches and flies for South America and can be reached at pescacommosca@uol.com.br.

TUBE MATUKA

Tube: Plastic 1/8-inch O. D., 1 1/2 inches long, with silicone hook sleeve

Thread: Black 6/0

Tag: Two turns of small, French oval tinsel, and two turns of black thread

Rib: French oval tinsel, small

Body: Red floss

Throat: Peacock herl

Wings: Two or four, white Black Laced hen saddles, 2 1/2 inches long, trimmed off on one side and tied in matuka style

From top: Tube Lula-Squid; Tube Ghost; Tube Matuka; Tube Lula-Squid (yellow eyes)

Hackle: One white Black Laced hen saddle dyed red and one
   white Black Laced hen saddle, wound in separately
Cheeks: Jungle cock
   Head: Black ostrich herl
   Hook: Size 6 to 2/0, 3XS to 5XS

Step 1: Put the plastic tube on your vise. Tie in the black thread
   at the rear end of the tube, leaving 1/4 inch to slide on the
   hook sleeve after the fly is completed.

Step 2: Tie in the French oval tinsel and make two tight turns,
   then tie off with two turns of black thread. Do not trim off the
   tinsel as it will form the rib.

Step 3: Advance the thread to the front of the tube and tie in the
   red floss, leaving 1/4 inch of bare tube for the hackle and head.
   Wrap a floss body that is 3/16 inch in diameter at the front
   end. The body starts to taper at its midpoint, and ends up
   slightly more than 1/8-inch diameter at the back. Tie down the
   floss at the front and trim excess.

Step 4: Wind the thread 3/8 inch back onto the floss body, and
   tie in the peacock herl. Advance the thread to the front again.
   Wind the peacock herl forward, tie it down, and trim excess.

Step 5: Trim the paired white Black Laced hen saddles by cutting
   away 1 1/2 inch from the butt of one side, leaving the black-
   edged tips about an inch long. In front of the herl, tie down the
   white Black Laced hen saddles with curves facing inward. Trim
   butts.

Step 6: Wind the French oval tinsel rib over the Black Laced hen,
   the floss, and the herl at 3/16-inch intervals, tie down and trim.

Step 7: Tie in red-dyed Black Laced hen saddle and the white
   Black Laced hen saddle in front of the wing butts with curves
   facing the rear. Wind the red saddle around the tube as a wet-
   fly hackle. Tie down and trim the saddle.

Step 8: In front of the red hackle, wind the white Black Laced hen
   saddle. Tie down and trim excess feather.

Step 9: Tie in jungle cock feathers as cheeks.

Step 10: Tie in the black ostrich herl and wind it on for the head.
   Tie down and trim the herl.

Sergio releases a peacock bass.

Step 11: Whip finish and varnish wraps.
Step 12: Slip on the hook sleeve.

This is a highly adaptable fly. I've fished it with success in Brazilian rivers, lakes, and salt water. It works particularly well on snook. The rod weight normally depends on the size of the fly, but I like to play tennis with a soccerball: little rod/big fly. I use Teeny and intermediate sinking lines in rivers and lakes, and Teeny and full-sinking lines in salt water.

TUBE GHOST

Tube: Plastic 1/8-inch O. D., 1 1/2 inches long
Thread: White 3/0
Tentacles: Eight to 12 white saddle hackles, 4 1/2 inches long, colored with permanent marker
Body: Two sections of white deer hair, spun and clipped. First section, with the eyes, is about 1/3 the length of the second.
Eyes: Prismatic or Audible eyes, 1/4 to 3/8 inch in diameter
Front fins: White marabou, tied in short on either side at front of body
Weight: Nickel cone head, 7/16-inch diameter
Hook: Size 1 to 2 X strong (to add weight), length standard to 2 XS

I fish this fly in salt water when the squid are schooled up and spawning. I divided the deer-hair body into two sections to get more movement in the water. Rod weight depends on the size of the fly, but I usually use an 8- or 10-weight and a full, fast-sinking line. The Lula-Squid is meant for all saltwater game fish.

TUBE LULA-SQUID

Tube: Plastic 1/8-inch O. D., 1 1/2 inches long
Thread: Black
Tag: Flat silver tinsel
Body: Yellow floss
Ribbing: Copper wire
Bellywing: Ten or 12 peacock herls, 1 3/4 inches long, under a sparse bunch of white bucktail
Underwing/Throat: Three small, staggered bunches of white hackle fibers tied on top and bottom of tube. Bunches are angled to the rear.
Wing: Golden pheasant crest feather with 2 or 3 white saddle hackles on each side, tied in cove style
Cheeks: Golden pheasant tippet feathers and jungle cock
Hook: Size 6 to 3/0, 3XS to 5XS

I fish this fly in salt and freshwater, lakes or rivers. The hook can ride point up or down.

CHAPTER
19

DAG MIDTGÅRD

Oslo, Norway

I was born in 1971 on the west coast of Norway and as a young child I spent holidays at the river bank watching my grandpa and my uncle fish for salmon with either a worm or with a float and a fly. My introduction to fly-fishing was with a spinning rod!

At the age of seven or eight, while my uncle was out fishing, I tied my first flies. He did not allow me to use his gear when he was at home. Only when I got my own fly-tying kit, rod, and reel at the age of 11 could I tie regularly. I caught my first salmon, which weighed almost two pounds, the same year I got my fly-tying kit. Since then I have favored the use of the fly over the worm or spoon — to be honest, I've never had any luck with either, and when the fish aren't biting I always enjoy casting my fly rod.

I made my first tube flies from the inner tubes of Bic ballpoints. The pens were cheap and easy to get, but removing the ink was always messy. From the age of 15 or 16 on, I started regularly selling hair-winged flies to shops in Oslo, both on tube bodies and on hooks. It wasn't until 1996-97 that I began tying the majority of my flies on tubes. I still tie hair-winged flies on large Spey hooks in the winter, usually after rereading my two favorite books by Hale and Pryce-Tannatt, as I normally do before Christmas.

A lingering problem with small tube flies has always been proportionality. One-eighth-inch O. D. tubes work fine for bodies and heads on large flies, but they make smaller, low-water flies bulky, clumsy looking, and very bad swimmers. I have spent five years working on a tube-fly concept and materials that make it possible to tie perfectly proportional large and small flies. I developed paired sets of tubing, Large, Medium, and Small. Each set consists of an outer and an inner tube. The Large inner tube is 0.75 mm I. D./1.9 mm O. D.; outer tube is 1.95 mm I. D./2.95 mm O. D. The Medium inner tube is 0.63 mm I. D./1.7 mm O. D.; outer tube is 1.75 mm I. D./2.5 mm O.D. The Small inner tube is 0.5 mm I. D./1.5 mm O. D.; outer tube is 1.5 mm I. D./2.2 mm O. D. Midgar Small and Medium tubing is designed for tying flies 1 1/4 inch and shorter. My fly plate includes large and small versions of the same patterns to illustrate the effect.

The sample flies have full-dress, Atlantic salmon style bodies tied on the outer tubing with small, neat thread heads or small cone heads slipped on the much skinnier inner tubing. Tying can also be done mostly on the inner tubing, this creates a very slim body profile and a tiny head. With these materials and techniques tying a fly on a tube is identical to tying on a regular salmon-fly hook.

From top left: Purple Light (Large); Purple Light (Small); Golden Light (Small); Golden Light (Large); Silver Grey (Large); Silver Grey (Small)

The first two books I read on fly-tying were *How to Dress Salmon Flies* by T. E. Pryce-Tannatt, and *Salmon Flies* by Poul Jorgensen. I adapted many of their ideas into my early tying, the only difference being that I have always used hair materials instead of the feathers they advocated. However, my very favorite tying book is still J. H. Hale's *How to Tie Salmon Flies*. This book came out in 1892, but was reprinted later, and is still available from time to time in well-stocked book shops. Hale's book covers almost everything there is to know about tying a salmon fly except the use and preparation of hair and flash materials, and how to combine them to form a nice-looking wing.

PAL MUGAAS

Over the last 20 years the use of softer and softer hair for salmon-fly wings has taken hold in Scandinavia. I am a product of this tying style, plus some classic thoughts from Hale and Pryce-Tannatt.

It is hard to say what actually sparked my patterns, but I have always been jealous of friends who took many salmon on Rapalas and other wobblers while I stood fishless with my fly rod. Since the mid-1990's I have tried to tie my flies in the same shape as the thin and mobile Rapala. Where Swedish tiers talk about wing width and movement, I have been more interested in wing *height* and movement. I extensively taper the entire wing, using from four to seven wing sections of different lengths and thicknesses.

When the fly runs through the water, the movement is from the shoulder back to the tip of the wing.

After I started fishing tube flies, I soon realized that a short body is required to keep the fly swimming straight and stable in moving water. If the body is too long, the rear end of the tube points down at the stream bed. My rule of thumb is that the tube body should not be longer than 1/3 of the total wing length; this applies to wing lengths up to 11 or 12 cm. The wing should be heavily tapered and thick to balance the tube body and the cock hackles should be long and densely packed. The combination of layered, soft hair wings and long hackles from the second body section to the shoulder and between the wing sections makes a dense, strong fly that moves wonderfully in flowing water.

Wherever I fish, I use tube flies. I retrieve them quickly as I feel that fish take the fly much better when a fly is speeding through the water. Although I have had good results fishing all sections of pools, I have had the best success where the water is running very fast, at the beginning or end, and especially the latter. Often people do not fish that far forward or back in a pool because they think the water is moving too quickly to hold salmon, or because their flies skate on the surface in such fast water. In the very early morning these places can produce some very exciting fishing. Salmon that have migrated upward in the river during night wait there until day light forces them to hide in deeper places in the pool. Because the fly moves so quickly through this fast water, I miss some strikes, but even so I get a kick as the water explodes. If I am lucky I hook the fish on the next cast.

When fishing tube flies, I usually cast 90 degrees across the river, holding the line tight to get the highest speed possible on the fly. When a fish takes the fly I hold the rod and line tight at an angle of 30 to 45 degrees so the rod absorbs that first hard hit, and the fish hooks itself.

In the past 8 to 10 years I have concentrated fishing the River Gaula and the River Namsen, but I also travel to Finnmark to fish the Alta and smaller rivers. On these smaller rivers I chase fresh grilse using dry flies and small tube flies with my 9-foot, 5-weight rod. The prices there are very affordable, too: NOK 2-300 per day/USD $35-50.

To hold my tube-fly bodies in the vise I make my own tube-fly tool. It is simply a thin needle fastened with thread and Zap-A-Gap to the top of a tube-fly hook or a double hook with a down eye. I slip the needle into the innertubing of the already assembled tube body, then I push the rear end of the body over the hook eye so the tube will not spin during tying. The size of hook and needle varies according to the size of tubing I am using.

Currently I run a fly-fishing store in downtown Oslo that specializes in gear and fly-tying materials for salmon and sea trout. I sell my tube-fly tubing, tube-fly cone heads and Tempelhair to tiers all around the world. No minimum purchase is required. If you visit my web pages, www.midtgardfluefiske.no and www.midgartubeflies.com, you can see pictures of how the tubing is put together and how I tie my tube flies. Email: dag@midtgardfluefiske.no.

PURPLE LIGHT

Tube: 2 inches of Midgar innertubing and 1 inch of Midgar outertubing with 1/2-inch overlap. The rear end of the outertubing is the hook sleeve. The body on the larger version of the sample flies is 1 3/16 inch long, including cone head. Smaller fly's body is 1 inch long,with a thread head.

Tag: Small oval silver tinsel

Butt: Black silk floss, heavily twisted, or dubbed seal fur

1st body section: 3/5 satin embossed silver tinsel

1st under-wing section: White Tempelhair, 1 inch long

2nd body section: 2/5 purple ice dubbing

Body hackle: Black, long, cock hackle

2nd under-wing section: White Tempelhair, slightly longer and thicker than the first under-wing section

1st over-wing section: Bright purple Tempelhair, approximately same thickness as the white, and slightly longer

Flash: Steelhead ice Angel Hair, a few strands

Collar hackle: Black, long, cock hackle

2nd over-wing section: Black Tempelhair, slightly longer than previous wing section, thickness approximately 2/5 of total wing

Horns/topping: 3 or 4 peacock herls dyed black

Sides: Small, thin jungle cock extending almost to the butt

Thread head: Black Gudebrod size 10/0

Cone head: Midgar black nickel. For the larger fly use 1/4-inch diameter; for the smaller fly use 5/32-inch diameter.

Hook: Single, double or treble

Step 1: Join the two sections of tubing together with an overlap of 1/3 to 1/2 of the body length and slide them onto the needle tool. After connecting the tubes put a small drop of Zap-A-Gap on the join area of the inner and outertubing, then wrap thread over the outertubing before the glue dries. The pressure of the thread cemented by the Zap-A-Gap is what holds the two tubes together. Whip finish and trim the thread. Wait until the glue sets before tying.

Step 2: Attach tying thread 3/16 inch from the end of Medium tubing and tie in oval silver tinsel. Wind on the tag, tie down, trim excess. Wind on the butt of black spun silk floss.

Step 3: Tie in the satin embossed silver tinsel, advance thread 5/16 inch along body. Wrap tinsel forward, 3/5 of body length, tie down, and trim excess.

Step 4: Tie in first white Tempelhair wing section.

Step 5: Tie in body hackle.

Step 6: Dub on the purple ice for the 2nd body section. It should cover 2/5 of body and heavily taper down to the innertubing where the rest of the fly will be tied. Wind body hackle over dubbing four or five turns, tie down, and trim excess.

Step 7: After second body section and body hackle are made, brush the dubbing with a male Velcro. This spreads the dubbing between the hackle fibers. It also makes a smooth transition from the inner and up to the outertubing so the second wing section lies flat against the dubbing body and forms a strong and dense wing.

Step 8: Tie in second under-wing section of white Tempelhair, slightly longer and thicker than the first section.

Step 9: Tie in the first over-wing section of bright purple Tempelhair, same thickness as the two bunches of white hair combined, and slightly longer.

Step 10: Tie in a few strands of steelhead ice Angel Hair, slightly longer than purple wing.

Step 11: Tie in a doubled, black cock hackle and wind it four to six turns from the purple wing section down to the innertubing to cover the tie-in spot for the previous wing sections. This makes the front of the tube wide and strong. It also makes it easy to build a small, nice-looking thread head after tying in the last over wing.

Step 12: Tie in second over-wing section of black Tempelhair, slightly longer than previous wing section, approximately 2/5 of total wing thickness. Fasten the hair down with with 3 to 4 turns of thread, then remove 2 or 3 turns, apply Zap-A-Gap to the thread, then rewind it.

Step 13: Tie in horns/topping of 3 or 4 peacock herls dyed black.

PÅL MUGAAS

Step 14: On either side, tie in small and thin jungle cock feather extending almost back to the butt.

Step 15: When I finish the fly off with a thread head, I make it with Zap-A-Gap-soaked thread. After I whip finish and the glue is dry, I cut the inner and outertubing at the head with a razor blade to approximately 2 mm (3/32 inch) from the base of the wing section. Then I apply one or two additional coats of Zap-A-Gap to the head so the wraps will not loosen while fishing.

Step 16: For a cone head, I finish the last wing section with 2 to 4 parallel thread wraps, then cut off the wing butts as close as I can to the last thread turn. It is important that the last over wing section is tied in by a maximum 3 to 4 thread turns so there is no space between last wing section and cone head. I put a drop of Zap-A-Gap in front of the wing, then push the cone head into place. Some cone heads need to be drilled out to fit the innertubing, or you can use Midgar Tube Fly Cone heads, that are predrilled to fit the different innertubing sizes I offer. After the cone is in place, I cut the innertubing 2 to 3 mm in front of the cone head, and melt the tubing with a lighter. The innertubing crimps backwards as it melts, holding the cone in position. Clear the innertubing hole with a needle.

I named this fly Purple Light because it has been very productive in evenings when the bluish light turns to purple, just before dark. It was inspired by the Purple Job, a pattern devised by a friend of mine, Allen Tucker. Allen only dresses his flies on short brass tubes, with no body or hackle, and just a plain wing. I used his white and purple color combination, added a little silver and black to make a variant.

GOLDEN LIGHT

Tubing: 2 inches of Midgar innertubing, 1 inch of Midgar outertubing. The innertubing is inserted into outer tubing with 1/2 inch-overlap. The rear end of outer tubing is the hook sleeve. The body on the larger version of the fly is 1 3/16 inch long, including cone head. Smaller fly has a 1 inch body and thread head.

Tag: Small oval silver tinsel
Butt: Black silk floss
1st body section: Marigold silk floss
Ribbing: Oval silver tinsel
2nd body section: 2/5 purple ice dubbing
Body hackle: Black, long, cock hackle
1st wing section: Marigold Tempelhair
2nd wing section: Hot orange Tempelhair
3rd wing section: Black Tempelhair
Collar hackle: Black, long, cock hackle
Sides: Small, thin jungle cock feathers extending almost back to the butt
Cone head: Midgar black nickel. For the larger fly use 1/4-inch diameter; for the smaller fly use 5/32-inch diameter.
Hook: Single, double or treble

This fly uses same tying procedure and principles as the Purple Light. Its body is based on the famous Jock Scott. I like this fly at sunrise and sunset when the light is yellow and warm. It has proven itself in low water conditions on the River Gaula and the River Alta, producing many nice salmon from 2.5 to 8.8 kilos (5.5 to 19.4 pounds).

SILVER GREY

Tube: Midgar Medium or Large. The overlap of outertubing on innertubing is 1/3 as long as the finished body length. Body length should be approximately 1/3 of total wing length. Use thread to taper down from the outertubing to the innertubing and make a smooth, even under layer for the flat metal silver tinsel of the body. The body on the larger version of the fly is 1 3/16 inch long, including cone head. Smaller fly's body is 1 inch long, with a thread head.
Tag: Small oval silver tinsel
Butt: Black silk Lagartun or Pearsalls floss, twisted after it is tied in, then wrapped in 4 to 5 turns
Body: Satin embossed silver tinsel
Ribbing: Medium oval silver tinsel
Body hackle: Black, long, cock hackle
1st under-wing section: White Tempelhair
2nd under-wing section: Lemon yellow Tempelhair
3rd under-wing section: Lime green Tempelhair
Collar hackle after 3rd under-wing section: Badger chinese cock hackle doubled and wound 5 to 6 turns to cover tie-in spot for the three under-wing sections
Side wing and 1st over wing: Natural grey Tempelhair
2nd over wing: Natural grey Tempelhair
3rd over wing: Black neck Tempelhair and brown dyed Tempelhair from the neck with black tips, often found on the same skin patch. Remove almost all the under fur before tying in.
Sides: Small, thin jungle cock extending almost back to the butt
Cone head: Midgar black nickel. For the larger fly use 1/4-inch diameter; for the smaller fly use 5/32-inch diameter.
Hook: Single, double or treble

After the fly is finished, brush the wing 40 to 50 times with a male Velcro to get all fibers, flash, hackle, and hair mingled together.

The tying procedure for this fly is a little bit more complicated and time-consuming than for the Purple Light and Golden light. I developed it in order to reproduce the subtle color combinations found on classic Atlantic salmon flies from the Victorian era. I also wanted to make a wing strong enough to keep its shape in fast-running water but that still had good movement.

I tie these tube flies in different hues, using sharper and brighter colors and materials in the bodies and wings for flies intended to fool newly-run fish, and duller color shades for wing and body for fish that have been in the river for a time.

RICH MURPHY

Georgetown, Massachusetts

I taught myself to fly-cast and tie rudimentary freshwater flies when I was eight years old. I caught my first trout on a fly the following spring using a mayfly spinner pattern I copied from an old *Field & Stream*.

I started saltwater fishing with live and cut bait. I'd set up two or three monster spin- or bait-casting rods on sand spikes, and then sit and wait for something to happen. I always brought a fly rod along, filling in the time between strikes fly-casting and catching near-shore fish. As the seasons passed I realized I was having more fun fly-fishing and I left the bait rods at home.

Seventeen years ago, I began commercially tying Deceivers and other saltwater flies, and my own patterns. After three years of part-time tying, I was producing my own patterns exclusively to the tune of 40 gross a year.

In the winter of 1995, at the suggestion of the late Bill Peabody, I submitted six patterns to Umpqua Feather Merchants, hoping to move from burn-out mass production into fly design. I received a form letter six months later gently informing me that I didn't make the cut and asking me to try again next year.

In the fall of 1996, I met Umpqua's sales representative and was recruited into the company's Northeast Specialty Program. Per the program contract, I prepared instructional media and construction specifications for four of my patterns which were mass produced in Thailand and test-marketed by Umpqua in fly shops in the Northeast and Middle Atlantic states. A year later, on the basis of the strong customer response, all four Specialty patterns — Conomo Special, Steep Hill Special, RM Shortfin, and RM Flatside — were included in Umpqua's 1997-1998 catalog.

Between 1998 and 2002, Umpqua picked up four more of my patterns: RM Needlefish, RM Rattlesnake, Pamet Special, and the RM Spitfire.

In February 2001, Umpqua invited me to their factory in Chiang Mai, Thailand ("Thai-a-Fly") to do one-and-a-half weeks of advanced instruction in modern saltwater fly-tying to the essential production personnel.

I still do custom tying for a faithful client base, and I write about fly-tying and fly-fishing. I have been published in *Saltwater Flyfishing*, *Fish and Fly* magazine, *Fly Tyer*, and in an interesting Japanese periodical, *Flyrodder*.

I have also recently completed a book, *Fly Fishing for Striped Bass*. It will be published by Wild River Press, a division of Riversong Communications. The scheduled release date is June 2006 (ISBN 09746427-2-X).

Over the last five years, I have taught an average of 25 saltwater fly-tying classes a year, including free classes for the Massachusetts Chapter of United Fly Tyers. I have appeared as a featured tier for Umpqua at industry trade shows in Salt Lake City and Denver, as well as venues on the East Coast, including Somerset, New Jersey, Wilmington and Marlborough, Massachusetts, and Providence, Rhode Island.

I usually start the fishing season in the Bahamas in mid-March for bonefish, permit, tarpon, jacks, and barracuda, and end it in late December chasing stripers and tunas in North Carolina. From early April to late November, I fish the Northeast. I usually

can get out on the water five to seven times a week during that interval.

I live in Georgetown, a small town very near the northeast coastline of Massachusetts, with my lovely wife Lucy and our two faithful bad dogs, the Duck and Tahoe. I pay our mortgage by consulting as a Professional Civil Engineer (P.E.).

RM SHORTFIN SQUID

Tube: Plastic HMH Salt Water TU-KSW, 1/8-inch O. D., 6 inches long

Thread: White flat-waxed nylon

Tentacle assembly: 6 to 8 gray or white ostrich herls, 4 to 6 inches long; two 1/16- to 1/8-inch diameter bunches of blue dun marabou 2 to 3 inches long; 7 to 10 strands of rainbow Krystal Flash; and 2 to 4 strands of pearl-barred Sili-Legs

Head: Large-diameter clear EZ Body, 2 inches long

Eyes: Silver Prismatic stick-on, 3/8-inch diameter

Cement: 5-minute epoxy and super glue

Body: 1/2-inch-wide clear FLEXO tubing, 9 inches long

Fins: Rainbow Krystal Flash, 1 to 3 inches long, over blue dun marabou, one bunch on each side

Hook: Gamakatsu Circle Octopus 6/0 to 8/0

Step 1: Cut about a 2-inch piece of large-diameter clear EZ Body. Turn one end into itself forming a trumpet-like extended conical shape, to form the head cone. This folding operation can be facilitated with a thin blunt object like a Philips head screwdriver.

Step 2: To form the tentacle assembly, bind together 6 to 8, 4- to 6-inch-long gray or white ostrich herls; two 1/16- to 1/8-inch diameter, 2- to 3-inch-long bunches of blue dun marabou; 7 to 10 strands of rainbow Krystal Flash; and 2 to 4 strands of pearl-barred Sili-legs with about ten turns of thread turns. Whip finish, trim the tag ends of the material, add a drop of super glue on the joint, but do not cut the thread.

Step 3: With a bodkin, push the tentacle assembly about 5/8 inch inside the head cone. Start a series of tight, touching turns or barrel wraps on the cone with thread about 1/2 inch from its wide end , and wind about 1/4 inch toward it, binding the tentacle assembly to the inside walls of the cone. Whip finish and apply and spread a drop of super glue over the thread wraps. After it's cured, flatten the completed head with pliers, apply colors of your choice to the cone so it covers the length of inserted tentacle assembly with permanent-ink markers, and apply a thin coat of 5-minute epoxy to both sides. When the epoxy begins to gel, apply and align 3/8-inch or 1/2-inch Prismatic eyes, pre-coated with epoxy and cured, on opposite sides of the head cone. Allow to cure.

Step 4: Place a 6-inch-long, 1/8-inch O. D. plastic tube onto a mandrel and secure it in your vise. Neatly barrel-wrap the entire length of the tube. Lightly coat the thread with super glue. Position the completed head assembly so the eye extends beyond, or is cantilevered off, one end of the tube and the remainder of the assembly lays over the tube. Start a barrel wrap at the forward end of the assembly and wrap along the tube to the eyes' overhang, then back to the starting point.

Step 5: Slide a 9-inch piece of 1/2-inch-wide clear FLEXO over the forward end of the tube and tie down its leading edge just in front of the head assembly. Tie in a 6-inch length of pink, medium chenille at the same point. Wrap the chenille down to the eyes and back to the original tie-in point. The chenille should cover the head assembly tie-in point. Tie off, whip finish, and trim off the excess chenille. Apply a drop of super glue to the thread wraps.

Step 6: Push the free end of the body over itself, so that the edge of the doubled FLEXO touches the base of the Prismatic eyes. Hold the FLEXO in that position and compress its free end to expand its diameter over the length of the tube to 1 1/4 inches. This should not require much force at all. Pinch and hold the expanded FLEXO against the tube at the front end. Mark the compressed FLEXO where it hangs over the front of the tube. Allow the FLEXO to relax so you can cut it at the mark without cutting the tube.

Step 7: Push the FLEXO toward the eyes until the free end of the tube is exposed. Start a barrel wrap on the exposed tube, and then allow the FLEXO to relax until its trimmed end is over the free end of the tube. Compress the FLEXO, making the ends match up, then, holding it against the tube, start a barrel wrap, binding it to the tube. Wrap about 3/4 inch toward the rear of the tube, and then return to the starting point. Apply a drop of super glue to the wraps, but do not cut the thread. This expanded length of FLEXO simulates a live squid's mantle, which constitutes about 2/3 of its total body length.

Step 8: Apply color to the FLEXO mantle. I use pale blue over blush pink, pale brown over milky white, and bright red over pale orange color schemes.

From top: RM Shortfin Squid (Large); Conomo Special; RM Flatside 3 Tube; RM Shortfin Squid (Small)

Short Fin Squid in repose are pale brown over their entire dorsal surface and pale white over their entire ventral. However, they can change colors quickly like a chameleon, to camouflage themselves and also in reaction to stress. In response to attack they turn mostly red. Both the pale blue or bright red/pale orange color schemes simulate the squid in the process of making that color change.

Step 9: Tie in 5 to 7 strands of 1- to 3-inch-long Krystal Flash over a 1/16- to 1/8-inch-diameter bunch of marabou on each side of the FLEXO tie-in point at the front end of the tube.

The color of both the Krystal Flash and the marabou should complement the color of the FLEXO mantle. For instance, rainbow Krystal Flash over blue dun marabou with a pale blue/blush pink body, or red Krystal Flash over pale orange marabou with a red/orange body.

Step 10: Whip finish and cut the thread. Apply a thin coat of epoxy to the wraps and let it cure.

Shortfin Squid are a Northwest Atlantic species whose life span ends after a single spawning cycle. These squid spawn offshore in early winter, between Bermuda and Cape Hatteras, N.C. After the new larvae hatch, they are transported north by the Gulf Stream to the offshore limits of the Gulf of Maine. On the way, the larvae metamorphose into 1 1/4-inch mantle length, free-swimming "young of the year"(YOY) juveniles.

Shortfin spend virtually all of their time capturing and consuming prey — they have to. In order to spawn the following winter, the YOY must grow from 1 1/4 inch to about 6 inches in mantle length. If the YOY do not grow sufficiently over the summer, they will not spawn, and become holdovers. Sex and size-segregated schools of holdovers migrate north from the spawning ground, generally following the same timing and tracking the YOY.

In early April, both YOY and holdover schools begin to move inshore onto the Northeast's continental shelf and feed voraciously. By then, the YOY are 1 1/2 to 2 1/2 inch in mantle length. The holdover schools, though numerically much smaller than the YOY, and consist of much larger individuals, 7 to 9 inches in mantle length.

As the YOY grow, they feed on progressively larger finfish prey. The holdovers compete for the same finfish forage as large predatory marine fish. In October, their forage time in near-shore north Atlantic waters ends and all Shortfin schools begin their terminal spawning migration south along the edges of the Mid-Atlantic Bight.

These flies imitate the holdover population, which, by competing for the same prey as larger striped bass, bluefish, and bluefin tuna, often as not become prey themselves.

The blue over pink version is about 6 inches in mantle length and the brown over white is about 5 1/2 inches. Both mantles are way too long to tie directly on a reasonably light, commercially available, long-shanked hook. Mounting them on tubes is the answer.

RICH MURPHY

I fish this pattern relatively high in the water column, using a 12-inch strip, punctuated with a pause. The hit usually comes on the re-initiation of motion. An important feature of this pattern is its resilient texture, neither too hard or too soft, which is very much like the natural bait. Predatory fish will hold these flies in their mouths longer before rejecting them, giving an angler a few extra seconds to make a hook-set.

CONOMO SPECIAL

Tube: Plastic HMH Salt Water TU-KSW, 1/8-inch O. D., 4 inches long

Thread: White flat waxed nylon

Tail: Opal Mirage over gold Krystal Flash over red Krystal Flash over natural yak hair about 14 inches long

Spreader: Pearl EZ Body 1/2 inch wide

Collar: Natural yak hair

Wing: Herring Back Ultra Violet Krystal Flash over long natural peacock herl over ultra-marine Super Hair over olive yak hair over Peacock Ultra Hair over sea foam green Super Hair over long pink bucktail. Use a black permanent marker to make 1/4-inch-wide vertical stripes set about 3/4 to 1 inch apart the length of the wing, like those of an Atlantic mackerel.

Flash: Red Krystal Flash beard, gray ghost over shrimp pink Krystal Flash side highlights

Head: Pearl EZ Body 1/2 inch wide

Eyes: Silver Prismatic stick-on, 1/2-inch diameter

Hook: 10/0 Trey Combs Big Game

I developed the Conomo Special to imitate a variety of herring-type baitfish, including Atlantic menhaden, alewife and blue back herring which migrate north in spring and early summer then south in the fall along the Northeast's inshore waters. The pattern is named for a deep, rock ledge-sided channel near the mouth of the Essex River in Essex, Massachusetts which cow-sized striped bass favor as an ambush chokepoint on the ebb of the tide. I use this fly for larger striped bass, bluefish, and small bluefin tuna. It is a big-profile fly, 14 inches long, 5 inches high, and 2 1/2 inches deep. It is too large to tie on a hook, again mounting it on a tube solves that problem.

This pattern features two uses of EZ Body (a braided mylar and nylon tubing): as a spreader tied on the tube between the tail and wing materials; and for the fly's head. The three polyester reinforcing strips embedded in the EZ Body should be removed prior to tying.

The spreader flares the collar and wing materials around the tail, creating a large, three dimensional silhouette with minimal materials. This creates a fly very light for its size, and very flexible. Both characteristics add to the pattern's castablility. The benefit of a low throw weight is obvious; the pattern's flexibility allows it to turn over smoothly and quickly at the end of a backcast. If the pattern were stiffer, its aerodynamic drag would delay the turn over and ruin the cast timing.

The spreader goes on the tube after the tail is in place. Slide the length of EZ Body over the front end of the tube and tie it down ahead of the tail's thread wraps. Push the rest of the EZ Body over the tube, the tie-in point, and itself. The doubled-over edge should stop just in front of the tail's thread wraps. Wrap down the free end of EZ Body ahead of the first tie-in point and barrel wrap back over it. The EZ Body should form a flat-sided cone 1/2 to 3/4 inches wide at its base.

The EZ Body head forces the collar and wing material to flare over the spreader, and provides an aerodynamic platform on which to mount the pattern's eyes.

After the collar and wing are tied on the tube, attach one end of the EZ Body in front of their thread wraps. Push the rest of the EZ Body towards the spreader, making the material double over on itself. Keep pushing until the doubled-over edge just about touches the doubled-over end of the spreader, then with the fingers of one hand, pinch and hold the free end against the tube about 1/2 inch from the initial tie-in. Use the fingers of the other hand to manipulate the EZ Body into a symmetrical, flat-sided, elliptically-shaped head. When you get the right shape, start a barrel wrap just ahead of your finger pinch. Then wrap the thread toward the front end of the tube about 1/8 inch. Whip finish and trim thread. Apply a coat of super glue over the wraps and the excess EZ Body and section of tube extending beyond the whip finish. Carefully trim off the excess EZ Body and protruding tube.

RM FLATSIDE 3 TUBE

Tube: Plastic HMH Salt Water TU-KSW, 1/8-inch O. D., 6 inches long

Thread: White flat waxed nylon

Keel weight: Lead tape

Internal frame: Large clear EZ Body. Leave in the polyester reinforcing strips. Orient the EZ Body so the strips are in the same plane as the hook shank, bend, and point. Apply super glue to the strips to stiffen them.

External skin membrane: Loco Foam Pearl Sili Skin, thick, cut as a rough rectangle, folded over the EZ Body, and then trimmed to shape with sharp, clean scissors.

Color: Bronze with a black ocellation spot behind eye. Apply primary color as a stripe on the adhesive side of the Sili Skin with a permanent-ink marker.

Tail: White Arctic fox

Eyes: Silver Prismatic stick-on, 1/2-inch diameter

Hook: Gamakatsu Circle Octopus 6/0

The Flatside 3 Tube imitates a young Atlantic menhaden, blue back herring, or alewife. In the fall, Northeast inshore waters can be choked with acre-wide schools of YOY of these species migrating south and offshore. Individuals range in length from 1 1/2 to 6 inches. They are a favored prey of stripers, bluefish, false albacore, bonito, and bluefin, yellowfin, and skipjack tuna.

This fly does very well fished along the edges of schools of herring being blitzed by predators. I let it sink a bit in the water column, then retrieve it with short erratic strips like an injured bait separated from the safety of the school.

CHAPTER
21

BERND NICKOLEIT
Thumby, Germany

When I first took up fly-fishing more than 20 years ago, I chased after nearly every species of fish with the long rod. After a decade, I discovered my true passions: Atlantic salmon and sea trout in Scandinavia's rivers, and Baltic sea trout. I have written articles on tube flies for the fly-fishing and tying magazines *Fliegenfischen* and *Fisch und Fliege*, and for the last eight years I have run a small fly-fishing school in my spare time near Marburg, fishing the River Luhn for trout and grayling. I demonstrate tying techniques for modern Atlantic salmon and sea-trout flies at fly-fishing and tying shows in Germany, and do private teaching.

One of my favorite rivers is the famous Mörrum in Sweden, but I also like the small Danish sea-trout rivers. There is much to discover and enjoy in Scandinavia: unspoiled nature, and migrating wild salmon and sea trout. I fly-fish the coastal waters of Germany, Sweden, and Denmark as well. The smell of salt water, the crying gulls, blue sky, strong wind, and the chance for a big, ocean-fresh sea trout on a fly is balsam for my soul.

Ninety percent of my river fishing for salmon and sea trout is done with tubes. There are many reasons for this, but one of the most important is the fact that I can tie my favorite patterns/sizes in many different weights/sink rates using plastic tubes with or without cone heads, and aluminum, brass, or copper tubes. In the last few years some interesting tube variations have appeared on the market, including deep-water tubes, low-water tubes, brass bottle tubes, and US tubes. "US" stands for Ulf Sill, a German living near the river Mörrum. He designed these short, extra-heavy, straight tubes for salmon fishing in that river. US tubes are distributed by the Fly Company. Also quite heavy for their size, deep-water tubes are tied without a body; their short length (3/8 inch) allows the wing to move freely.

My tube tying has been profoundly influenced by the newer Scandinavian styles. One trend in Scandinavia is to tie on very short tubes and fish them with a so-called "flying treble," a hook that is not fixed to the tube. A very-small-diameter silicone sleeve is slipped on the leader between the fly and hook eye. After the hook is tied on, the sleeve goes over the knot and hook eye. The sleeve protects the knot and allows the fly to slide freely on the leader. The hooking performance of a flying treble is excellent, and during the fight the fly isn't damaged. Another advantage of this approach: the wing of the free-sliding fly doesn't tangle in the treble.

For years I relied on the Kamasan B-990 Tube Fly Treble hook, but now I combine my flies with Partridge's new Salar Tube Fly Hook designed by Michael Frödin of Sweden. This high-quality treble is available in black, gold, and silver to match and

From top: Swedish Salmonizer; Bernd's G. P.; Call of the Sea; Rapala Fly

complement the basic color of the fly. A General Practitioner with a gold hook looks very nice, indeed.

One last, but very important thing. If you use natural materials in your flies, please take a serious look at their source. Don't use materials from endangered species. If you tie with jungle cock, be sure the feathers are from farmed birds and have a CITES document, or use substitutes like those made by Mustad, Norway.

I live in the northern part of Germany, only minutes from the coast, where I work as a veterinarian specializing in small-animal surgery.

SWEDISH SALMONIZER

Tube: Two sizes of plastic tubing (I use the Frödin Tube system), joined. A 1 1/4-inch length of 3/32-inch (2.5 mm) O. D. rear tube and a 5/8-inch length of 1/16-inch (1.5 mm) O. D. plastic tube that fits inside it. Joined length is 1 7/8 inch.
Tag: Medium oval gold tinsel
Tail: Hot orange Glow Brite yarn
Butt: Hot orange Glow Brite yarn
Rib: Medium oval gold tinsel
Rear body: Gold Holo Flat Braid
Front body: Salmon red Korsika Salmon dubbing
Rib hackle: Orange cock hackle
Wing: Three bunches of Arctic fox hair, two orange and one black, mixed with orange, electric blue, and yellow flash material (Angel Hair and/or Gliss 'n' Glow)
Sides: Domestic jungle cock
Front hackle: Black, long and soft
Cone head: Gold, 1/4-inch diameter
Hook: Gold Partridge Salar Tube Fly treble, size 4 or 7

Step 1: Permanently fix the small tube inside the larger one with a drop of gap-filling super glue (you can also use hot glue or epoxy), then cover the overlap with tying thread and whip finish. Put the joined plastic tubes on your tube vise.

Step 2: Attach tying thread and wind three to four turns of medium oval gold tinsel for the tag.

Step 3: Follow with a tail of hot orange "Glow Brite" yarn (Veniard), then tie in a butt of the same material.

Step 4: Tie in a length of medium oval tinsel for the ribbing and the Holo Flat Braid.

Step 5: Wind the rear half of the body with the Holo Flat Braid.

Step 6: Make a dubbing loop, and with Korsika Salmon dub form the front half of the body. You can substitute any other other dubbing you like, e.g., the new and effective UV Dubbing. or SLF Salmon and Steelhead from Partridge.

Step 7: Tie an orange badge cock hackle butt first at the front of the body, then wind it backwards as a rib, towards the tag. Use the oval gold tinsel to tie down the hackle (crossing over technique) and wind the tinsel forward to the front of the body.

Step 8: Tie in three bunches of Arctic fox hair — well brushed beforehand and mixed with some flash material like Angel Hair or Gliss 'n' Glow. Start with a small bunch of short orange hair,

then a bunch of larger, longer orange, and finish off with a little shorter black hair, so you get a teardrop-shaped wing.

Step 9: Tie in a pair of domestic jungle cock feathers on the sides.

Step 10: On the thin inner tube, wind a collar of soft, black saddle hackle. This blends the cone head in nicely.

Step 11: Whip finish and cut the thread. Slide a cone head over the thin tube. Super glue it in place, then cut and melt the protruding tube.

CALL OF THE SEA

Tube: Plastic, 3/32-inch (2.5 mm) O. D., 1 1/2 inches long
Tag: Oval silver tinsel
Butt: Hot orange Glo Brite yarn
Tail: Poly Bear in golden crest color
Rear 2/3 body: Black Holo Flat Braid
Front 1/3 body: Black booby Korsika Salmon dub
Ribbing: Oval silver tinsel and purple cock hackle
Wing: Blue-dyed squirrel tail under black Arctic fox, mixed with electric blue Angel Hair
Sides: Domestic jungle cock
Front hackle: Blue-dyed silver pheasant breast feather
Head: Blue Body Wrap covered with Liquid Glass (Veniard)
Hook: Gold Partridge Salar Tube Fly treble, size 4 or 7

BERND'S G. P.

Tube: Plastic, 3/32-inch (2.5 mm) O. D., 1 1/2 inches long
Feelers: Orange polar bear (came from an animal that died in a zoo)
Eyes: Black Fly Eyes (monofilament stem)
Shellback: Two orange-dyed breast feathers from golden pheasant
Body: Korsika Salmon dub in G. P. Orange flash
Ribbing: Oval gold tinsel and orange cock hackle
Head: Red thread, covered with Liquid Glass
Hook: Gold Partridge Salar Tube Fly treble, size 4 or 7

RAPALA FLY

Tube: US 1/8-inch O. D. copper tube 5/8 inch long with a thin plastic liner tube that protrudes 1/4 inch from the front end. The Fly Company supplies both components; you have to assemble them yourself. Melt a nub on one end of the plastic tube before sliding it through the copper tube. The nub end is the butt of the fly body. The fly's wing, sides, and hackle are all dressed on the thin, protruding plastic tube.
Body: The bare copper tube forms the fly body.
Hackle: Hot orange tied in behind and in front of the wing
Wing: Three or four bunches of fluorescent orange Arctic fox, mixed with orange and pearl green Gliss 'n' Glow and electric blue Angel Hair
Sides: Domestic jungle cock
Head: Red thread, covered with Liquid Glass
Hook: Gold Partridge Salar Tube Fly treble, size 4 or 7

HÅKAN NORLING
Viksjö, Sweden

The old people in my family were sailors and fishermen so I suppose fishing is in my genes; having always fished I honestly can't remember when I did it the first time. I had never seen anyone cast a fly rod when I bought one at age 12. I tied my first 1000 fly order when I was 14 for the old Swedish fly-tying master Per-Olof "Flug-Pelle" Persson. In the 1980's and the beginning of the 1990's I worked as a guide in Norway, mostly on the Gaula River, a very creative period for me with a lot of fishing. I met fly-fishers from all over the world. It has been my privilege to fish some of the best salmon rivers on the planet, but there are still places left to go, and I hope to visit them someday.

I stopped tying flies professionally five years ago. Having done it for so long (about 25 years) I cannot say I miss it much. Currently, I work as a sales representative for Guideline AB/Aktiv Fritid in Sweden, a new challenge in many ways; my only regret is that my fishing time is now limited.

In 1985 I was looking for some long goat hair to make an order of Sunray Shadows when Margrete Thompsen, the original Swedish master fly-tier, told me there was no goat hair in stock, but she had something else that could be useful to me that she called Tibetan jackal dog. When the hair arrived it looked terrible and was too short for the Sunrays. I dyed some of it black and dark brown and tied the first original Tempeldog before my friend Michael Frödin and I went on our annual autumn trip to the River Em in Sweden. I will never forget the sight of that fly in the water. It looked like it would swim away with my leader. The wing was alive and moving in a way I had never seen with any other hair. At that time we were using mostly squirrel, bucktail, and goat hair. Since then, a lot has happened. Without exaggerating too much, the style of flies that

Michael and I developed over the next 10 years set the standard for salmon flies fished in Scandinavia today.

The hair that I call Tempeldog is actually dog hair. It has always been difficult to find, although during the 70's it was quite common to use dogs to make fur coats. There is no other hair material that even comes close to it in texture and movement in the water. Not long ago I saw a TV documentary from China showing the treatment of the animals used for the skin market. It was really nasty to watch and I have decided not to use or sell dog hair anymore. The best alternative is farmed fox hair, but that is also very difficult to find in good quality.

In my opinion the quality of the material used for a fly determines how well it fishes. The salmon don't care if you have travelled around the world and use tackle worth thousands of dollars; they are only interested in the fly. The fish see the fly from below, so in my opinion it's important for a tube fly to have a good silhouette and movement. It's also important to balance the weight of the fly and hook size against the strength and the speed of the current; if you properly make these adjustments your flies will "fish" better and catch more fish.

My choice of fly line depends upon water level, temperature, the speed of current, and when and where I'm going to fish. I carry a selection of shooting heads and poly leaders with me so I can fish efficiently under all conditions. Two-handed fly rods of 12 to 15 feet and shooting heads are standard equipment for salmon and sea-trout fishing in Scandinavia and they are usually necessary to cast the flies we use. The surroundings are also important. Is there open space for overhead casts? Or is it bushes and trees all the way down to the water? Will I need short and heavy shooting heads for Spey casting, or a longer but a class lighter line for distance casting? One thing to keep in mind: The choice of fly line (shooting head) is often more important than the choice of the fly. It's all about presentation, getting the fly where you want it, at a level where it will interest a fish, and making it fish instantly.

For the past five or six years, the fly-tying trend in Scandinavia has turned to cone heads and weighted tubes. Again, the weight of the fly and the hook size determine how these flies fish. If you balance a fly correctly, it will "swim" and move naturally in the current.

PLASTIC TUBE SYSTEM

Michael Frödin and I worked independently and jointly to develop this product line which is distributed by Guideline AB, Sweden (See Appendix for address). It consists of four different diameters of tubing that fit together. The tubing comes in fluorescent orange, fluorescent red, fluorescent chartreuse, fluorescent yellow, black and clear.

X-Small: Fits inside the Medium tube, and is used with Small and X-Small cone heads

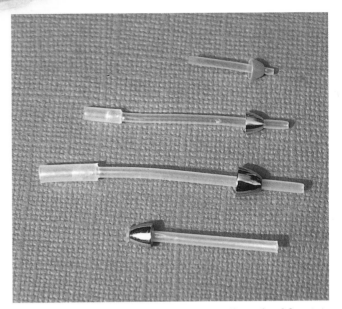

From top: X-Small tube with X-Small or Small cone head for mini tubes; X-Small and Medium tubes for fixed hook with Small gold cone head; Large and Small tubes for fixed hook with Medium silver cone head; Small tube with cone head pointing backwards.

Small: Fits inside the Large tube and is used with Medium and Large cone heads

Medium: For fixed hooks (The hook eye fits directly into the tube without a silicone or rubber sleeve) in sizes 8 to 6. Fits over the X-Small tube.

Large: For fixed large hooks (The hook eye fits directly into the tube without a silicone or rubber sleeve) in sizes 4 to 2. It fits over Small tubing.

With this system you can use a piece of Large tubing in the back for the hook, and tie the body and wing on the Small tube, or you can tie a full body on the Large tube and finish the head on the Small tube. The same goes for the use of Medium/X-Small.

CONE HEADS

There are several brands of cone heads on the market. It's important that the hole in the cone is large enough for plastic tube you are using. The best tubing is slightly thicker than the diameter of the hole and you have to stretch the tube until it's thin enough to fit inside. After the fly is tied slide the cone back and release the stretched tubing. The cone is held in place without glue.

I use two types of cone heads and beads, brass and tungsten. The brass are usually available in gold, silver, copper, black and fluorescent colors (orange, chartreuse, red) in sizes X-Small, Small, Medium, and Large. Tungsten cone heads also come in gold, silver, black and in fluorescent colors (orange, chartreuse, red) in sizes X-Small, Small, Medium, and Large. A Small

From top: Black Greenhighlander Tempeldog; Red Tempeldog; Original Tempeldog; Black and Silver Tempeldog; Marlodge Tempeldog; Grey Tempeldog with tungsten cone head

MEASURED WEIGHTS OF	
Brass Cone Heads	Tungsten Cone Heads
Small = 0.19gr	Small = 0.56gr
Medium = 0.34gr	Medium = 0.82gr
Large = 0.45gr	Large = 1.09gr

Mustad Treble	Partridge Salar Double-Tube Hook
Size	Size
4 = 0.65gr	2 = 0.55gr
6 = 0.45gr	4 = 0.40gr
8 = 0.31gr	6 = 0.32gr
10 = 0.20gr	8 = 0.23gr

MEASURED WEIGHTS OF FLY TREBLES AND DOUBLE HOOKS		
Partridge Salar Treble	Partridge Treble	Kamasan Treble
Size	Size	Size
3 = 0.77gr	4 = 0.50gr	4 = 0.85gr
5 = 0.55gr	6 = 0.35gr	6 = 0.50gr
7 = 0.42gr	8 = 0.27gr	8 = 0.40gr
9 = 0,32gr	10 = 0.18gr	10 = 0.31gr
11 = 0.20gr	12 = 0.15gr	12 = 0.19gr
13 = 0.13gr		

tungsten cone weighs almost as much as a 1/2-inch long brass tube. A Medium tungsten cone weighs as much as a 3/4-inch tube and the Large weighs as much as a 1-inch tube.

Using this system, it is possible to create more than 30 variations of a single tube-fly pattern. I currently carry about 10 patterns in different colors and weights that cover most water conditions.

As a general rule, a fly will swim better if it is the lightest combination of cone head, tube, and hook for the speed and strength of the currrent. If the fly looks like it is going to swim away with your leader, you know you've found the right combination. It takes experimentation with different textures of hair, synthetic material, hackle, tubes, and cones in all speeds of current to learn how the flies will behave.

I can be contacted by email at h.norling@telia.com.

ORIGINAL TEMPELDOG

Tube: Medium and X-Small Tube System plastic tubes weighted with a strip of zonker lead tape. Combined tube length is 2 inches; X-Small protrudes about 1/8 inch from front on finished fly
Thread: Black
Tag: Oval gold tinsel No.15
Butt/Tail: Fluorescent orange Shimmer
Rib: Oval gold tinsel No.17
Body: 2/3 gold tinsel; 1/3 Ice Dub, UV black and peacock mixed
Body hackle: Hoffman silver badger dyed hot orange

Front hackle: Metz Soft Hackle dyed black or Hoffman Chickabou body feather
Wing: Dark brown Arctic fox mixed with strands of Angel Hair (pheasant tail, dark orange and gold holographic), black Arctic fox on top
Shoulders: Few strands of fine gold, red and Sunburst Flashabou alongside the wing
Cheeks: Jungle cock
Head: Black thread
Hook: Partridge Salar gold treble

Step 1: Put joined Tube System tubes on your vise. Attach tying thread. About 3/8 inch from the rear end of the tube tie in oval gold tinsel. Wrap three turns forward for a tag. Tie down and trim.
Step 2: Tie in flat gold tinsel, wind forward 1/8 inch, tie down but do not trim.
Step 3: Tie in fluorescent orange Shimmer. Wrap a butt 1/8 inch long over the flat tinsel. Finish with material on top of tube, fold it back to form a 1-inch-long tail. Trim excess.
Step 4: Tie in No. 17 oval gold tinsel and orange-dyed silver badger hackle by its tip.
Step 5: Wind flat gold tinsel forward to 2/3 of body length. Tie down, trim excess.
Step 6: Wrap a short strip of zonker tape over the front 1/3 of the body. Form a dubbing loop for the Ice Dub/UV black and peacock and wind dubbing over tape. Tie down and trim excess.
Step 7: Wind hackle forward over the entire body, tie down and trim butt. Rib body with oval gold tinsel. Tie down and trim.

Step 8: Here is the basic technique for tying Tempeldog style wings. The wing normally consists of three sections. The first section should be the shortest.

Select a bunch of Arctic fox hair, in the case of the Original Tempeldog, dark brown. Tie in the wing section with hair points facing forward. Add strands of fine Flashabou. Bend the hair section backwards, and tie the wing down with 6 or 7 wraps of thread.

The tied-down wing butt will create a little head on the tube. Hide it with a turn or two of soft hackle, in this case black.

Tie in another section of hair longer than the first hair section, in the case of the Original Tempeldog, again dark brown fox. Hair points should again face forward. Add Angel Hair. Bend the section backwards, and tie the wing down with 6 or 7 wraps of thread.

Tie in another soft hackle, again black.

Tie in a third hair section longer than the other two, in this case black fox.

Step 9: Add Flashabou to the sides and tie in the jungle cock. Form a small, neat head on the protruding X-Small tubing with black thread. Whip finish. Varnish the head.

The Original Tempeldog has taken more big fish than I can count. It fishes well in any river with coloured water. I like to use the zonker tape for weight it because it allows me to finish off with a small, neat head. When the holographic colours and mixes of Angel Hair came on the market years ago they gave my flies a new appearance and life.

GREY TEMPELDOG
WITH TUNGSTEN CONE HEAD

Tube: Small plastic tubing with a piece of Large tubing inserted as a hook sleeve. Combined tube length is 2 inches.
Thread: Black
Tag: Oval silver tinsel No.15
Butt/Tail: Fluorescent green Shimmer
Underbody: White floss
Body: A strip of Mirage sheet wound over a layer of Lagartun flat braid, holographic silver
Rib: Oval silver tinsel No. 17
Body hackle: Hoffman silver badger
Front hackle: Widgeon
Underwing: Few strands of fine silver holographic Flashabou mixed with yellow, white, green Arctic fox
Midwing: Natural fox, mixed with strands of Electric Yellow, Blue Ice Angel Hair and fine silver holographic Flashabou
Topwing: Dark brown Arctic fox under black fox
Shoulders: A few strands of fine Sunburst and olive Flashabou
Cheeks: Jungle cock
Head: Tungsten cone head, Medium
Hook: Partridge Salar treble silver

The tungsten cone head concentrates a lot of weight at the nose of this fly. Because there isn't much room to finish the head, it's necessary to hide the butts of the wing material behind at least two front hackles. It is also very important that you finish the fly with a small neat head before you slide on the cone. Leave 2 to 3 mm of bare tube protruding from the nose of the cone. To make sure the hole stays open, insert a needle into it before you melt the tube. I'm using the Partridge Salar hook, which comes in black, gold, and silver and is a part of the fly's color scheme.

BLACK GREENHIGHLANDER TEMPELDOG

Tube: Slipstream brass tube, type D, 1/2 inch long
Thread: Black
Tag: Oval gold tinsel No.15
Hackle: Highlander green cock hackle
Front hackle: Yellow cock hackle
Underwing: Mirage Accent mixed with orange, yellow, green Arctic fox
Midwing: Electric Yellow Angel Hair, lime and fine holographic gold Flashabou
Topwing: Dark brown Arctic fox under black fox
Shoulders: Fine holographic gold and green Flashabou
Cheeks: Jungle cock
Head: Black thread
Hook: Partridge Salar treble black

This is a very good pattern for a sunny day and slightly coloured water. I made the first of these "Half-inchers" some 15 years ago. In the beginning I wanted a fly that would work as a jig but I soon discovered other benefits of this type of tube. First of all, the fly starts to fish almost from the moment it hits the water. Second, in fast water the fly doesn't skate across the surface.

The best way to fish this tube is with a "free swinging hook." Take a small piece of Medium plastic tubing and slide on the leader between the hook and the fly. Push the tubing over the hook eye. Do not connect the tubing to the fly. The tubing keeps the knot from turning in the hook eye and makes the hook ride straight behind the fly. If single or double hooks are used with this rigging they will ride upside down with the hook points hidden inside the wing, which means you will not get snagged so easily if you are fishing deep. Another advantage is the lack of leverage in the fish's favor after it is hooked. The "free swinging" hooks can also be used with cone heads if the current permits. If the water is slow, I prefer a fixed hook.

MARLODGE TEMPELDOG

Tube: Small tube for the body; Medium tube for a hook sleeve. Combined tube length is 2 inches
Thread: Black
Tag: Oval gold tinsel No.15
Butt/Tail: Fluorescent green Shimmer, UV black Ice Dub, and 2 small jungle cock feathers

Underbody: White floss

   Body: A strip of Mirage sheet wound over a layer of Lagartun holographic silver flat braid. The body is divided in half by a section of mixed peacock and black Ice Dub 1/4 of body length.

   Rib: Oval silver tinsel No. 17

Underwing: Mixed blue, red, yellow Arctic fox

Midwing: Electric Yellow, red, and Blue Ice Angel Hair

Topwing: Dark brown and black fox

Shoulders: A few strands of fine red and blue holographic Flashabou, and Blue Mirror Flash

Front hackle: Fuchsia and Kingfisher blue Metz soft hackle

   Cheeks: Jungle cock

    Head: Large red cone head

    Hook: Partridge Salar treble, silver

This pattern combines the classic Marlodge and Silver Wilkinson salmon flies. Their colors have been catching fish for at least a hundred years.

RED TEMPELDOG

Tube: Medium plastic tube 3/4 inch long and Medium tungsten cone head, attached by melting tubing as usual. Tube is then placed on mandrel for tying in a reverse position, with the nose of cone head to the rear, at the back end of the body. Body is tied on tube from the back of cone head forward

   Thread: Black

   Body: Holographic silver Ice Dub, spun with dubbing twister and teased out

Underwing: Mirage Accent Flash, fine holographic red and gold Flashabou mixed with hot orange Arctic fox

Midwing: Mixed strands of red and Electric Yellow Angel Hair and fine silver holographic Flashabou

Topwing: Coral Arctic fox

   Hackle: Orange and black cock hackle

Shoulders: Two large jungle cock feathers

    Head: Black thread

    Hook: Partridge Salar treble black

This is a very good pattern for large, fresh fish. It has several 40-pounders to its credit. I also like to tie it on a 1-inch-long aluminium tube and fish it on a floating line.

Why do I tie this tube with the cone head in a reversed position? In my experience, flies tied with large and medium-sized cone heads at the front don't fish as well as flies tied with good-quality hair, a good front hackle, and finished with a small, neat thread head. On a very short tube it doesn't matter whether the weight is in front or in the back of the fly. Reverse mounting the cone head allows me to finish off the tube with a small thread head. I fish this fly with a free-swinging hook.

BLACK AND SILVER TEMPELDOG

Tube: Medium and X-Small tubes, unweighted. Combined tube length is 2 inches; X-Small protrudes from front about 1/8 inch on finished fly.

   Thread: Black

   Tag: Oval tinsel No. 15

Butt/Tail: Fluorescent orange Shimmer

   Rib: Oval Silver Tinsel No. 17

   Body: Rear 2/3 is a layer of white floss, covered with layer of Lagartun flat braid, holographic silver. Cut Mirage sheet in a strip and wind it over the holographic tinsel. Front 1/3 of body is a mix of olive and peacock Ice Dub.

Body hackle: Black cock hackle

   Wing: Black Arctic fox mixed with a few strands of fine silver and red Flashabou and orange Mirror Flash

Front hackle: Black Metz soft hackle

   Cheeks: Jungle cock dyed hot orange

    Head: Black thread

    Hook: Partridge Salar treble silver

If I had to choose one pattern to fish with, the Black and Silver would be it. It's a fly that works everywhere, in a wide variety of sizes. You'll notice that this fly is unweighted. One of the reasons I started to weight my flies was to get a better turnover of the leader, something that is difficult with a light tube. But Guideline's new Power Taper Shootingheads kick over so well it's a piece of cake to use unweighted flies again, and they fish very well.

TONY PAGLIEI

East Lansing, Michigan

TONY PAGLIEI

I started fly-tying and fly-fishing in 1976 along the shore of Lake Erie in western New York at age 12. In 1978, a local fly shop gave me the opportunity to start my commercial fly-tying career. Through the late 70's and early 80's I spent most of my free time chasing stream trout and small-mouth bass on the fly. After graduating from high school, a newly-found fishing friend introduced me to Great Lakes fly-fishing and I traded in 12-inch stream trout for 12 pounds of raging steelhead, the occasional king salmon, lake-run brown trout, tiger musky, and common carp.

I currently reside in central Michigan with my wife, Diadre and our two children, Taylor Ann and Cole Anthony. My entire family enjoys the sport of fly-fishing and the art of fly-tying. Their love and support fuels my career and passion for fly-fishing. Our geographical location couldn't be better. Michigan is known as the "Great Lakes State" but I call it "Paradise for the Modern Fly Fisher"!

I am a member of the HMH/Kennebec River Fly & Tackle Company and Gudebrod, Inc., National Pro Staff Advisory Teams. These companies have given me the opportunity to consult and develop new products for the fly-tying industry. I've published articles in *Fly Tyer*, *Warmwater Fly Fishing*, *Fly Fishing and Tying Journal*, and *North American Carp Angler*. Jim Bedford and I coauthored *The River Journal: Grand River*, published by Frank Amato Publications, May 2001.

During the winter months, I travel around the Great Lakes region giving lectures and seminars on tube fly-tying. I also own my own business, the T. Pags Company, which manufactures and distributes tube fly-tying products, Convertible Tube Flies, and produces fly-tying videos (Tying Convertible Tube Flies with Tony Pagliei: Volumes 1 and 2; Tying Flies for Golden Bones; Guide Patterns for Common Carp; Tying and Fishing Tube Flies for Smallmouth Bass; and Tying Flies with Ultra Braid). We also produce an online webcast featuring streaming video on fly-fishing/fly-tying around the Great Lakes Region titled "The Modern Fly Fisher." For more information, log on to www.modernflyfisher.com or www.tubeflies.com. Email: info@tube flies.com.

I would like to express a special thanks to Mark Mandell and Les Johnson for their inspiration. Back in 1995, I purchased their book, *Tube Flies: A Tying, Fishing and Historical Guide*. It exposed this open-minded fly tier to a whole new world! Several of the book's featured tiers dressed their trailing hooks, which made a lot of sense to me. So much, in fact, that I created the Convertible Tube Fly, an interchangeable system of heads tied with (or without) cones, beads, or dumb bells, and dressed trailing hooks that allow a fly-fisher to quickly alter colors, size, action, and sink rate to match the food source and water conditions. For example, a Woolly Bugger tube fly with a marabou-dressed trailing hook can be transformed into a leech/worm fly by switching to a hook dressed with

a long, hackle tail. This translates into fewer fly boxes in the vest, less time at the vise, and more time on the stream catching fish.

CONVERT-A-HEX

Tube: T. Pags Custom 1-inch blank with olive HMH Junction Tubing hook sleeve
Thread: Tan Gudebrod 6/0
Gills: Pheasant rump hackle
Wingcase: Natural goose quill
Thorax: Cream dubbing
Legs: Gray dun hen saddle
Eyes: Monofilament or lead dumb bells

NYMPH TAIL

Hook: Mustad C67S size 8
Thread/Ribbing: Tan Gudebrod 6/0
Tail/Shellback: Natural ostrich herl
Abdomen: Cream furry foam

BUGGER TAIL

Hook: Eagle Claw L118 size 8
Thread: Tan Gudebrod 6/0
Tail: Gray dun chickabou

NYMPH HEAD

Step 1: Begin by placing the HMH Tube Fly Tool in the vise. Then insert the small mandrel into a 1-inch custom tube blank and tighten down securely.

Step 2: Start the thread slightly in front of the junction tubing and continue to bind the junction tubing down with thread.

Step 3: Tie in a clump of webby pheasant rump fibers over the top of the junction tubing. Then tie in a 1/4-inch-wide piece of goose quill for the wingcase.

Step 4: Dub around the base of the fiber groups then tie in a hen saddle hackle. Bring your thread forward and palmer the hackle forward 2 or 3 turns.

Step 5: Tightly secure a set of eyes in front of the hackle and cover your thread with some additional dubbing.

Step 6: Bring the goose quill forward and tie down in front of the eyes. Whip finish and apply head cement, then with a razor blade cut the remaining tubing away. With a butane lighter, you can melt back the tubing to finish the head.

NYMPH TAIL

Step 1: Start the thread behind the eye of the hook and wrap a solid thread base to the barb of the hook. Leave the thread tag in place to be used as ribbing.

Step 2: Tie in four ostrich herl fibers over the barb of the hook. Trap the remaining fibers back to be used later to form a shellback.

Step 3: Securely wrap a strip of furry foam in the back and wind forward then bring the ostrich herl over the top to create a shellback.

Step 4: The tag piece of thread is now ribbed forward. Tie down the thread, whip finish and head cement.

BUGGER TAIL VARIANT

Step 1: Start the thread behind the eye of the hook and wrap a solid thread base to the barb and return to the front.

Step 2: Select 2 chickabou feathers about 3/4 inch long, trim and tie in behind the eye of the hook. Securely form a thread head, whip finish and head cement.

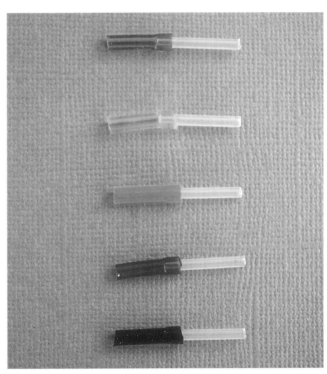

Colored junction tubes (hook sleeves) from HMH

If a weighted nymph is desired, I add mini dumb bell eyes. I use mono eyes for my unweighted versions, and 4/32 inch (1/100 oz.) and 5/32 inch (1/50 oz.) for the weighted version. I flatten all dumb bell stems with a pair of pliers before tying them. With an elongated stem, I can wrap the eyes below the half-way point on the hard tubing, which balances the head properly. Otherwise, the weighted nymph will swim upside down. I hand-paint the lead or

From top: The Wiggle Worm; The Wiggle Worm hackle leech tail; The No Body Matuka with Arctic fox tail; The No Body Matuka thread tail; Convert-A-Damsel with nymph tail; Convert-A-Damsel bugger tail; Convert-A-Hex with nymph tail; Convert-A-Hex bugger tail; Convert-A-Stone with nymph tail; Convert-A-Stone bugger tail; Frank's Jig Fly; Frank's Jig Fly curly tail lead substitute dumb bell eye to match the specific colors of each nymph.

Another way to add weight is by the selection or style of trailing hook. I primarily use Daiichi and Eagle Claw hooks because they are strong, sharp, and offer several straight-eyed style choices. The Daiichi X510 and Eagle Claw L118 series make great tube hooks for Great Lakes salmon and steelhead. They are super sharp and made of heavy wire which helps sink nymphs and other tube-fly patterns.

Convertible nymphs give you the option of realistically imitating the species in the water system or of creating an attractor pattern (mini Woolly Bugger) by switching to the bugger tail. The bugger tail provides more color contrast and movement, which can be a critical factor in high water conditions.

CONVERT-A-STONE

Tube: T. Pags Custom 1-inch blank with black HMH Junction Tubing hook sleeve
Thread: Black Gudebrod 6/0
Wingcase 1: Black pheasant rump hackle
Wingcase 2: Black pheasant tail
Thorax: Black dubbing
Legs: Black hen saddle
Eyes: Monofilament or lead dumb bells

NYMPH TAIL

Hook: Eagle Claw L084 size 8
Thread/Ribbing: Black Gudebrod 6/0
Tail: Black goose biots
Abdomen: Black furry foam

BUGGER TAIL

Hook: Daiichi 1650 size 8
Thread: Black Gudebrod 6/0
Tail: Black chickabou

CONVERT-A-DAMSEL

Tube: T. Pags Custom 1-inch blank with light olive HMH Junction Tubing hook sleeve
Thread: Tan Gudebrod 6/0
Wingcase 1: Light olive chickabou
Wingcase 2: Olive ostrich herl
Thorax: Light olive dubbing
Legs: Olive hen saddle
Eyes: Monofilament or lead dumb bells

NYMPH TAIL

Hook: Eagle Claw L084 size 10
Thread/Ribbing: Tan Gudebrod 6/0
Tail: Olive ostrich herl
Abdomen: Olive furry foam

BUGGER TAIL

Hook: Daiichi 1650 size 10
Thread: Tan Gudebrod 6/0
Tail: Light olive chickabou

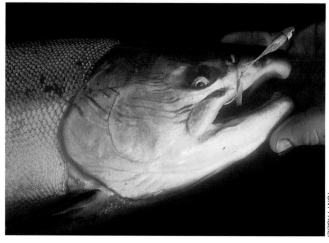

THE NO BODY MATUKA

Tube: HMH Premium 1 inch aluminum with clear HMH Junction Tubing hook sleeve
Thread: White and fluorescent red Gudebrod 3/0
Rear Wing: White Arctic fox
Front Wing: White Arctic fox
Hackle Collar: Cream saddle hackle

Hook #1: Mustad C67S size 4
Thread: Fluorescent red Gudebrod 3/0
Tail: White Arctic fox

Hook #2: Eagle Claw L084 size 4
Body: Fluorescent Gudebrod 3/0 thread or floss

TONY PAGLIEI

This leech fly pattern has proven very effective for steelhead throughout the Great Lakes region. Swinging this tube fly with a down-and-across presentation in tailouts of pools and runs will produce violent strikes. The bonus convertible factor with this tube comes with the second trailing hook and the choice of thread or floss body. By changing the trailing hook, you achieve a Spey-styled tube with brightly colored tag ends that can be changed to meet the water or sunlight conditions.

THE WIGGLE WORM

Tube: T. Pags Custom 1-inch blank with black HMH Junction Tubing hook sleeve
Thread: Black Gudebrod 6/0
Hackle collar: Black saddle hackle
Head: Oval Jiggy head, Small or Medium

Hook #1: Eagle Claw L118 size 4
Thread: Black Gudebrod 6/0
Tail: Red large Ultra Braid
Thorax: Black rabbit fur dubbing

Hook #2: Daiichi 2451 size 4
Tail: Four black saddle hackles with pearl Flashabou

The Wiggle Worm tube fly was created to directly compete with the "rubber/plastic worm industry" and all of those folks who fish with spinning and/or bait-casting tackle on the rivers and streams of North America for smallmouth bass. Pat Dunlap from Cascade Crest Tools and I figured out a way to braid ultra chenille or vernille to form a three-ply braid. This new material called "Ultra Braid" is available in every rubber-worm-matching color and it's the best material to imitate the body of a terrestrial worm (night crawler). Tail colors and tail lengths can be adjusted streamside along with its interchangeable hackle leech tail as well. No smallmouth bass in North America is safe if you have a few Wiggle Worms in your arsenal!

FRANK'S JIG FLY

Tube: T. Pags Custom 1-inch blank with chartreuse HMH Junction Tubing hook sleeve
Thread: Fluorescent green Gudebrod 3/0
Hackle collar: Fluorescent green marabou plume with pearl Flashabou
Eyes: Painted lead dumb bells, 1/24 to 1/100 ounce
Head: Fluorescent green rabbit fur dubbing

Hook #1: Eagle Claw LO84 size 6
Thread: Fluorescent green Gudebrod 3/0
Tail: Fluorescent orange marabou

Hook #2: Daiichi 1650 size 6
Thread: Fluorescent green Gudebrod 3/0
Tail: Large fluorescent green Fly Tail
Body: Fluorescent green Furry Foam

One of the cool things about being a fly tier is that we are able to name our own creations. This tube fly is named in honor of my hometown fishing buddy, Frank Zak. Frank and I have been fishing the waters of New York State together for almost a quarter of a century. He has been my mentor on this spectacular fishery and his fly creations put a smile on my face every time we wet a line.

Frank's Jig Fly is a marabou Clouser variant. The sink rate can be modified by using different sizes of dumb bells on the head section. I mix and match rear sections using natural and fluorescent colors, and add a curly "Fly Tail" for good measure. If I had to pick just one tube fly to catch fish to feed my family, this is it.

TONY PAGLIEI

SACHA PUETZ

Hemer, Germany

I was born in 1971 in Hemer, Germany, where I still live with my girlfriend, Britta, and our dog, Alice. I first became fascinated with fly-fishing in 1985 when I saw two anglers casting for grayling and trout on my home water, the River Volme. From then on, one thought ran through my mind: "I want to learn fly-casting and fly-fishing."

I bought a rod, reel, and fly line and went down to the river and caught my first grayling and trout. I soon learned fly-tying and started creating my own patterns for the rivers Volme, Lenne, and Hoenne near my home. I have been fly-tying and fishing for over 16 years, having learned everything on my own, never having taken fly-fishing or tying classes.

In 1989, I travelled for the first time to fish the Swedish River Mörrum, and caught my first sea trout and salmon. I didn't have much money at the time so I tied my tube flies, glittering bodies and bucktail wings, on plastic tubes taken from Q-tips. Those early days began my special passion for the salmon fly.

Since 1998 I have tied at many fly-fishing shows in Germany and other European countries, most notably the British Fly Fair in England, Danish Fly Festival in Kolding, Denmark, and the Fly Fair in Hattem, the Netherlands, just to mention a few of the nine European countries where I have demonstrated the art of fly-tying. My greatest accomplishment thus far was taking part at the Flytying Symposium and the Somerset Show in New Jersey in January. In national and international fly-tying competitions, my best results have been the silver medal for hairwing salmon flies

and a bronze medal for fully dressed salmon flies at the Mustad Scandinavian Open in 2003 and the gold and silver medal in 2004 at the same competition. I attended the British Fly Fair and demonstrated the tying of some of my flies.

I also had success in Ken Sawada's Flytying Competition (Japan). Out of 400 entries from around the world, Sawada selected the 40 best flies. Out of the 40 flies, 20 are then chosen for the "Artworks" award. Out of the 20, ten are selected as "Better Artworks," and from that group a Grand Prix winner is named. Ken Sawada chose my fly as the Grand Prix winner in 2003. At the Irish Open Fly Tying Championship in 2004 I was overall winner with two gold, two silver, and two bronze medals. In general, flies for competitions have to be more detailed than the ones used for fishing; proportion and precision are important to the judges, as well as the selection of colors and the originality of the fly.

The German artist, Thomas Kubitz, chose some of my classic salmon flies and tube flies for creating a calendar for 2002 (classics) and 2003 (tube flies). Along with a few famous American tiers, I contributed a fly (Dusty Miller) to the ALS Society poster project which raised money for that organization.

My tube flies aren't inspired by the work of any specific tiers; my inspiration comes from reading general tying articles in magazines and books. The size of the tube flies I fish depends on the water temperature, depth, and clarity. All my patterns can be tied on small as well as large tubes. Fishing for sea trout, salmon, and occasionally pike, I use both single-handed (9-foot for 8- or

From top left: Shades of Blue; Fire Woman; SP Speylight; Ninety Nine; Casting Shadow

9-weight) and double-handed rods (12- to 15-foot for 8- to 11-weight).

CASTING SHADOW

Tube: Aluminum, 1/8-inch O. D., 3/4 inch long, with a plastic liner tube, 1/3 longer than the aluminum

Tag: Fluorescent pink thread

Body: None

Thread: Black UNI 8/0

Wing: Sparse, 2 3/4-inch underwing of purple over orange polar bear (substitute Finnish raccoon), topped by 3 1/2 inch of sparse red Angel Hair and purple Krystal Flash, topped by 5 1/4 inch of sparse, dark pink polar bear (or Finnish raccoon)

Throat: Claret and purple hen hackle

Cheeks: Two jungle cock feathers

Head: Black thread

Finish: Varnish

Hook: Partridge treble size 9 with a 3/8-inch piece of silicone tubing over the eye

Step 1: Carefully melt a collar on one end of plastic liner tubing, then wrap forward a 3/32-inch-long tag of fluorescent pink thread. Whip finish. Varnish the thread. Let dry.

Step 2: Slip the aluminum tube over the liner so the butt is against the tag, then put the joined tubes on your mandrel. Attach black thread on the protruding liner at the front of the metal tube. This will lock the metal tube in place. On top of the tube, using as few turns of thread as possible, tie in the sparse 2 3/4-inch orange underwing, then top it with sparse bunch of purple, the same length.

Step 3: On top of the purple, tie in ten strands of 3 1/2-inch-long red Angel Hair and the same amount of purple Krystal Flash.

Step 4: Wind in the throat of a few turns of claret and purple hen hackle.

Step 5: Top the wing with 5 1/4 inches of sparse, dark pink polar bear or Finnish raccoon.

Step 6: Tie in the jungle cock cheeks.

Step 7: Build a small neat head with thread. *Do not varnish.* Remove from mandrel. Trim excess liner to 1/16 inch and carefully melt a front collar.

Step 8: Finish with several coats of varnish on the head.

FIRE WOMAN

Tube: Plastic 1/8-inch O. D., 1 1/2 inches long, with a plastic liner tube that protrudes about 1/2 inch from the front end of the larger tube — this is trimmed and melted after the fly is tied as in the Casting Shadow. Finished tube overall length is 1 3/4 inch.

Thread: Black UNI 8/0

Tag: Four turns of fine oval gold tinsel, and orange floss, covering 1/8 inch of tube

Tail: Red Arctic fox, 1 1/4 inches long

Butt: Black herl, one turn

Rear body: Dark orange floss, covering 7/16 inch of tube

Front body: Red floss, covering 11/16 inch

Rib: Fine gold oval tinsel

Throat: Red-dyed badger hackle and orange-dyed guinea fowl

Underwing: Orange Finnish raccoon and red Finnish raccoon with red Angel Hair, 2 3/4 inch long

Wing: Red Arctic fox with black tips mixed with red and orange Angel Hair, 3 1/2 inch long

Cheeks: Four jungle cock feathers

Horns: Three strands red holographic tinsel

Head: Black thread

Finish: Varnish

Hook: Partridge X4S size 11

I often mix the softer, longer Finnish raccoon with Arctic fox hair because it gives me better volume and action in the current. This big, colorful tube fly is meant for springtime fishing in cold, high, and fast water.

I "sign" most of my tube flies with four jungle cock eyes. If the fly is above or below the salmon, it can't see the eyes on the side; that's why I put them top and bottom. Because of the materials, this is a very mobile pattern, productive in fast and slow water.

SP SPEYLIGHT

Tube: Plastic 1/8-inch O. D., 1 1/2 inches long, with a plastic liner tube that protrudes about 1/2 inch from the front end of the larger tube — this is trimmed and melted after the fly is tied as in the Casting Shadow. Finished tube overall length is 1 3/4 inch.

Thread: Black UNI 8/0

Tag: Four turns of fine oval silver tinsel, and golden yellow floss, covering 1/8 inch of tube

Tail: Yellow Arctic fox, 1 1/4 inches long

Butt: Black herl, one turn

Body: Golden yellow floss, rear half of tube; black floss, front half

Rib: Fine silver oval tinsel

Throat: Blue ear pheasant and guinea fowl
Underwing: Sparse, 3 1/2 -inch-long, brown Arctic fox
Wing: Sparse, 3 1/2-inch-long, dark brown bear with black tips
Sides: Two coq de leon feathers and two jungle cock feathers
Horns: Two strands of peacock herl
Hook: Loop Black Nickel size 6

This fly is productive year around and is one of my favorite flies for evening. I also tie the pattern on metal tubes, but just the main wing and throat hackle, leaving out the complicated body.

SHADE OF BLUE

Tube: Plastic 1/8-inch O. D., 1 1/2 inches long, with a plastic-liner tube that protrudes about 1/2 inch from the front end of the larger tube — this is trimmed and melted after the fly is tied as in the Casting Shadow. Finished tube overall length is 1 3/4 inch.
Thread: Black UNI 8/0
Tag: Four turns of fine oval silver tinsel, and royal blue floss, covering 1/8 inch of tube
Tail: Blue and purple SLF hank, 1/2 inch long
First butt: Black herl, one turn
Rear half of body: Flat silver tinsel, fine oval silver tinsel rib
Midbody veil: Blue and purple SLF hanks, 1/2 inch long, top and bottom
Second butt: Fiery red SLF dubbing
Front half of body: Purple floss ribbed with fine oval silver tinsel.
Front veil: Blue and purple SLF hanks, 1/2 inch long, top and bottom
Throat: Light blue hackle and purple hen hackle
Underwing: Sparse, light blue Arctic fox, 3 inches long, topped with a few strands of electric purple Angel Hair

Wing: Sparse, dark blue Arctic fox with black tips, 3 1/2 inches long, topped with blue Angel Hair
Cheeks: Four jungle cock feathers
Hook: Partridge Treble size 11 silver

This is an amazing fly for springtime fishing very clear and cold water. I also tie the pattern on metal tubes, but just the main wing and throat hackle, leaving out the complicated body.

NINETY NINE

Tube: Plastic 1/8-inch O. D., 1 1/2 inches long, with a plastic-liner tube that protrudes about 1/2 inch from the front end of the larger tube — this is trimmed and melted after the fly is tied as in the Casting Shadow. Finished tube overall length is 1 3/4 inch.
Thread: Black UNI 8/0
Rib: Strung, dark red sparkle dubbing
Body: UNI 6X AXXEL pearl
Underwing: Six, 3-inch-long peacock herls, dyed purple
Wing: Four, 3-inch-long orange-dyed grizzly saddle hackles, two to a side, tied cove style
Rear hackle: Orange mottled marabou feather over a couple of turns of black saddle hackle
Throat: Grey hen fibers
Front hackle: Coq de leon feather
Cheeks: Four jungle cock feathers
Hook: VMC black treble size 6

I tie the black saddle hackle under the marabou to keep the fibers from compressing against the body of the fly, which gives better action in the water. This pattern works well in both fast and slow water. It is good in bright sunlight in spring and summer.

TANYA ROONEY

Portland, Oregon

In 1985 my dad began teaching me to fly-fish on the Sandy and Upper Clackamas rivers around Oregon's Mt. Hood, with occasional trips to the Deschutes, Kalama, and Lewis rivers. Every once in a while he suggested that I learn to tie my own flies. I never gave it much thought until later that year when I received some money from him for an unrelated reason, and it occurred to me that I could use it to buy myself a fly-tying kit. So off to the local sporting goods store I went, and I wound up with a good old Thompson vise and enough stuff to tie my first mosquito pattern. I still have that fly! I have no idea how it ever managed to float when fished because it looked like a blimp with a bad haircut, but catch trout it did, and I'm proud of it.

At age 15 I started tying flies commercially for local stores and a distributor who sent my work all over the U. S. I began my tying career with dry flies for trout, but over the years have focused primarily on steelhead/salmon patterns, and some salt water, too.

While still a teenager I was asked to make up some sample patterns of Borden's Krystal Bullet on tubes, but no one ever explained to me what they were for, so my education in the world of tube flies was postponed until the latter part of 2000, when I began tying tube flies on a regular basis for The Fly Fishing Shop in Welches, Oregon. Since then, I've also tied custom, steelhead, trout, pike, and saltwater tubes, replicating unique patterns for stores or individuals when they couldn't get what they wanted from the big companies — either standard flies with a tweak here or there, or new, locally hot patterns. I stopped tying commercially in 2005 to focus on homeschooling my two children, though I still enjoy tying for myself. I have lived in Portland since 1993, when I married my husband, James.

Initially all my tube flies were tied on plastic, but I soon began experimenting with improvements to brass tubes. This led to the development of my custom-flared, linerless tubes which I now sell commercially through my company, Rooney Tube Works. We manufacture brass tubes in 1/8-inch O. D. ("heavy brass") and 3/32-inch O. D. ("light brass"). They are handmade and handpolished, guaranteed to be burr-free to keep the leader from chafing and fraying. They are flared at one end to eliminate

Clockwise from top: R. F. T. Squid; R. F. T. Leech; Dapper Dan; Marabou Practitioner; Leah Marie; Derrick's Sculpin

thread slippage when tying the fly head. We make brass and 1/8-inch O. D. plastic tubes in lengths from 1 to 3 inches. They all fit on a 1/16-inch O. D. mandrel.

The challenge for me now is adapting conventional patterns to tubes and designing new patterns that tubes make possible, such as larger streamers, saltwater patterns, etc. As far as ideas for original patterns go, a number of my own designs came into being because someone else was wishing aloud. There are so many gorgeous flies out there, I feel as though all I can really do in most cases is try to improve upon what already exists. My R. F. T. (Reasonable Facsimile Thereof) Squid is an example of this. After hearing more than one friend complain about heavy, hard-to-cast squid patterns I decided to come up with something much lighter. And even I couldn't believe how realistic it looked when I tested it in my bathtub. When fished with slight tugs on the line, it pulses along like the live item, and is deadly in Alaska for sea bass.

The influences on my tying have been so many it would be difficult to list them — all the excellent fly-tying publications I've ever read, all the awesome articles I've found on the web, anyone whose shoulder I've peered over at a tying show. I'm always eager to learn something new. I can be reached at www.rooney-tubeworks.com.

R. F. T. SQUID

Tube: Rooney Light Brass (this fly can be tied in any size or color) 2 inches long, with a 1/2-inch hook sleeve attached
Thread: White 3/0 and 6/0
Tail flash: Twelve 3-inch-long strands of fine pearl Flashabou (or flash material of your choice)
Tail/tentacles: One long, wispy, white marabou feather
Eyes: Deep See dumb bell, 7/16-inch diameter, inset with 3-D silver Hareline Mirage Dome eyes, 3/8-inch diameter
Head: Four, full wispy white marabou feathers
Mantle: One fluffy white marabou feather
Finish: 5-minute epoxy
Hook: Daiichi X452 stainless steel size 4

Step 1: Place a 2-inch-long light brass tube with hook sleeve attached on your vise.
Step 2: Attach 3/0 thread right behind the hook sleeve and add a dozen strands of flash of your choice, depending on the color of squid you are tying. Tie on one very long wispy marabou feather at the butt end and palmer it on to make the tail (tentacles). Trim excess.
Step 3: With ample figure-eights of thread tie on a 7/16-inch Deep See dumb bell with 3/8-inch silver 3-D eyes. Whip finish and cut the thread and epoxy the wraps, being careful not to get any glue on the marabou. I wet the marabou before gluing so it doesn't float around.
Step 4: After the epoxy is dry, attach the 6/0 thread (I use 6/0 to keep the head small) approximately 1/2 inch from the front

end of the tube. Tie in and palmer forward four full, long, wispy marabou feathers in close consecutive wraps, one feather at a time; each one directly in front of the last, leaving about 1/8 inch of space at the head for the last feather which comes later.

Step 5: Whip finish and cut the thread. Moisten your fingers, grab all the marabou, and pull it back over the eyes. While holding the marabou down, put a loose wrap or two of thread around the marabou and slide the thread loop back over the marabou to a point just in front of the eyes. Tighten down on the thread, whip finish, and cut the thread. You can carefully epoxy this spot, too.

Step 6: Attach the 6/0 thread at the front of the tube, tie in one more marabou feather (fluffy, not wispy, is better in this case), and wrap it three or four turns. Trim excess. Whip finish and cut the thread. Pull this single feather forward over the front end of the tube and pinch it off short — about 1/2 to 3/4 inch long. Smooth it back over the body to complete the fly.

This fly can be fished with floating and sinking lines. It has caught sea bass, steelhead, and even brown trout. Anything that eats squid seems to go for it.

DERRICK'S SCULPIN

Tube: Rooney Heavy Brass 2 inches long, with silicone hook sleeve
Thread: Black UNI 6/0 for the body; black UNI Big Fly for the head
Tail: Natural rabbit strip, 4 inches long
Body: Natural rabbit strip, 6 inches long, wrapped forward
Fins and head: Natural deer hair spun and packed tightly, then trimmed wide and flat
Finish: Griffin's Brand head cement from Hareline Dubbin
Hook: Daiichi 2451 size 4

This fly was originally tied for freshwater pike in Canadian lakes. It can be tied in large sizes, and tying it on a plastic tube eliminates some of the weight, and of course the size of the hook is up to the fisher.

R. F. T. LEECH

Tube: Rooney Light Brass or plastic 1 1/2 inches long, with silicone hook sleeve
Thread: Black UNI 6/0
Tail: Black rabbit strip, 2 inches long
Body: Three black marabou feathers, palmered
Eyes: Lead dumb bell, yellow and black, medium
Head: Black Angora goat dubbing
Finish: Head cement
Hook: Daiichi X510 size 4 or 6

The R. F. T. Leech can be fished in either fresh or salt water. Locally, it is used in rivers and lakes to catch steelhead and trout.

MARABOU PRACTITIONER

Tube: Rooney Light Brass 1 1/2 inches long, with silicone hook sleeve

Thread: Orange Danville 6/0

Tail: Sparse bunch of orange bucktail, 3 inches long, topped by three or four strands of orange Krystal Flash, and one large dyed-orange pheasant flank feather

Body, 1st half: One hot orange marabou feather, topped by one hot orange schlappen, topped by a strand of large oval gold tinsel for the rib

Underbody: Dubbed fluorescent fire orange Angora goat

Eyes: One large dyed-orange golden pheasant tippet, trimmed (see instructions), and one dyed-orange pheasant flank feather

Body, 2nd half: One hot orange schlappen, large oval gold tinsel ribbing

Underbody: Dubbed fluorescent fire orange Angora goat

Back: Two pheasant flank feathers; one 2 inches long, the other slightly shorter

Hackle: One medium-sized mallard flank feather

Finish: 5-minute epoxy

Hook: Daiichi 2451 size 4 or 6

Step 1: Put the Light Brass tube and silicone hook sleeve on your vise and attach thread.

Step 2: Tie in a sparse bunch of orange bucktail, topped by three or four strands of orange Krystal Flash, and one large dyed-orange pheasant flank feather tied on flat over the bucktail and flash.

Step 3: Tie in one hot orange marabou feather, topped by one hot orange schlappen, topped by a strand of large oval gold tinsel for the rib. Dub an underbody of fluorescent fire-orange Angora goat and bring it forward to the midpoint of the tube. Wind the ribbing forward in three even wraps and tie off. Holding the marabou and schlappen together, wrap them forward in three turns, using the ribbing as a guide. Tie off and trim excess rib and feather, but do not cut the thread.

Step 4: Take one large, dyed orange golden pheasant tippet and cut out the middle of the tip so you are left with a V-shaped tippet to form the eyes. Tie the tippet flat over the body, extending about 1/2 inch beyond the end of the tube. Tie in one dyed-orange pheasant flank feather on top of the tippet.

Step 5: Tie in more ribbing, another hot-orange schlappen, and more dubbing. Wind the body forward about 3/8 inch, then wind on the rib and palmer the feather, leaving about 1/8 inch of space at the front of the tube for the final materials. Tie down and trim excess.

Step 6: Tie one long pheasant flank feather flat on top of the tippet eyes, and a slightly shorter flank feather on top of that.

Step 7: Select one medium-sized mallard flank feather, strip off the fibers from the left side of the feather, tie the feather in tip first, and put on three turns at the head.

Step 8: Whip finish the head, trim thread, and epoxy.

I added marabou to the original Practitioner pattern because I felt that it was too static. Marabou gives the fly a lifelike motion in the water.

DAPPER DAN

Tube: Rooney Light Brass 1 1/2 inches long, with silicone hook sleeve

Thread: Black Danville 6/0

Tag: Fine oval silver tinsel

Ribbing: Fine oval silver tinsel and one royal blue saddle hackle palmered forward

Body: Three roughly equal sections of dubbing: a section of kelly green Angora goat, followed by a section of royal blue Angora goat, followed by a section of Root's Dubbing Enhancer, dark blue

Collar: Chartreuse saddle hackle, then royal blue saddle hackle

Wing: Two 2-inch-long, royal blue saddle hackles tied cove style, then two turquoise saddle hackles slightly shorter, then two chartreuse saddle hackles slightly shorter

Cheeks: Jungle cock

Finish: Head cement

Hook: Daiichi X510 size 6

This fly is an attractor pattern for steelhead and cutthroat in local rivers.

LEAH MARIE

Tube: Rooney Light Brass 1 1/2 inches long, with silicone hook sleeve

Thread: Black Danville 6/0

Ribbing: Fine oval gold tinsel and one hot-pink saddle hackle palmered forward

Body: Three roughly equal sections of dubbing: a section of hot-pink Angora goat, followed by a section of purple Angora goat, followed by a section of Flashabou dubbing enhancer, in dark purple

Collar: One hot-pink saddle hackle

Wing: Two 2-inch-long, hot-pink saddle hackles tied cove style, then two dark purple saddle hackles slightly shorter, then two more hot-pink saddle hackles slightly shorter

Cheeks: Jungle cock

Topping: One golden pheasant crest

Finish: Head cement

Hook: Daiichi X510 size 6

The Leah Marie is a steelhead, salmon, and cutthroat pattern for local rivers. It is tied in the same body style as the Dapper Dan. These two patterns are based on the color schemes of already popular steelhead flies.

DERRICK ROTHERMEL

Kamloops, British Columbia, Canada

I learned to fish for pike growing up on the great prairie flatland of Alberta. It wasn't until I joined the Royal Canadian Air Force in 1964 that I was introduced to fly-fishing and tying by a colleague, Bill Waller. Fly-fishing for pike was almost unheard of at the time; dedicated patterns were few, if any. Using the metallic shield from coaxial cable, I developed some durable flies of my own. They stood up to the razor-sharp teeth of pike, but as you can imagine, were awful to cast.

Seven years ago I realized that successful fly-fishing for pike doesn't depend on complex patterns, but rather having available a variety of fly colors, sizes, and weights to match changing feeding preferences. This meant I had to tie and carry an enormous number of flies on my trips to northern Canada for large pike. Then I arrived at the idea of tying tube flies in three-part combinations. With a series of five modular tubes for tails, bodies, and heads I had up to 125 combinations of different pike flies. And I could easily alter the color and size of a fly by simply changing one or more of the components. When modular tubes are strung on the wire leader used for pike fishing, the fly can be either cast or trolled.

My first tube flies were created using the plastic cores from Q-tips, however these were found wanting. When the amount of material required to build the bulk of a pike fly was tied to the core, the tightly cinched thread wraps often collapsed it. To counter this problem, I started tying flies on hobby store brass tubing (used in model aircraft building). I cut the brass stock to length, inserted the plastic tubing from the Q-tips, and then melted the ends to keep the liner in place. It was an extremely labor-intensive process. Around this time I met Bob Kenly, a tube-fly guru, who liked my ideas and innovations and became very supportive. Through Bob, I was introduced to Tanya Rooney (See Chapter 25: Tanya Rooney), who has her own fly-tube manufacturing business. Rooney Tube

Clockwise from top: Black Back Shiner Variant; Perch Minnow; Black Back Shiner; White Minnow; Multi-Piece Pike Fly head section (black); Multi-Piece Pike Fly body section (orange; purple); Multi-Piece Pike Fly tail section (orange); Red/White Pikeabou; Egg Sucking Black Leech

Works now supplies all my thin-wall brass tubes. Although the Rooney Light Brass tubes aren't much heavier than plastic tubing, they do increase the speed and efficiency of tying, eliminate the collapse under thread pressure, and are useful even for popper heads. The major benefit, though, is that the tube sections better withstand the savage strikes of pike and their teeth.

I tie flies for pike fishing, not just for fun. Mention pike and I get excited; mention big pike and I am like a kid in a candy store. My largest pike to date on a tube fly was a 55-inch monster out of the Yukon Territories in 1998. And I am back there every spring with a good supply of tube flies looking for an even bigger one.

I use a Renzetti vise for tying large pike tubes, but I've found that the standard tube attachment occasionally lets go, allowing the tube to spin — and the fly-in-progress to unwind and fly apart. To correct this, I created a screw-in adapter head with a small, cross-set screw. The tube is inserted into the head and screwed down solidly so no amount of thread pressure will cause it to spin.

You can visit my Web site at http://members.shaw.ca/mrpike.

RED/WHITE PIKEABOU

Tube: Rooney Light Brass, 3/32-inch O.D., 1 1/2 inches long, with silicone hook sleeve

Thread: Red Danville's +

Flashtail: Six strands, silver or pearl 3-D holographic Flashabou, 6 inches long

Tail: Six 6-inch-long, red neck hackles

Wing: Six 4-inch-long white marabou plumes

Eyes: Silver Prismatic stick-on, 5/32-inch diameter

Head: UNI-Stretch thread, Chinese red

Glue/Finish: Head cement, Sally Hanson's Hard As Nails, and 5-minute epoxy or Soft Body

Hook: Eagle Claw 254 in 3/0, or any good, small-eye bait hook

Step 1: Insert the Rooney Light Brass tube into the hook sleeve, put it on your vise, and wrap the junction with thread to secure it.

Step 2: Tie in three red neck hackles on one side of the tube, just ahead of the junction, with the curves facing out. Apply head cement.

Step 3: Tie in three red hackles on the other side of the tube, making sure they are the same length. Apply cement.

Step 4: Add flash material down each side and cement. I prefer the wide saltwater 3-D holographic in silver or pearl, but any color will work as long as it has a bit of sparkle. I've even used Christmas tree tinsel: pike are not fussy.

Step 5: At about the middle of the tube, tie in the butt of the first marabou plume flat on top, with the curve facing down. Tie in the other two plumes on the sides, also curve facing inward. Apply cement.

Step 6: Rotate the tube 180 degrees. Tie in the butt of the first marabou plume flat on top, with the curve facing down. Tie in the other two plumes on the sides, also curve facing inward. Whip finish and trim thread. Do not apply head cement as it discolors UNI-Stretch thread.

Step 7: Wrap a neat head with red UNI-Stretch thread, and whip finish.

Step 8: Coat head with Sally Hanson's Hard As Nails.

Step 9: Apply stick-on eyes to the sides of the head.

Step 10: After the Hard As Nails has dried, epoxy the head and eyes and rotate the fly on a wheel until it has cured.

I've been using bunny bugs on pike with great success for 30 years. There are two drawbacks to these rabbit-strip patterns: they are heavy and unpleasant to cast when soaked and pike always chew the heck out of them. While preparing for a 1995 trip to Watson Lake in the Yukon Territories, I decided that there had to be something that would do the same job as bunny strip and not feel like I was casting my wet wool sock. I started to experiment with other materials. I had seen marabou, of course, and liked the action it gave, but never thought it would hold up to pike. Then I decided to develop a tube fly combining marabou with 6-inch neck hackles.

Pikeabous tied on tubes hold up far better than the old style bunny flies. The fly disconnects from the hook eye on the strike and slips up the leader, out of reach of pike jaws and teeth. I tie the pattern in several sizes from 4 to 6 inches, and 6 to 8 inches, and in all sorts of color combinations. The Yellow & Red version (substitute yellow marabou for white, and black Danville's + for red) is an exceptionally deadly combination. Pikeabous have become my most productive fly.

I fish Pikeabous on top of the water with a skipping retrieve, or let them sink and retrieve them in short or long strips.

EGG-SUCKING BLACK LEECH

Tube: Rooney Light Brass, 3/32-inch O.D., 1 1/2 inches long, with silicone hook sleeve
Thread: Black Danville's +
Flash tail: Six to eight strands of black pearl flash
Tail: Six black saddle hackles, 5 inches long
Wing: Six, 3-inch-long bunches of black marabou

Eyes: Silver Prismatic stick-on, 5/32-inch diameter (optional)
Head: Orange or Chinese red UNI-Stretch thread
Glue/Finish: Head cement, Sally Hanson's Hard As Nails, and 5-minute epoxy or Soft Body
Hook: Eagle Claw 254 in 3/0, or one of their bait hooks if I need an extra-short shank

In 1974 I was fly-fishing for pike in Brazeau Reservoirs in Alberta and having no luck. In desperation I switched to spinning gear and lures and still had no luck. I had purchased a bag of rubber bass worms, so I decided to try them. I put on a 6-inch black rubber worm and cast it towards a weed bed and POW! I had myself a nice pike. My partner decided to try other colors of rubber worms, and no success; this while I was catching a pike every other cast. When he switched to black, he starting catching pike, one after another. We decided to clean an eight-pounder and check its stomach. Right away I noticed it had no canine teeth. Its belly was full of black leeches from 6 to 8 inches long, and freshwater shrimp. This pike had a lake full of baitfish to feed on, but it was only eating eating leeches and shrimp.

It didn't take long to catch several more pike, and when we examined their mouths we found that none of them had any canine teeth. All were caught on the black rubber worm. I had my fly kit with me so I tied up some black bunny tail flies, matching the leech as best I could. Bingo, they worked! But the pike kept biting off the tails. We were at the lake long enough to see the pikes' teeth come in full and we watched their feeding habits switch over to attractor-colored flies and bait patterns. Even so, the black leech was still productive.

Over the years, I have experimented with other materials for a leech pattern. I settled on feathers and marabou for the same reasons I use them in the Pikeabou: light weight, good action, and when tied on a tube, they survive pike teeth. When all else fails, this pattern usually works for me.

BLACK BACK SHINER

Tube: Rooney Light Brass, 3/32-inch O.D., 2 inches long, with silicone hook sleeve
Thread: Clear nylon
Belly: Sparse bunch of 4 1/2-inch-long, white Flat "N" Fine (substitute FisHair)
Back: Sparse bunch of 4 1/2-inch-long, black Flat "N" Fine (subsititute FisHair)
Lateral line: Six to eight strands of pearlescent or metallic flash material on each side
Eyes: Silver Prismatic stick-on, 5/32-inch diameter
Head: Black UNI-Stretch thread
Glue/Finish: 5-minute epoxy, Hard As Nails, Soft Body (over eyes as well)
Hook: Eagle Claw 254 in 3/0, or any good, small-eye bait hook

BLACK BACK SHINER VARIANT

Tube: Rooney Light Brass, 3/32-inch O.D., 2 inches long, with silicone hook sleeve

Thread: Clear nylon
Flash tail: Twenty strands of black Krystal Flash, 6 inches long
  Tail: Six 6-inch-long white saddle hackles, tied in cove style
  Belly: Tapered, 3-inch-long bunch of white "fun fur" (aka Craft Fur)
  Back: Tapered, 3-inch-long bunch of black "fun fur"
Shoulder: One grizzly saddle hackle, each side, 3 inches long
Shoulder flash: Six to eight 3-inch-long strands of pearl Krystal Flash, each side
  Eyes: Yellow Prismatic stick-on, 3/8-inch diameter
  Head: Clear nylon thread
Glue/Finish: 5-minute epoxy, Hard As Nails, Soft Body (over eyes as well)
  Hook: Eagle Claw 254 or small-eye bait hook

PERCH MINNOW

  Tube: Rooney Light Brass, 3/32-inch O.D., 2 inches long, with silicone hook sleeve
Thread: Clear nylon
  Tail: Six 4-inch-long, yellow-dyed grizzly saddle hackles, tied cove style, with a 3-inch-long grizzly saddle on each side
  Body: Small bunch of 2-inch-long, green "fun fur" on top of tail. The rest of the body is made up of 2-inch-long bunches of yellow "fun fur," tied in top and bottom and then flattened vertically to make a wide side and a very thin cross section. Top and bottom of the yellow fur are barred with black felt pen.
Lateral line: Six to eight strands of pearlescent Krystal Flash
  Eyes: Silver Prismatic stick-on, 3/8-inch diameter
  Head: 5-minute epoxy (on eyes as well)
  Hook: Eagle Claw 254 or small-eye bait hook

WHITE MINNOW

  Tube: Rooney Light Brass, 3/32-inch O.D., 2 inches long, with silicone hook sleeve
Thread: Clear nylon
  Tail: Six 4-inch-long, white saddles, tied in cove style
  Body: Sparse, tapered, 3-inch-long bunches of white "fun fur," tied in top and bottom and then flattened vertically to make a wide side and a very thin cross section.
Shoulder: One grizzly saddle each side, 3 1/2 inches long
Lateral line: Six to eight strands of 4 1/2-inch-long pearlescent Krystal Flash, each side

  Eyes: Prismatic silver stick-on, 3/8-inch diameter
  Head: 5-minute epoxy (on eyes as well)
  Hook: Eagle Claw 254 or small-eye bait hook

MULTI-PIECE PIKE FLY

TAIL SECTION

  Tube: Rooney Light Brass, 3/32 inch O.D., 2 inches long, with silicone hook sleeve
Thread: Black
Flash tail: Fine silver holographic tinsel
  Tail: Six 6-inch-long orange (or white, gray, purple, yellow, chartreuse, pink, red, black) saddle hackles, tied with curve facing out
  Body: Black rabbit fur, 3/4 inch long, tied around the tube; sparse, 1 1/2-inch-long collar of fine silver holographic tinsel; 3/4-inch-long, orange rabbit fur, tied around the tube
  Collar: Sparse, 1 1/2-inch-long, silver holographic tinsel
  Head: Black thread
Finish: Head cement
  Hook: Eagle Claw 254 or small-eye bait hook

BODY SECTION

  Tube: Rooney Light Brass, 3/32-inch O. D., or plastic tube, 1 1/4 inches long, *without* silicone hook sleeve (no hook-eye connector is necessary)
Thread: Black
  Sides: Four 2 1/2-inch-long, orange (or white, gray, purple, yellow, chartreuse, pink, red, black) marabou plumes, tied two to a side, with curve facing inward
  Head: Black thread
Finish: Head cement

HEAD SECTION

  Tube: Rooney Light Brass, 3/32 inch O. D., or plastic tube, 1 1/4 inches long, *without* silicone hook sleeve (no hook-eye connector is necessary)
Thread: Black
  Sides: Orange (or white, gray, purple, yellow, chartreuse, pink, red, black) marabou plumes or bunches of rabbit fur, 1 1/4 inches long, tied around the tube.
  Eye: Doll's eyes, 5/16-inch diameter
  Head: Black thread
Finish: Head cement

This is my "pike kit." I use it for walk-in trips: less weight and bulk to carry.

MASAHITO SATO

Tokyo, Japan/Cambridge, Massachusetts

KOJI YAOITA

I am a freelance writer and a correspondent for a Japanese fishing magazine, *Fly Rodders*. I've lived in Cambridge, Massachusetts for almost six years. In Japan I enjoyed largemouth bass and bluegill fishing, but most of the time I was enthusiastic about fly-fishing for *yamame*, or Cherry salmon, which are native to Japan, Korea, and Taiwan, and *iwana*, a Japanese species of char.

More than 20 years ago, when I started fly-fishing I also started fly-tying, my first fly was a Royal Coachman with quill wings. I made over 100 Royal Coachmans for practice, but I never fished them on rivers because the quill wings looked so fragile, and they were all size 10 and too big to use.

Although I had been fly-fishing for many years when I came to the United States, I had never tried fishing salt water. After moving to a suburb of Boston, which is a mecca for the fun of striped bass fishing, my fishing life changed dramatically. Now, just five percent of my fly-fishing is for trout, another five percent is warmwater fishing, and once a year I go to the Margaree River in Canada for Atlantic salmon. The rest of my fly-fishing is dedicated to salt water, and especially to stripers.

I became interested in tube flies while researching an article for a Japanese fly-fishing magazine on the HMH tube-fly tying kits. When I sent an e-mail to John Albright, the HMH CEO, asking him if I could write story on his company's products, he immediately shipped me one of the kits. I also received an e-mail from him that said I did not have to send it back, that I could keep it for myself. As soon as I got the kit, I tied several tube flies, took photos and sent them off to Japan. The kit included a tube-tying video and I was amazed at the number of tube flies for saltwater fishing. The video convinced me of the value of tube flies. Now, almost all of my saltwater flies are made on a tube fly system that I invented. I've also been working on a tube fly system for trout and bass which is a scaled-down version of my saltwater system.

In the course of my journalism work, I've met and interviewed many well-known fly-fishermen: Jack Gartside, Dick Talleur, Bob Popovics, Nick Curcione, Poul Jorgensen, Harrison R. Steeves III, David Skok (See Chapter 31: David Skok), Joe Humphreys, Joan Wulff, Mark Sedotti, Bill Catherwood, and Ed Koch. All of these great people have influenced and improved my tying and fishing, but Jack and Bob have probably influenced me the most, and I am still learning from them.

The first pattern I tied on a tube was Jack's Beast Master General, which has a spun and clipped deer-hair head, a marabou midsection, and a Lefty's Deceiver tail. At the time, I was using Jack's fly a lot because it worked so well on stripers. When I fished a prototype tube conversion, I realized there were some things I didn't like. The tube put the hook a little further back than on the conventional fly, which meant the tail materials had more of tendency to wrap and foul over the shank. Without a counterbalance — such as dumb bell eyes — the hook always

rode point down. Also, the thick butts of the saddle hackle were tied on the bigger-diameter junction tube, which made the bunch look even thicker and less pleasing to the eye, and set the wing position higher than when the pattern is tied on a hook. During the off-season, I considered ways to improve the design.

The Beast Master General consists of a saddle hackle tail, marabou that is hackle-wrapped over the base of the tail, more wound marabou for a body, and a clipped, deer hair head. I realized that these components could be separated into two sections, with the tail and the first spun marabou tied on the hook, and the second marabou and the head tied on the tube. With this design, the tube is much shorter, and the tail materials do not wrap around the hook. And the completed tube fly looks more like Jack's original.

After I finished the fly, it occurred to me that if I made the head and body sections in different styles and colors, I could interchange them at will. To vary the sink rate and presentation, I tied four types of heads: popper, slider, epoxy, and jig. I tied each head and tail section in black, white, and chartreuse. The tube fly head sections can be used with an undressed hook as a independent fly. Because I wanted to be able to use the dressed hook tail part independently as well, I put eyes on it and tied it back towards the bend of the hook, like tarpon fly. I can quickly assemble 19 different flies using these seven components. I think that the combination of these parts can cover 80 percent of striper fishing. When the water is very clear, I add gray to the list of colors for tail and collar.

In the course of developing this tube fly system, I changed some of the Beast Master General's materials. In my version, the tail has a single saddle hackle tied in as a flat wing. A single feather moves more naturally from side to side, unlike a Deceiver tail which moves up and down. A single saddle also moves more freely and gives the tail a thin profile like a sand lance or silverside. I like Whiting American saddle hackle because the butt is stiff and thick enough to prevent the wing from fouling, and the rest of the stem is thin and soft, giving good action. I use Finnish raccoon in place of marabou because it doesn't tear as easily and has similar action when wet. I substitute closed cell foam for the original spun deer hair because it is more durable and has better buoyancy for slider and popper heads.

I normally tie floating Silverside and Baby Bunker patterns on hooks, but sometimes fish will nip at the fly from the rear, and to get a solid hook set, the point must be moved further back. Finding hooks in the right size with shanks long enough to accomplish this is difficult, if not impossible, and moving the hook to the rear creates balance problems on the retrieve. For these reasons, I started tying tube fly conversions, but with a different approach: the hook is directly fixed to the tube. Instead of threading the tippet through the tube and tying it to the hook eye, the tippet is threaded through and tied to a split ring that fits inside the junction tubing. HMH plastic tubes are very strong and

flexible; the tippet will break before the fly does. These patterns are derived from Jack's Floating Minnow and Captain Joe Blados' Crease Fly.

My tube fly system (finished tails and interchangeable heads) is available for purchase from W. S. Hunter & Co, 113 Storrs Street, Concord, New Hampshire 03301, Tel: 888-889-0004.

MASA'S TUBE-FLY SYSTEM

FINNISH RACCOON DECEIVER FLAT WING TAIL SECTION

Hook: Gamakatsu SL12 or Varivas 990S size 1/0 or 2/0
Thread: Danville's flat waxed nylon, the color depends on the tail and wing color
Tail: Sparse 2 1/4- to 3-inch-long bunch of white (black or chartreuse) bucktail, under a single, 4 to 4 1/2-inch-long white (black or chartreuse) Whiting American saddle hackle with marabou left on
Lateral Flash: Pearl Flashabou, 3 to 4 inches long, six strands over the tail
Wing: Sparse, 2 1/2-inch-long white (black or chartreuse) Finnish raccoon, topped by sparse, 3 1/2-inch-long bunch of dark green Angel Hair
Topping: Sparse, 3 1/2-inch-long bunch of dark green Angel Hair
Eyes: Silver Mylar stick-on, 1/16-inch diameter
Finish: 30-minute epoxy

Step 1: Put the hook in your vise and attach the thread near the bend, tarpon style, leaving about 3/8 inch of bare shank to the hook eye. Tie a very sparse bunch of white bucktail on the hook shank with four or five loose wraps of thread. Push the bucktail down with your thumb, forcing it to spread evenly around the hook shank, then tighten the thread and wrap down with several turns.
Step 2: Choose a hackle about 4 to 5 inches in length and tear off the fluff about 1/4 inch from the base of the stem. Leave most of the fluff on.
Step 3: Flatten the base of the stem with pliers parallel to the hackle fibers.
Step 4: Tie in the hackle flat-wing style over the bucktail.
Step 5: Tie in a sparse bunch of pearl Flashabou over the hackle. Make the flash a little bit shorter than the hackle.
Step 6: Cut a piece of hair from a Finnish raccoon zonker strip and tie it over the Flashabou. The raccoon hair should be about 2/3 the length of the hackle.
Step 7: Tie a sparse bunch of Angel Hair over the raccoon. It should be a little longer than the raccoon.
Step 8: Whip finish a small, neat head, then put a stick-on eye on either side of the head with super glue. Let dry.
Step 9: Apply 30-minute epoxy to the head and eyes.

Clockwise from top: Masa's Tube Fly System Deep Sinking Head; Baby Bunker; Masa's Tube Fly System General Head; Silverside; Masa's Tube Fly System Popper Head; Masa's Tube Fly System Sheet Foam Subsurface Head

GENERAL HEAD

Tube: HMH plastic 1/8-inch O. D., 3/8 inch long, with 1/2 inch of vinyl hook sleeve Total combined length is 3/4 inch. When tubing is joined, cut excess to leave 1/8 inch of the plastic sticking out in front.

Thread: Danville's flat waxed nylon, the color depends on the tail and wing color

Back flash: Sparse bunch of 3 1/2-inch-long, pearl Flashabou tied over the belly of the tube

Belly: Sparse, 2 1/2-inch-long, white (black or chartreuse) bucktail tied on the belly and sides of the tube

Wing: Sparse, 2 1/2-inch-long, white (black or chartreuse) Finnish raccoon, topped by sparse, 3 1/2-inch-long bunch of dark green Angel Hair

Eyes: Silver Mylar stick-on, 1/4-inch diameter

Finish: Epoxy

DEEP-SINKING HEAD

Same materials as the General Head, except I finish the fly by slipping a 3/8-inch eyed-cone head (I use a brand called Jiggy Head, size large, silver) over the end of tube, set it in place with super glue, then melt the excess protruding plastic tube to hold it in place. I cover the cone head and wraps with a thin coat of 30-minute epoxy.

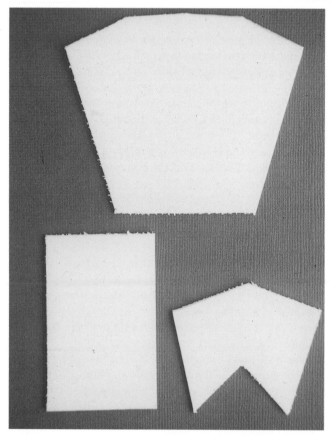

Top: popper back template. Lower left: popper bottom. Lower right: popper core.

SHEET-FOAM SUBSURFACE HEAD

The combined (plastic and hook sleeve) tube length for this head is 1 inch. After tying the bucktail/Finnish raccoon/Angel Hair portion on the tube, cut a head shape from 2 mm and 1/8-inch sheet foam, 1 1/4 inch wide and 1/2 inch long. Apply super glue to the tube and one side of the foam, center the width of the foam on top of the tube, and fold it down to form the head. After the super glue dries, I mark the top of the head with green permanent marker, then cover the foam and thread wraps with a thin coat of epoxy.

SHEET FOAM POPPER

Tube: Same as the other heads, except the combined (plastic and hook sleeve) tube length on the popper is 2 inch

Belly: Sparse 3 1/2-inch-long, white bucktail

Back flash: Sparse, 3 1/2-inch-long, fine pearl Flashabou

Wing: Sparse, 3 1/2-inch-long, white Finnish raccoon

Head core: White 6 mm sheet foam, midline 1/2 inch long, sides 3/4 inch long, (see photo for core shape) wrapped around the tube, super glued, and painted red.

Popper head: Two sections of 2 mm white sheet foam (see photo for shapes). The section that folds over the back and sides is 1 3/8 inch long by 2 inches wide. The bottom section is 1 1/8 inch long, 1/2 inch wide at the front end and 3/16 inch at the rear.

Eyes: Silver Mylar stick-on, 5/16-diameter, and 1/4-inch diameter, solid, black plastic taxidermy eyes with plastic stems. I cut the stems in half because they are a little bit long. I put a hole in the center of the Mylar eye, apply super glue to the back of the plastic eye and stem, then insert the stem in the hole. I super glue the stems into the popper head.

Finish: Spread a thin coat of super glue on the entire head. I think this treatment is necessary to protect the head and eyes.

Hook: Gamakatsu SL12 1/0, 2/0 or Varivas 990S 1/0, 2/0

Captain Joe Blados' Crease Flies were the inspiration for my sheet-foam slider and popper heads.

BABY BUNKER

Tube: HMH 1/8-inch O. D. plastic tube, 2 1/4 inches long, and 1-inch long vinyl hook sleeve. The combined length is 3 inches

Tail: Gray marabou fluff, tied on top and bottom of hook sleeve, 1/2 inch long

Hook: Tiemco TMC600SP 6/0, attached to tube with thread and super glue. This is done before the rest of the fly is tied

Body floating core: Closed-cell white foam 2 mm cut to shape (it forms the head and gill plate, and top of body), folded over the tube and super glued

KOJI YAOITA

Body flash: Pearl Mylar ribbon, found in craft stores, cut to shape, folded over the foam core and super glued

Body skin: Clear EZ Body Braid, 1/2 inch wide. Work with a long piece of braid, and cut it after the fly is tied.

Thread: Clear monofilament

Eyes: Silver Mylar stick-on, 3/16-inch diameter

Gills: Red permanent marker

Gill plates: Nail polish, super frost platinum

Back: Bronze Prismacolor permanent marker

Finish: 30-minute epoxy

Split ring: The tippet is tied to this instead of the hook eye. It must be larger than the outer diameter of the hard plastic tube, and more than 20-pound test. The ring slips inside the hook sleeve.

SILVERSIDE

Tube: HMH 1/8-inch O. D. plastic tube, 3 1/4 inches long, and 5/8-inch-long vinyl hook sleeve. The combined length is 3 1/2 inches

Tail: Gray marabou fluff, tied on top and bottom of hook sleeve, 1/2 inch long

Hook: Varivas 990S 1/0, attached to tube with thread and super glue. This is done before the rest of the fly is tied.

Body core: White 2 mm sheet foam, 1 3/4 inch long, 1 inch wide, folded over and super glued to cover approximately 1/2 of the tube

Body flash: White Mylar ribbon, found in craft stores, cut to shape, folded over the foam core and super glued

Body lateral flash: Two strips of silver 1/16-inch Mylar ribbon, one to a side

Body skin: Clear Corsair braided tubing, produced by Jack Gartside, 1/2 inch wide. I always work with a long piece of braid, and only cut it after the fly is finished.

Thread: Clear monofilament

Eyes: Silver Mylar stick-on, 1/8-inch diameter

Gills: Red permanent marker

Gill plates: Nail polish, super frost platinum

Back: Bronze Prismacolor permanent marker

Finish: 30-minute epoxy

Split ring: The tippet is tied to this instead of the hook eye. It must be larger than the outer diameter of the hard plastic tube, smaller in diameter than the hook sleeve (it slips inside the hook sleeve), and more than 20-pound test.

I usually use a 10-weight rod for the tube-fly system and the Baby Bunker and Silverside flies, but an 8-weight will work, too.

DARREN SCAIFE

Santa Rosa, California

I was born in Ukiah, California, a small town 120 miles north of San Francisco. My earliest fishing memories take me back to hot summer afternoons on Clear Lake and Lake Mendocino with my grandmother Kate, all 4 foot 10 inches of her, yelling for me to slow down as I ran ahead carrying her fishing gear. When I grew older I started chasing winter steelhead and salmon on the many rivers and streams that cross Northern California and Southern Oregon.

I started tying flies 14 years ago after a Christmas in Montana when I was fortunate enough to meet Berney Griffin, of Griffin Tools, who was a close friend of my ex-father-in-law. I got a tour of Berney's workshop, and left with a selection of professional-grade tying gear. Since I didn't own a fly rod, yet, I tied Glo Bugs to throw with my bait-casting rod. After tying Glo Bugs in just about every color and size, I decided to expand my horizons and come up with the greatest steelhead lure to ever hit the water. When that didn't work as well as hoped, I put away the fly-tying gear and reverted to bait-fishing. Shortly after my thirtieth birthday I was in a little fly shop in Silverdale, Washington, called The Morning Hatch

where I met Mike Croft (See Chapter 9: Mike Croft). I had no idea who I was talking to, all I knew was that he was the first person who had anything positive to say about the experimental steelhead lure I showed him. The following fall I bought a reel for the first of many fly rods.

I have been tying with confidence for ten years now, everything from trout to billfish flies. My favorite patterns are for salt water. I began tying tubes after seeing some of Mike Croft's flies for Baja. I do most of my commercial and personal tying on tubes.

A few years ago I started using bulk coilhose tubing manufactured by Freelin-Wade. This tubing is nylon, virtually clear, and very strong. With a little effort, it can be straightened by bending it against the natural curve of the coil; no heating or stretching is necessary. Epoxy and super glue bonds to it, and a 100-foot coil costs a mere eight cents a foot. Because it is nylon and pliable I can work the eye of the hook in the end of it, eliminating the need for a hook sleeve. The tubing comes in different sizes and wall thicknesses, and can be purchased through air-hose or hydraulic-hose suppliers. It is primarily used in the medical field.

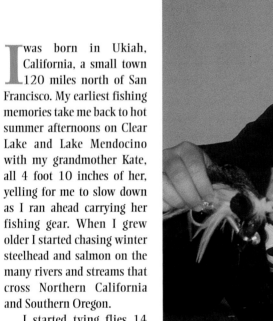

From top: Tuna Treat (purple); Tuna Treat (green); Tuna Treat (pink); Striper Float Fish (rainbow trout); Float Fish (rainbow trout parr); Danna Banana (black and gold); Danna Banana (rainbow trout).

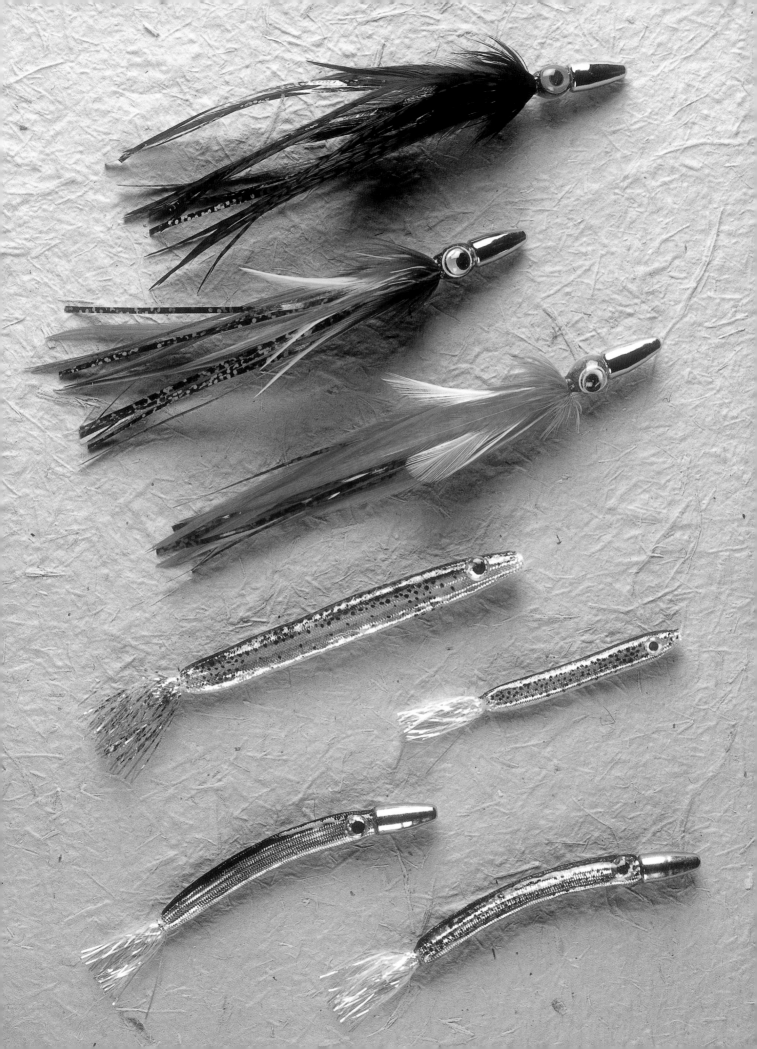

Some of my tube patterns incorporate silver chain tabs, which are used in jewelry making to finish off bracelets and neck-laces. They can be found in craft stores and bead catalogues. Chain tabs are lighter than cone heads, and they have a more elongated shape. They add just enough weight to balance out the hook — keeping the fly horizontal in the water — and a whole lot of flash.

After living ten years in Washington State I moved back to Northern California two years ago to be close to family. I now live in Santa Rosa where I operate a small fly company called FlyMax, where I specialize in tube flies for salmon and other saltwater game fish. I can be contacted at dsflymax@sbcglobal.net.

DANNA BANANA

Tube: Freelin-Wade nylon 11, .125 O. D./.093 I. D, 4 inches long
Thread: White
Body: Silver Mylar braid, medium
Tail: Pearl Mylar braid, small, 3/4 inches long, unraveled
Eyes: Silver 3-D stick-on, 1/4-inch diameter
Underhead filler: Yarn or thread
Head: Silver chain tab. This bullet-shaped, light-weight, hollow metal cone can be found at most craft and bead stores. It only comes in one size.
Paint: Waterproof markers. I use Zig Memory System, Sharpie, and Eberhard Faber Design 2 Art Markers.
Glue: Super glue and a thin, water-based head cement

Finish: 5-minute Devcon epoxy
Hook: Partridge MM3STBN tube fly hook or Owner thin wire, live bait hook, size 6 to 1

Step 1: Start with a piece of the nylon tubing that is 4 inches long. If the tubing that is used comes off a coil do not straighten it. This curve gives the fly a spinning, darting action on the retrieve.

Step 2: Cut a piece of medium silver Mylar braid 1/2 to 3/4 inch shorter than the tube and a piece of small pearl Mylar braid 1 inch long and remove the core material from both.

Step 3: This step can be done by hand or on a vise. Slip one end of the silver Mylar braid over the rear of the tube 1/2 inch and secure it with tying thread. Whip finish and trim thread. Coat the thread with enough super glue to bond it to the tube but don't get glue on the braided Mylar. Let dry. Invert the Mylar braid over the tie-in point (turning it inside out) and up the tube, then secure it with thread at the head of the tube, 1/2 to 3/4 inch from the end. Do not pull the Mylar braid tight against the tube; push it to the rear to form an air pocket between it and the nylon tube. Whip finish and apply super glue.

Step 4: Next, slip the small pearl Mylar braid over the tail end of the tubing and secure it as close to the silver braid as possible with a couple of thread wraps and a spot of super glue. The fewer the thread wraps, the more natural the appearance.

Step 5: Trim the front of the tube so that when the chain tab is put on it will cover the tie-down point of the Mylar at the head. Use yarn or thread to build up the tube under the chain tab and make a snug fit. Coat yarn with 5-minute epoxy and glue on the chain tab. Let cure.

Step 6: Now it's time to paint the body. A thin coat of head cement may be applied over the Mylar braid in order to prevent bleeding of colors; however, you may want the colors to bleed. On the rainbow trout version I use a black Sharpie for the spots; Olive Drab(D-79) Design 2 Art Marker for the back; and Hot Pink Design 2 Art Marker for the pink. Some experimentation is necessary, here. After the color is applied, coat the body with head cement to lock it in; when it dries, overcoat with 5-minute epoxy.

Step 7: Stick on the eyes and coat them with 5-minute epoxy.

The Danna Banana has been fished in Puget Sound, San Francisco Bay, Lake Mendocino, San Pablo Bay, and outside Noyo Harbor on the Mendocino coast in Northern California. It has caught coho salmon, striped bass, large mouth bass, smallmouth bass, and rock fish. When this chain-tab head pattern is dressed on a 3 inch tube it has a very natural-looking, neutral buoyancy in the water. I like to fish it on a clear intermediate-sink line.

TUNA TREAT

Tube: Freelin-Wade nylon 11, .125 O. D./.093 I. D., 2 inches long, with silicone hook sleeve

Thread: White 6/0; metallic rod winding thread (color to match wing)

Flash: Saltwater Flashabou, six 5-inch-long strands, tied 360 degrees around the tube. I use pearl for a blue fly, holographic red for a hot pink fly, holographic dark green for a green fly, holographic purple for a purple fly

Underwing: Six 2 1/2-inch-long saddle hackles tied around the tube. Choose colors that will contrast and complement the wing color – hot pink with dark blue; red and white with hot pink; chartreuse with emerald green; lavendar with dark purple

Wing: Eight 5-inch-long saddle hackles, long and thin, tied around the tube

Collar: Short, webby saddle hackle to match wing color

Head: Wrap 3/8 inch of tube ahead of collar with metallic thread and epoxy on a silver chain tab

Eyes: Plastic doll's eyes or 3-D stick-on, 3/8-inch diameter

Finish: 5-minute epoxy over metallic thread and eyes

Hook: Owner live bait or any good-quality short-shank saltwater hook, size 3/0 to 5/0

These flies came about in 2003 after a construction company client asked if I tied flies for albacore fishing. I told him I hadn't ever tried, but if he gave me a week I could come up with something. While doing the research, I found some albacore lures in an offshore-trolling catalog, and it hit me: I would tie scaled-down, attractor flies to mimic them. Not only will the Tuna Treat catch albacore, but other species of tuna as well. It also works on a variety of other game fish, including dorado, bonito, blue runner, and salmon. It is light enough to cast and can also be trolled.

FLOAT FISH

Tube: Freelin-Wade nylon 11, .125 O. D./.093 I. D., 2 1/4 inches long

Thread: 8/0 white

Ballast: Three strands of lead from lead-core trolling line, the same length as the fly, inserted into the Mylar braid on the underside of the tube

Body: Medium pearl Mylar braid, 1 1/2 inches longer than tube to make the tail

Paint: Color with waterproof markers to imitate baitfish or small trout (See Tying Instructions for the Danna Banana, Step 6)

Eyes: Silver 3-D stick-on, 1/4-inch diameter

Glue: Super glue and a thin, water-based head cement

Finish: 5-minute epoxy

Hook: Partridge MM3STBN tube-fly hook, sizes 6 to 1

Air trapped between the Mylar braid and the tube and sealed in with the epoxy gives this fly its buoyancy. Before I secure the ends of the Mylar to the tube I twist together the three strands of lead and slip them inside the braid, then I tie the braid to both ends of the tube creating a hollow body. I put a drop of super glue on the outside of the hollow body to attach the lead to the inside of the braid. Thus keel-weighted, the water the fly will always swim upright; with a floating line it can be dead-drifted or twitched on the surface.

These flies have worked well night-fishing trout in lakes. Bass and stripers take this freshwater fly.

STRIPER FLOAT FISH

Tube: Freelin-Wade nylon 11, .125 O. D./.093 I. D., 4 inches long

Thread: 8/0 white

Ballast: Four strands of lead from lead-core trolling line, the same length as the fly, inserted into the Mylar braid on the underside of the tube

Body: Large pearl Mylar braid, 2 inches longer than tube to make the tail

Paint: Color with waterproof markers to imitate baitfish or small trout (See Tying Instructions for the Danna Banana, Step 6)

Eyes: Silver 3-D stick-on, 3/8-inch diameter

Glue: Super glue and a thin, water-based head cement

Finish: 5-minute epoxy

Hook: Partridge MM3STBN tube-fly hook or Owner thin wire live bait, sizes 1 to 2/0

This is a larger version of The Float Fish designed to target striped bass in freshwater lakes.

CHAPTER 29

JURIJ (YURI) SHUMAKOV

Moscow, Russian Federation

March 5, 1956 – August 20, 2006

I was born in 1956 in Stavropol City, Northern Caucasus region of the Russian Federation, formerly the USSR. I started fishing when I was six or seven years old and my father often joked about my true origins because for four generations no one on either side of my family had been even remotely interested in fishing. At first Dad followed me at a safe distance, hiding just out of sight to make sure I could manage different situations on the waterside. I also learned to swim quite early, when I was only three or four, which wasn't too difficult for me since my astrological sign is Pisces (fish). After that first summer of tight surveillance, Dad left me to fish in the company of my friends.

When I completed my military service in 1976, I entered Moscow State Lomonosov University, and in 1984 I graduated from the department of biology as a microbiologist. An excellent and broad education in etiology and entomology, and many field trips and experiments gave me a unique view of fish and their environment.

Until 1986 I fished mostly with spinning gear. That year I bought a reprint of a very old book, *Fish of Russia* by Sabaneev. The first edition was published before the Russian Revolution and Sabaneev is a Russian fishing patriarch who first described all the methods and techniques of fishing, as well as most of the fish species in Russia. When I read the chapter about fly-fishing, I was fascinated both by the flies and the method. The first flies I tied were mostly for pike and perch, and I fished them with a spinning rod and leader fly in the front of a spoon. The results were remarkable, and made me even more interested in the subject.

At that time, fly-fishing was an almost unknown discipline in the Soviet Union. Fishing shops rarely carried anything related to the sport and only a few enthusiasts had "real" fly-fishing stuff. After I caught my first fish with home-made fly-gear there was no turning back.

In 1988, I joined a small group of Moscow fly-fishers; a year later we formed the first Moscow fly-fishing club. We have to thank many American fly-fishermen, like Leon Chandler, who

Clockwise from top: Russian Bullet; Rusty Skittle; Kolander; Night Rainbow; GP Wanted; Black Sheep; Sunny Day; Black Pyramid; Belly Gunner

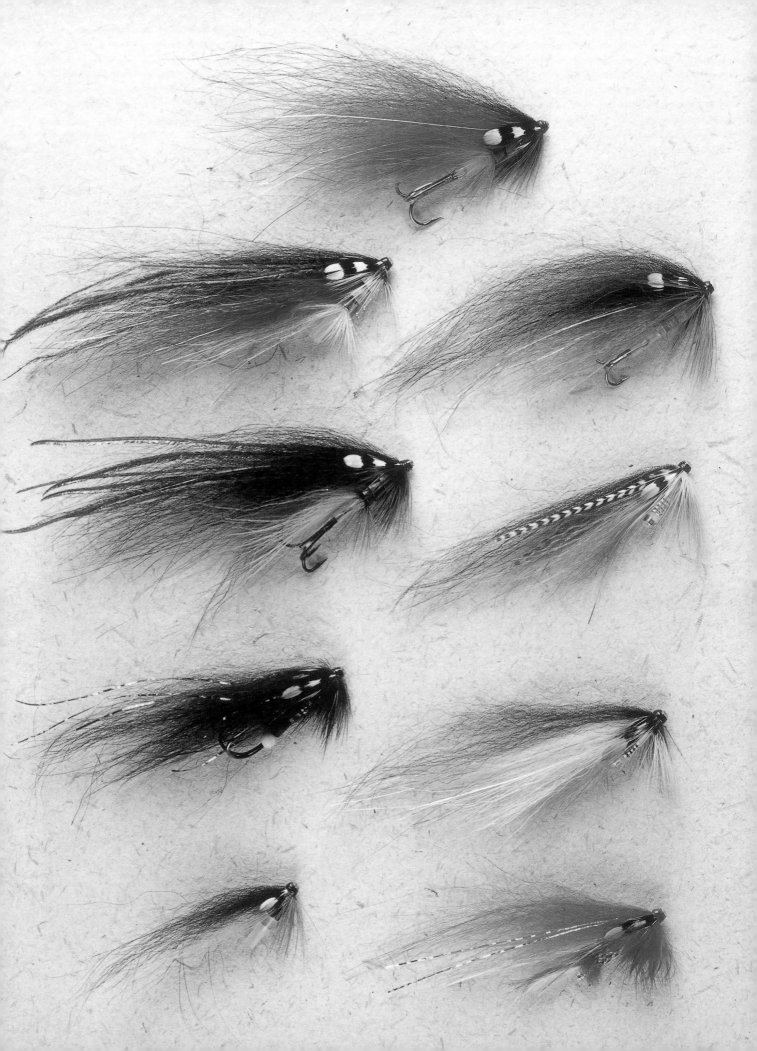

donated equipment, tying materials, tools and knowledge, and helped us to build our club. Big companies such as G. Loomis, Martin, and Cortland kindly provided us with blanks, rods, lines and reels because those were hard times in Russia and we didn't have the money to buy the gear. The first Americans who visited Russia in the early 90's and helped start clubs in Moscow, St. Petersburg and Murmansk would hardly recognize the fly-fishing scene there today. Most of the first-generation club members have become professional fly tiers, casting instructors, guides, fishing journalists, owners of fly-fishing shops or fishing tourist agencies, and all of us continue to promote fly-fishing as the most positive kind of fishing. We now have fly-fishing pages in all of the Russian fishing magazines as well as our own national fly-fishing magazine, *Nahlyst* (*Fly Fishing*).

In 1992 I defended my PhD thesis and in 1993, I was invited to Lund University in the south of Sweden for post-doctoral training. Since then I've worked as a microbiologist at Lund University. With my Swedish friends and colleagues, I fish many rivers, lakes, and "put and take" reservoirs, not counting hundreds miles of first-class coast line for sea trout and other species.

After moving to Sweden, I discovered the Scandinavian style of tube fly-tying. An article in *Trout and Salmon* magazine by the world famous Swedish tier Häkan Norling (See Chapter 22: Häkan Norling), the inventor of the Templedog tube fly, opened up a whole new world for me. Norling's innovations and those of

an equally famous Swedish fly-tier, Michael Frödin, heavily influenced my early tube tying. In the south of Sweden many local tiers are working in the Scandinavian style and exchanging ideas; they are an important resource for my fly-tying. I have fished tube flies with great success since 1995 in rivers on the Russian Kola Peninsula and in Kamchatka, as well as Sweden.

When I closely examined the flies I tied on short, half-inch commercial tubes, I noticed that in a moderate current they ride with their noses tipped up and their hook ends hanging down, which looks unnatural. This problem can be partially fixed by adding a compact, wound hackle at the rear end of the tube — on Mörrum style tubes the hackle is tied on the plastic liner before it is inserted into the metal body. The hackle helps to hold the rear part of the body up; it works like a horizontal underwater wing (hydrofoil).

Another way to minimize the tendency of the rear of the fly to hang down is to use thick, stiff monofilament that won't bend under the weight of the tube and hook. Tippet material for the spring fishing on Mörrum is 0.40 to 0.50 mm because the salmon can be really huge and the rocks are sharp. Thick monofilament is also useful for evening and night fishing for sea trout, but it is much less productive in clear summer water with small summer tube flies.

In spite of these solutions, I kept returning to the question: Why create an imbalance in the first place?! After months

YURI SHUMAKOV

made in brass and aluminium. This model is suitable for low-water fishing and was designed for those who prefer to tie on a metal neck instead of a plastic liner.

The "Summer Arrow" body is the shortest in my collection. It is 8 mm in length and made from brass only. It is intended for small summer patterns. It has enough weight to hold a fly in fast water where salmon are often found at that time of year.

All my patterns use domesticated Caucasian silver goat (Serebrjanka) hair in their wings. This natural hair has a texture similar to Arctic fox and the translucency of polar bear.

Since 1996, I have been tying commercially, mostly custom orders for particular rivers and situations.

I don't think tube flies are the answer in every case, but they are very productive at the beginning of the season when the weather is cold. More often than not, the easily fishable stretches of rivers are overcrowded; with my tube flies, I can catch salmon in inconvenient or "impossible" places.

A case point: Spring fishing the Kola Peninsula's rivers and Mörrum I found myself casting over salmon holding in the throats of pools under wild white water. (Fish tend to stay in places where it feels comfortable for them, not for fishermen.) Convential hook-tied and tube flies were simply washed away before the fish had a chance to see them. To fill this gap in the "ammunition," I developed the Russian Bullet tube fly, which has a body made of different sizes of cone heads. The Russian Bullet pattern and its variants sink rapidly and present correctly even under waterfalls.

pondering the problem, three potential shapes came to me. It took a few months more to find someone to produce the tubes and then to fine-tune their balance. The result was five different body shapes in two weights, brass and aluminium. The rear diameters of my tube bodies are standardized to accept thin and thick silicone hook sleeves.

The brass "Skittle" body has enough weight at the front end to push the fly down and hold it firmly in the current; the rear part is much thinner diameter. This design helps keep the fly in proper position, either horizontal or slightly nose down. The front cone angles the wing to keep it away from the hook, preventing tangling. A variant of this body has three machined grooves on the rear, which can be painted different colors to increase attraction.

The "Weight Forward" brass tube is lighter than the Skittle, its weight is more concentrated at the front of the tube, and there are no grooves in the body. This tube was designed to fish slower waters. It's perfect for dusk and night fishing for sea trout when silhouette is more important than details.

My "Long Range" brass tube is meant to reach the deepest fish lies. To make the body's rear lighter, it has four machined grooves which can be painted. A friend who was the first to see this creation exclaimed in amazement, "It certainly is a fly, but it looks like Mepps!" Well, who said spinners don't catch salmon? The aluminium version of this body style is suitable for the low-water conditions and light dressing. Aluminum Long Rangers are my first choice for rivers that don't have much coloration, such as those in Norway.

The "JS bottle neck" tube has shorter body and is lighter than the Long Range. It has three grooves machined on the rear, and is

RUSSIAN BULLET

Tube: Plastic 2-mm O. D., 3/4 inch long, and a hook sleeve of 2.5-mm silicone tubing. Connected tubes have a 1 inch overall length

Thread: Black, size 10 Benecchi or 12 Gordon Griffith

Rear hackle: Five or six turns of cock feather dyed hot orange

Body: Two copper cone heads 7/32-inch diameter, and one brass cone head 1/4-inch diameter dyed orange

Tail: Tied in front of the rear hackle, two strips of orange Mirage Flashabou under a 1 1/4-inch long, sparse bunch of orange dyed Serebrjanka (Caucasian silver goat)

First wing section (tied in front of the first copper cone head): Few strands of red and copper Angel Hair, and a sparse, 2-inch-long bunch of hot-orange Arctic fox

Second wing section (tied in front of the second copper cone head): Few strands of red, black, and copper Angel Hair, and a sparse, 2 1/2-inch-long bunch of hot-orange Arctic fox

Third wing section (in front of the 1/4-inch orange cone head): Few strands of red and black Angel Hair, and a sparse, 3-inch-long bunch of Arctic fox dyed Mörrum orange

Front hackle: Five to six turns of badger cock feather dyed Mörrum orange

Fourth wing section (tie in front of orange-dyed badger): Few strands of red and black Angel Hair, and a very sparse, 3-inch-long bunch of rusty-brown Arctic fox. This section is reverse tied: the hair wing is first attached facing forward, then pulled back into the normal, rear-facing position and held in place with as few thread wraps as possible

Cheeks: Two jungle cock feathers

Head: Black thread

Finish: Varnish or head cement

Hook: Size 6 or 8 Kamasan treble or Loop double

Step 1: Take a plastic tube 25 to 30 mm (1 to 1 1/4 inch) in length and 1.8 to 2.0 mm O. D. and melt a collar on one end. Slip the silicone hook sleeve over the collar, put joined tubes on your mandrel, and the mandrel in your vise. Tube kits (properly sized hard tubing and hook sleeve) are available from The Fly Co., Denmark. Attach tying thread on the hook sleeve in front of the collar. This locks the sleeve in place. The hard plastic tubing must be free of thread or the cones won't slip on.

Step 2: Wind on the rear hackle, tie down with thread, and trim excess feather. Secure the thead with a whip finish or half hitch, cut the excess thread and apply a drop of varnish. All components must be tightly wrapped and with as few turns of thread as possible — this allows you to fit the cone heads very close together.

Step 3: Choose three cone heads. Some options: rear cone head is Small, middle is Medium, and front is Large; or Small, Medium, Medium; or Medium, Medium, Large. Make sure they slide freely onto the plastic tube. Paint the cone heads the desired color. A topcoat of transparent varnish will improve the hardness of the color layer.

Step 4: Apply a small drop of super glue on the plastic tube and thread wraps of rear hackle. Fit the smallest cone head over the front of the tube and push it back as close as possible to the hackle. Apply a few turns of the thread in front of the cone. In a couple of seconds the glue will hold the cone in place.

Step 5: Tie a couple of strands of flashy or holographic material. On top, tie in a small bunch of Arctic fox tail. Spread the fur with your fingernail over the top of the tube. This reduces the thickness of the tie-down area and increases wing volume, which is important for spring flies. Secure the thread with a whip finish or half hitch and cut the excess thread. I use a scalpel because it makes the cut very precise.

Step 6: Repeat Step 4 with the middle cone head.

Step 7: Attach the flash and second section of wing to the tube as in Step 5. The length of each succeeding wing section should be slightly longer than the last; this makes the silhouette proportional. Remember to distribute the hair over the top of the tube.

Step 8: Repeat Step 4 with the front cone head.

Step 9: Attach the flash and third section of the wing to the tube as in Step 5. Remember to distribute the hair over the top of the tube.

Step 10: Reverse-tie in the last wing section of Arctic fox . Wind a few turns of the front hackle on top of the thread wraps.

Step 11: Bend back the top wing and secure it as close as possible to the front hackle with a few turns of thread. Remember to distribute the hair over the top of the tube.

Step 12: On top of the wing, a few strands of synthetic flash or peacock can be added. Tie in jungle cock cheeks. Secure the thread with a knot and cut thread. **Do not apply varnish or cement!** It can burn in the next step.

Step 13: Next, one of the most delicate operations — the melting of the tube's front collar. Take the tube off the vise and remove the mandrel. Cut off excess plastic tube at the front with a scalpel or sharp knife, leaving a stub no longer than 1 to1.5 mm. Insert the mandrel (or a needle) into the plastic tube's front end. The metal mandrel prevents the plastic from melting too quickly and possibly burning. Carefully smooth back the fly materials and hold them tightly in your fingers. Fire-up your lighter and heat the stub of plastic tube in the lowest part of the flame, turning it quickly from side to side. A perfect collar will form. Take away the heat at once. After the plastic hardens, remove the mandrel from the front, and reinsert it into the rear of the tube and put it back on your vise.

Step 14: Attach black thread and form a small, neat head behind the collar. Whip finish, trim thread and apply a couple of coats of varnish.

BLACK PYRAMID

Tube: Plastic 2-mm O. D., 5/8 inch long and a hook sleeve of clear, 2.5-mm O. D. hard tubing

Thread: Black, size 10 Benecchi or 12 Gordon Griffith

Rear hackle: Five to six turns of red-dyed cock feather

Body: One 5/32-inch diameter (4 mm) brass cone head dyed black, and two 3/16-inch (4.8 mm) brass cone heads dyed black

Tail: Tied in front of the rear hackle, two strips of yellow Mirage Flashabou under a 1 1/4-inch-long, sparse bunch of yellow-dyed Serebrjanka (Caucasian silver goat)

First wing section (tied in front of the smallest black cone head): Few strands of red and yellow Angel Hair, and a sparse, 2-inch-long bunch of red Arctic fox

Second wing section (tied in front of the first 3/16-inch black cone head): Few strands of red, black, and deep blue Angel Hair, a sparse, 2 1/2-inch-long bunch of black-dyed Arctic fox

Third wing section (in front of the second 3/16-inch cone head): Few strands of red, black, and deep blue Angel Hair, and a sparse, 3-inch-long bunch of Arctic fox dyed black

Front hackle: Five or six turns of red-dyed cock feather

Fourth wing section (tied in front of red-dyed cock): Few strands of peacock herl and a very sparse, 3-inch-long bunch of black-dyed Arctic fox. This section is reverse tied: hair wing first tied facing forward, then pulled back into the normal, rear-facing position and held in place with thread wraps.

Cheeks: Two jungle cock feathers

Head: Black thread

Finish: Varnish or head cement

Hook: Size 6 or 8 Kamasan treble or Loop double

BELLY GUNNER

Tube: Plastic 2-mm O. D., 5/8 inch long and a hook sleeve of clear, 2.5-mm O. D. hard tubing

Thread: Black, size 10 Benecchi or 12 Gordon Griffith

Rear hackle: Five to six turns of natural white cock feather

Body: One 5/32-inch (4 mm) silver cone head, and two 3/16-inch (4.8 mm) silver cone heads

Tail: Tied in front of the rear hackle, two strands of silver holographic tinsel under a 1 1/4-inch-long, sparse bunch of natural white Serebrjanka (Caucasian silver goat)

First wing section (tied in front of the smallest silver cone head): Few strands of holographic silver Angel Hair, and a sparse, 2-inch-long bunch of Serebrjanka fur dyed blue

Second wing section (tied in front of the first 3/16-inch cone head): Few strands of dark blue, ocean blue and silver holo graphic Angel Hair, and a sparse, 2 1/2-inch-long bunch of blue-dyed Arctic fox

Third wing section (in front of the second 3/16-inch cone head): Few strands of dark blue, ocean blue, and silver holographic Angel Hair, and a sparse, 3-inch-long bunch of black dyed Arctic fox over a few strands of peacock herl

Front hackle: Five or six turns of natural badger cock feather

Fourth wing section (tied in front of badger hackle): Few strands of dark blue, ocean blue, and silver holographic Angel Hair, and a very sparse, 3-inch-long bunch of black-dyed Arctic fox. This section is reverse tied: hair wing first tied facing forward, then pulled back into the normal, rear-facing position and held in place with thread wraps.

Belly gun: A few short strands of pearl Krystal Flash tied under the body in front of third cone head

Cheeks: Two jungle cock feathers

Head: Black thread

Finish: Varnish or head cement

Hook: Size 6 or 8 Kamasan treble or Loop double

I fish the Russian Bullet and its variants on 1.5 to 2.5 m leaders with sinking lines, and on 3 to 4.5 m leaders with floating or sink-tip lines. My favorite lines are 13.5 m shooting heads from the Swedish GUIDELINE Company. I use fast or medium to fast action two-handed rods, 14 to 15 feet in length in 9- to 11-weight, and fast-action, 9.3-foot single-handed rods, 8- or 9-weight.

RUSTY SKITTLE

Tube: Plastic 2-mm O.D., 3/4 inch long liner that fits inside the metal tube body; and a hook sleeve of 2.5 mm silicone tubing that fits over the end of the tube body. Hackle, wing, cheeks and head are dressed on 4 mm (3/16 inch) of protruding liner tubing.

Thread: Black, size 10 Benecchi or 12 Gordon Griffith

YURI SHUMAKOV

Body: Machined brass, half-inch "Skittle" tube, 5-mm O. D.

Tag: Fluorescent red Glo-bright thread tied in the tube's rear groove. You can also use colored varnish.

First wing section: Two strands of orange Mirage Flashabou and a sparse, 1 3/4-inch-long bunch of Serebrjanka hair dyed light rusty brown

Second wing section: Few strands of light brown and copper Angel Hair and a sparse, 2 1/4-inch-long bunch of Serebrjanka hair dyed fiery brown

Front hackle: Five to six turns of orange-dyed badger cock feather

Third wing section (tied in front of badger hackle): Few strands of brown and copper Angel Hair, and a sparse, 3-inch-long bunch of Arctic fox fur dyed dark brown

Fourth wing section (tied in reverse technique): Few strands of brown Angel Hair, and a sparse, 3 1/2-inch-long bunch of Arctic fox dyed black

Topping: Few strands of fine, rippled hair in fiery brown color

Cheeks: Two jungle cock feathers

Head: Black thread

Finish: Varnish or head cement

Hook: Size 6 or 8 Kamasan treble or Loop double

SUNNY DAY

Tube: Plastic 2-mm O.D., 3/4-inch-long liner that fits inside the metal tube body; and a hook sleeve of 2.5-mm soft, black tubing that fits over the end of the tube body. Hackle, wing, cheeks and head are dressed on 4 mm (3/16 inch) of protruding liner tubing.

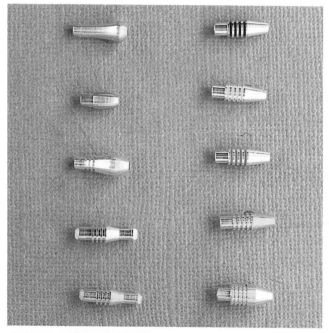

Left column, from top: WF; Summer Arrow; Skittle; JS Bottle Neck (aluminum); JS Bottle Neck (brass). Right column, from top: Long Range (aluminum, 4-mm O.D.) with painted grooves; Long Range (brass, 4-mm O.D.); Long Range (brass, 5-mm O.D.).

Thread: Black, size 10 Benecchi or 12 Gordon Griffith

Body: Machined brass, half-inch "Long Range" tube, 4-mm O.D.

Tag: Fluorescent green plastic bead slipped over hook shank

First wing section: Two strands of fine black holographic Flashabou and a sparse, 2 1/4-inch-long bunch of Arctic fox dyed black

Second wing section: Two strands of fine black holographic Flashabou and a sparse, 2 3/4-inch-long bunch of Arctic fox dyed black

Front hackle: Four to five turns of dubbed rabbit fur dyed black

Third wing section (reverse tied in front of dubbing): Two strands of fine black holographic Flashabou, and a sparse, 3-inch-long bunch of Arctic fox dyed black

Topping: Few strands of fine, rippled hair in greenish black

Cheeks: Two jungle cock feathers

Head: Black thread

Finish: Varnish or head cement

Hook: Size 6 or 8 Kamasan treble or Loop double

NIGHT RAINBOW

Tube: Plastic 2-mm O.D., 3/4-inch-long liner that fits inside the metal tube body; and a hook sleeve of 2.5-mm soft, clear tubing that fits over the end of the tube body. Hackle, wing, cheeks and head are dressed on 4 mm (3/16 inch) of protruding liner tubing.

Thread: Black, Size 10 Benecchi or 12 Gordon Griffith

Body: Machined aluminium, half-inch "Long Range" tube, 4-mm O.D. Grooves are painted with black varnish.

Tag: Fluorescent orange Glo-bright thread

First wing section: Two strands of orange Mirage Flashabou and a sparse, 1 1/2-inch-long bunch of Serebrjanka hair dyed orange

Second wing section: Few strands of holographic silver Angel Hair and a sparse, 2-inch-long bunch of natural white Serebrjanka hair

Third wing section: Few strands of holographic silver Angel Hair and a sparse, 2 1/2-inch-long bunch of natural brown Tempelhair

Front hackle: Five to six turns of badger cock feather

Fourth wing section (reverse tied in front of badger hackle): Few strands of holographic silver Angel Hair and a sparse, 3-inch-long bunch of dyed-black Arctic fox

Topping: Few strands of fine, rippled hair in greenish-black

Cheeks: Two jungle cock feathers

Head: Black thread

Finish: Varnish or head cement

Hook: Size 6 or 8 Kamasan treble or Loop double

BLACK SHEEP

Tube: Plastic 2-mm O. D., 3/4-inch-long liner that fits inside the metal tube body; and a hook sleeve of 2.5-mm soft, clear tubing that fits over the end of the tube body. Hackle, wing, cheeks and head are dressed on 3-mm (1/8 inch) of protruding liner tubing.

Thread: Black, size 10 Benecchi or 12 Gordon Griffith

Body: Machined brass, half-inch "Summer Arrow" tube, 4-mm O. D. I paint the weighted front of the body with black varnish and topcoat it with clear varnish.

First wing section: Two strips of yellow Mirage Flashabou and a sparse, 1 3/4-inch-long bunch of Serebrjanka hair dyed yellow

Front hackle: Five or six turns of kingfisher-blue-dyed cock feather

Second wing section (reverse tied in front of hackle): Few strands of yellow Angel Hair and a sparse, 2 1/2-inch-long bunch of dyed black Arctic fox

Topping: Few strands of fine, rippled hair in greenish black

Cheeks: Two jungle cock feathers

Head: Black thread

Finish: Varnish or head cement

Hook: Size 6 or 8 Kamasan treble or Loop double

GP WANTED

Tube: Brass 2-mm O. D., 1 inch long, with hook sleeve of 2.5-mm O. D. soft, clear tubing. Hackle, wing, cheeks and head are dressed on 3 mm (1/8 inch) of protruding liner tubing.

Thread: Black, Size 10 Benecchi or 12 Gordon Griffith

Tag: Five turns of fine, silver oval tinsel; five turns of yellow silk

Tail: Tied in two parts, 1/2 inch long, yellow and red SLF Hanks, sparse

Butt: Red-dyed ostrich

Rear 2/3 body: Red and silver braided tubing

Front 1/3 body: Red SLF dubbing

First section wing: Sparse, 1 1/2 inch long bunch of dyed yellow Serebrjanka hair

Second wing section: Two strands of silver holographic Angel Hair and a sparse, 2 1/4-inch-long bunch of red-dyed Serebrjanka hair

Front hackle: Four to five turns of dyed red cock feather, including soft, marabou-like butt

Third wing section (reverse tied in front of the hackle): Two strands of silver holographic Angel Hair and sparse, 3-inch-long bunch of dyed-red Arctic fox

Topping: Few strands of fine, rippled hair in fiery red

Cheeks: Two jungle cock feathers

Head: Black thread

Finish: Varnish or head cement

Hook: Size 6 or 8 Kamasan treble or Loop double

KOLANDER

Tube: Plastic 2-mm O. D., 3/4-inch-long that fits inside the metal tube body; and a hook sleeve of 2.5-mm soft, clear tubing that fits over the end of the tube body

Hackle, wing, cheeks and head are dressed on 4 mm- (3/16 inch) of protruding liner tubing.

Thread: Black, size 10 Benecchi or 12 Gordon Griffith

Body: Machined aluminium, type Halfincher "Long range" tube, 4-mm O. D. The grooves are painted with Glo fluorescent green varnish

Tag: Glo-Brite fluorescent yellow floss

First wing section: Two strands of orange Mirage Flashabou and sparse, 1 1/2-inch-long bunch of Serebrjanka hair dyed orange

Second wing section: Two strands of yellow Mirror Flash and a sparse, 1 3/4-inch-long bunch of Serebrjanka hair dyed yellow

Third wing section: Two strands of Come's Alive Ripple Flash in Mother of Pearl and a sparse, 2 1/4-inch-long bunch of Serebrjanka hair dyed insect green

First front hackle: Insect-green-dyed cock feather

Fourth wing section (reverse tied in front of the first front hackle): Two strands of olive Gliss&Glow ripple flash and a sparse, 3-inch-long bunch of Arctic fox fur dyed red-brown

Second front hackle: Yellow-dyed cock feather

Fifth wing section (reverse tied in front of second hackle): Two strands each of light copper and red Angel Hair, and a sparse, 3 1/8-inch-long bunch of dyed-black Arctic fox

Topping: Few strands of fine, rippled hair in greenish-black

Shoulders: Two grizzly neck hackles

Cheeks: Two jungle cock feathers

Head: Black thread

Finish: Varnish or head cement

Hook: Size 6 or 8 Kamasan treble or Loop double

Jurij (Yuri) Shumakov, 1956-2006

Yuri's sudden passing while fishing Russia's Kola Peninsula shocked and saddened all who knew him. Multi-talented and accomplished, he was a modern Renaissance man. Yuri's adventurous spirit, insight, and inspiration will be sorely missed. His family will continue to sell his products at www.shumakov tubes.com.

CHAPTER 30

CAM SIGLER, JR.
Vashon Island, Washington

Cam Sigler Jr. (center) and Cam Sigler Sr. (right) with a Guatemalan sailfish caught on a Jewel Tube.

My family has been in the fishing-tackle industry for 40-plus years. I started fishing and fly-tying at age seven. These days our company is primarily in the wholesale wader business, but we also produce three-piece fly rods, 8- through 16/17-weight, a three-piece teaser rod, and tube flies for billfishing. My dad's Big Game tube fly, developed in 1989, has been featured in many books, magazine stories, and TV shows, and it won the Mazatlan billfish tournament three years running, 1999 to 2001. The Big Game fly is a popper with a reversible foam head that can also be fished as a slider. Poppers are usually the ticket on sails, but at times they can be spooky

and won't break water to take a surface fly, so I decided to create a sinking tube fly as a change-up for those conditions.

In 1998 I began testing all the available commercial subsurface billfish flies. Testing flies is easy for me because our office fronts on Puget Sound. What I found was room for improvement. The Superhair used on many of the flies had three big drawbacks: a tendency for the wings to wrap and foul the hooks; the material was too stiff to move in a lifelike way in the water; and its texture could catch on the sandpaper surface of a fish's bill. You might think the latter isn't a bad thing, but a bill-fouled (as opposed to hooked) fish isn't IGFA-legal, and you can fight a sail

From top: Jewel Fly/California Sardine; Jewel Fly/Pink Squid; Jewel Fly/Green Mackerel; Jewel Fly/Mediterranean; Jewel Fly/Slimey Mack

for a long time only to have it self-release when the bill wrap works loose.

I abandoned Superhair for the main wing, switching over to holographic Flash, which has excellent movement and color in the water, and is very slick. That solved two of the three problems. In the end, the hook-fouling issue required Superhair, but only as a brace. Short bunches of Superhair tied to the top and bottom of the tube spread the main wing of Flash in a vertical plane, creating a deep, flat head and flowing body shape. The finished fly head is dipped in Softex which fixes the silhouette and keeps the flexible materials spread away from the hooks so they don't foul. To increase versatility, I leave enough bare tube sticking out of the nose of the fly to slip on a popper head or a metal cone.

I use a 90-degree offset with 6/0 Owner or Gamakatsu hooks tied on 100-pound Suffix shock and a 20-pound Mason bimini rigged to IGFA specs. If I'm not fishing according to IGFA rules, I rig the first of the two hooks ahead of the nose of the fly, and the trailer hook behind the head in normal fashion — this further reduces hook interference with wing movement. I fish the Jewel with rods 12-weight and up. I like a 500-grain sink-tip or shooting head to get down a bit and under the bubbles of the boat wake.

Fly-fishing for sails and marlin is usually done with a bait and switch technique. A live bait or trolled teaser lures the fish into range, is then jerked out of the water, and replaced by the cast fly. My Jewel tubes all have yellow eyes, which is different than the natural baits. In my experience, subtle differences can trigger selection and attack by game fish.

Billy Pate took some of my Jewel tube flies to Costa Rica in 1999 and used them to win the Quepos sailfish tournament. The same year, Jody Pate caught a two world-record white marlin, 109 and 89 pounds, on the fly in Morocco.

In February 2001, Scott Leon used this pattern with success on yellowfin tuna, fishing the Midnight Lump with Captain Damon McKnight of Super Strike Charters. "Lumps," as it is called locally, is a salt dome in about 600 feet of water (its top is at 300 feet) 30 miles from Venice, Louisiana, in the Gulf of Mexico. Scott had a selection of Jewel tubes with him, but the most effective pattern was pearl-dyed-over-black over pearl about 7 inches long that resembled the pogies (bunker, menhaden) they use for chum/bait. With the chum line going, Scott had the captain and mate fish conventional gear until they were sure tuna were under and behind the boat. Then he made a quartering cast across the current with his 16/17-weight and let the fly swing straight behind, running about 10 to 12 feet down. Two strips and he had a fish on. An hour and ten minutes later he landed a 65-pound yellowfin. After a rest he cast the fly again, and a few more strips gave him a second hook up, not a yellowfin but a blackfin. That tuna weighed 31 pounds back at the dock.

Scott fishes the Lumps for tuna several times a year. He loads his reel with 1000 yards of gelspun backing attached to Rio's 600-grain sinking Leviathan line (full length) with 4 feet of 50-pound butt looped to a standard big-game leader. The size of the class tippet and shock varies, depending on water clarity — the cleaner the water the lighter the line, and the less flashy the fly. Tuna have phenomenal eyesight, too much flash in the line scares them.

All of my Jewel flies are custom-tied to order. Working from photos of natural baits, I dye the materials and tie the flies to match. I can be reached at Flyfish@camsigler.com.

JEWEL FLY — CALIFORNIA SARDINE

Tube: Plastic, 1/8-inch O. D., 1 1/2 inches long, with silicone hook sleeve

Thread: White heavy nylon for the underbody; clear monofilament for the belly, back, and head

Underbody: Bunch of black Superhair, 2 1/2 inches long, 1/4-inch diameter, tied on the top of tube, 1/4 inch from the front; bunch of white Superhair, 2 1/2 inches long, 1/4-inch diameter, tied on underside of tube, same distance from front end. Both are tied in at 45 degrees.

Belly: Pearl holographic Flash, 8 inches long

Lateral stripe: Mixed bunch of red, purple, blue, and green, 1/32-inch-wide holographic tinsel, 8 inches long, on both sides

Back: Olive pearl Flash overdyed black, 8 inches long

Cheek/Gill Plate: Dyed-red, Black Lace hen saddles or Witchcraft red holograph ovals, 1 1/2 inches long

Eyes: Yellow Prismatic 3-D stick-on eyes, 1/2-inch diameter

Finish: Softex

Hook: Double Owner or Gamakatsu 6/0s, rear hook tied with a 90-degree offset

Step 1: Connect the plastic tube and hook sleeve and put on your vise. Attach heavy nylon thread and tie down the join area.

Step 2: On top of the tube, tie in a 1/4-inch diameter bunch of black Superhair, 2 1/2 inches long. The hair angle should be 45 degrees.

Step 3: Rotate the tube 180 degrees on your vise and tie in an equal bunch of white Superhair, also at a 45-degree angle. Whip finish, trim thread and cement. These short Superhair wings, top and bottom, spread out the back and belly materials, giving the fly a wider silhouette and more movement and flash.

Step 4: Attach monofilament thread. On top of the white Superhair butts, tie in the long pearl Flash belly.

Step 5: Rotate the tube 180 degrees. On either side, tie in the lateral stripes of mixed holographic tinsel.

Step 6: On top of the black Superhair butts tie in the olive pearl Flash overdyed black.

Step 7: On either side, tie in the red-dyed Black Laced hen saddles or Witchcraft red holographic ovals, then whip finish and trim thread.

Step 8: Stick on the 3-D eyes. Put a thin coat of epoxy over them and the thread wraps. Let cure.

Step 9: Dip the entire head, up to the edges of the red dyed Black Lace hen saddles or Witchcraft red holographic ovals (gill plate) in Softex.

I developed this pattern after coming back from a long-range trip out of San Diego. It is designed to resemble the California sardine, which the crew used as live chum to bring game fish into fly-casting range. This color scheme has worked well on billfish species in the Sea of Cortez and in Panama.

JEWEL FLY – PINK SQUID

Tube: Plastic, 1/8-inch O.D., 1 1/2 inches long, with silicone hook sleeve

Thread: White monocord for the underbody; clear monofilament for the belly, back, and head

Underbody: Bunch of red Superhair, 2 1/2 inches long, 1/4-inch diameter, tied on the top of tube, 1/4 inch from the front; bunch of white Superhair, 2 1/2 inches long, 1/4-inch diameter, tied on underside of tube, same distance from front end. Both are tied in at 45 degrees.

Belly: Pearl holographic Flash, 8 inches long

Back: Pink holographic tinsel, 8 inches long

Cheek/Gill Plate: Dyed red, Black Lace hen saddles or Witchcraft red holograph ovals, 1 1/2 inches long

Eyes: Yellow Prismatic 3-D stick-on eyes, 1/2-inch diameter

Finish: Softex

Hook: Double Owner or Gamakatsu 6/0s, rear hook tied with a 90-degree offset

JEWEL FLY – GREEN MACKEREL

Tube: Plastic, 1/8-inch O.D., 1 1/2 inches long, with silicone hook sleeve

Thread: White monocord for the underbody; clear monofilament for the belly, back, and head

Underbody: Bunch of olive Superhair, 2 1/2 inches long, 1/4-inch diameter, tied on the top of tube, 1/4 inch from the front; bunch of white Superhair, 2 1/2 inches long, 1/4-inch diameter, tied on underside of tube, same distance from front end. Both are tied in at 45 degrees.

Belly: Pearl holographic Flash, 8 inches long

Back: Green over equal bunch of yellow holographic tinsel, 8 inches long

Cheek/Gill Plate: Dyed red, Black Lace hen saddles or Witchcraft red holograph ovals, 1 1/2 inches long

Eyes: Yellow Prismatic 3-D stick-on eyes, 1/2-inch diameter

Finish: Softex

Hook: Double Owner or Gamakatsu 6/0s, rear hook tied with a 90-degree offset

JEWEL FLY – MEDITERRANEAN

Tube: Plastic, 1/8-inch O.D., 1 1/2 inches long, with silicone hook sleeve

Thread: White monocord for the underbody; clear monofilament for the belly, back, and head

Underbody: Bunch of black Superhair, 2 1/2 inches long, 1/4-inch diameter, tied on the top of tube, 1/4 inch from the front; bunch of white Superhair, 2 1/2 inches long, 1/4-inch diameter, tied on underside of tube, same distance from front end. Both are tied in at 45 degrees.

Belly: Pearl holographic Flash, 8 inches long

Back: Bunch of silver holographic tinsel, 8 inches long; topped by an equal-sized bunch of mixed blue and purple holographic tinsel, 8 inches long; topped by an equal-sized bunch of olive pearl Flash overdyed black, 8 inches long

Cheek/Gill Plate: Dyed red, Black Lace hen saddles or Witchcraft red holograph ovals, 1 1/2 inches long

Eyes: Yellow Prismatic 3-D stick-on eyes, 1/2-inch diameter

Finish: Softex

Hook: Double Owner or Gamakatsu 6/0s, rear hook tied with a 90-degree offset

I developed this color combination baitfish fly from a photo submitted by a client who was traveling to Italy to fish giant bluefin tuna in the Mediterranean.

JEWEL FLY – SLIMEY MACK

Tube: Plastic, 1/8-inch O.D., 1 1/2 inches long, with silicone hook sleeve

Thread: White monocord for the underbody; clear monofilament for the belly, back, and head

Underbody: Bunch of olive Superhair, 2 1/2 inches long, 1/4-inch diameter, tied on the top of tube, 1/4 inch from the front; bunch of white Superhair, 2 1/2 inches long, 1/4-inch diameter, tied on underside of tube, same distance from front end. Both are tied in at 45 degrees.

Belly: Pearl holographic Flash, 8 inches long

Back: Olive pearl Flashabou, same diameter as belly, 8 inches long, topped by an equal-sized bunch of olive pearl Flashabou overdyed black, 8 inches long

Cheek/Gill Plate: Dyed-red, Black Lace hen saddles or Witchcraft red holograph ovals, 1 1/2 inches long

Eyes: Yellow Prismatic 3-D stick-on eyes, 1/2-inch diameter

Finish: Softex

Hook: Double Owner or Gamakatsu 6/0s, rear hook tied with a 90-degree offset

I was fishing off Buddina Beach, on Australia's Sunshine Coast, with my friend Gavin Plats who owns Tie-N-Fly Outfitters. We were jigging up mackerel to use as tease baits and I couldn't help but notice how profusely the particular species bled — which is why Australians call them "Slimey." The red gills on this pattern are meant to mimic the blood. The Slimey Mack has worked well on billfish at Buddina Beach and Port Stevens, Australia.

DAVID SKOK

Winthrop, Massachusetts

DAVE SKOK

Although I have been tying flies for nearly twenty years, the tube fly is a new and exciting facet of the craft for me. Since I primarily tie saltwater flies, tube flies are most interesting to me as baitfish, squid, and crustacean imitations. I began fooling with tubes just a few years ago and I am glad that I have.

The most obvious advantage of a tube to me initially was the ability to swap hooks. Striped bass fishermen here in the northeastern portion of the United States are commonly fishing shorelines that have steep sandy beaches or jagged rocks behind them. Either will quickly ruin a hookpoint if an angler is not careful on the backcast. Many flies are discarded not because they are shredded, but because of damage to the hooks. Tubes afford anglers the opportunity to save a perfectly good fly by switching to a new hook.

Another advantage to the tube-fly scheme is the ability to switch color combinations without having to carry a truckload of different patterns. That was the thought behind the Flaming Tube Squid. Striped bass feeding on squid in swift-moving tidal rips are rarely selective to pattern, but are often picky about color. One day orange may be the hot color and then red the next. Fish will even switch their color preference as tide stages progress. Orange and pink seem to be the best colors over sandy-bottomed shoals, and red and purple over rocky reefs. White is the perennial favorite for night fishing. Anglers carrying one color of dressed hook and several tubes of different hair and hackle colors can make a quick change. All my patterns consist of a dressed hook and dressed tubes. The size and length of the fly can also be altered by stacking tubes on the leader. Tube squids should *not* be employed when there are good numbers of bluefish in an area. Often the tube will slide up the leader during the fight with a striper, turning it into a wiggling morsel that a toothy blue will grab, thereby severing the leader and losing both fly and fish.

The third and to me most interesting advantage to tube flies is the ability to tie slender-profiled flies without having to use a long-shank hook. The longer the length of a hook shank in relation to the size of the gap, the less effective it becomes in hooking and holding big fish. Long-shank hooks are typically not as strong as shorter models and the extra length gives fish greater leverage to work the point out of their jaws.

The earliest lobster patterns I tied were simply long-shank versions of Phil Chapman's rabbit tarpon flies. The fish ate them like crazy, but I was never satisfied with their performance due to the long hook. A short-shank hook and multiple tubes can be used to produce even longer carapaces.

THE SLOBSTER

Hook: TMC 600SP 3/0 or other short-shank hook
Thread: Clear fine monofilament
Feelers: Cream bucktail under slightly longer black bucktail
Claws: Two yellowish feathers from a golden pheasant skin; outside of which are two grizzly dyed-red saddle hackles; outside of which are two iridescent green

---

From top: Flaming Tube Squid (Chartreuse and Orange); Flaming Tube Squid (Orange and Purple); Flaming Tube Squid (Burgundy and Tan); the Slobster (or Skok's Lobster).

Bass love the Slobster!

feathers from a golden pheasant — all tied on the thick part of the stems, splayed out

Eyes: Two large, peacock-colored glass beads burnt into place on 60-pound mono, and coated with 5-minute epoxy

Innerbelly/hackle: One long shrimp pink and one long ginger variant saddle tied in by the butt and wrapped together to create a mottled effect, trimmed on top

Rostrum: Blended black and pale orange Slinkyfibre (3/4 black, 1/4 orange), tapered and tied slightly longer than the eyes

Legs: Several turns of coyote zonker strip, trimmed on top and bare hide darkened with a black permanent marker

Carapace: Blended black and pale orange Slinkyfibre (3/4 black, 1/4 orange), tapered and tied reverse-style

Finish: Head cement

Tube: Plastic, 1/8-inch O.D., 1 1/4 inches long

Thread: Clear fine monofilament

Back legs: Cream bucktail, tied long to hide the hook/tube junction

Middle legs: Several turns of badger zonker strip, trimmed on top and bare hide darkened with a black permanent marker

Front legs: Several turns of cream polecat zonker strip (rabbit or mink may be substituted), trimmed on top and bare hide darkened with a black permanent marker

Eyes: Lead dumb bell, medium (7/32-inch) — these can be painted cream or pale pink if desired. Dub cream polecat fur around the lead eyes.

Carapace: Blended black and pale orange Slinkyfibre (3/4 black, 1/4 orange), tapered and tied reverse-style

Finish: Head cement

HOOK DRESSING:

Step 1: Attach clear monofilament thread mid-shank and wrap rearwards to the point on the shank above the hook barb. Tie in a short bunch of cream bucktail over which is a slightly longer bunch of black bucktail.

Step 2: Select two pairs of feathers from the body of a golden or ring-necked pheasant and a pair of red-dyed grizzly saddle hackles 5 to 9 inches long. Strip the base of stems, taking care to not remove all of the marabou-like fluff. Align the feathers so the saddle hackle is sandwiched between the shorter, stiffer pheasant feathers. Marry the two bunches of feathers so that they are splayed (concave sides facing outward) and attach them to the hook shank at the same tie-in point as the bucktail. Be sure to tie in the feathers on the stiff part of stem to prevent hook fouling and to utilize the fluffy fibers as a cushion for easy mounting.

Step 3: Tie in a pair of eyes made from 60-pound monofilament, peacock glass beads and epoxy. The eyes should be tied in so that the curve of the mono places the eyes well above the feathers. The eyes should be made ahead of time, in bulk, by sliding the beads onto the mono and burning the mono so that a flame is sparked. Slide the bead down to extinguish the flame. Cut the mono leaving a stem about 1 1/2 inches long. Mix some 5-minute epoxy and roll the bead end in the puddle, covering it. Put the mono/bead eye on a drying wheel so it acquires a round shape. Many eyes can be made at once using the wheel.

Step 4: Tie in one long shrimp pink and one long ginger variant hackle at the same tie-in point as all of the above materials. Wrap the two feathers together so that a mottled pink/ginger effect is created. Tie off and trim away the top fibers.

Step 5: Create a blend of Slinkyfibre material that is 3/4 black and 1/3 orange. The fibers should be about 6 inches long. The blend is created by laying down a bunch of orange Slinkyfibre on a work space and then selecting a bunch of black fibers that is three times the thickness or quantity of the orange bunch. Blend the colors by making a pile of fibers with alternating layers of color. Repeat until the colors are thoroughly blended.

Step 6: Tie in a pre-tapered bunch of the blended Slinkyfibre on top of the hook shank so that the tips extend between and beyond the bead eyes. Trim excess.

Step 7: Take the excess Slinkyfibre blend and tie in the pre-tapered butt end on top of the hook shank facing forward, tight to the eye.

Step 8: Bring thread back towards the hook bend and attach a zonker strip from the belly of a coyote. Wrap the zonker strip forward to the hook eye so that the hairs flow towards and past the hook bend. Tie off and trim any excess zonker strip. Trim off the top fibers of coyote and darken the bare hide with a black Sharpie (or other permanent marker) pen.

Step 9: Take the pre-tapered bundle of Kinkyfibre that is hanging forward of the hook eye and reverse it. Bring your thread forward of the bundle and take turns to create a "wall" of thread that will cock the bundle rearwards towards the bend. Whip finish twice and apply head cement.

TUBE DRESSING:

Step 1: Insert 1 1/4-inch-long plastic tube into vise and start the clear mono thread at the rear of the tube. I've stopped using a hook sleeve to connect the tube and hook eye because I prefer to have the flex/joint separated…it looks just like a bending, escaping lobster.

Step 2: Advance the thread to the front of the tube and tie in a pair lead dumb bell eyes (eyes may be painted cream or pale pink if desired) on the bottom of the tube using figure-eight wraps.

Step 3: Advance thread rearward to original tie-down point and tie in cream bucktail on the bottom of the tube. The bucktail should be twice the tube length to hide the junction.

Step 4: Attach a badger zonker strip. Wrap the zonker strip forward so the hairs point towards and past the junction of the hook and tube. Tie off and trim any excess zonker strip. Trim off the top fibers of badger and darken the bare hide with a black Sharpie or other permanent marker.

Step 5: Tie in a pre-tapered bunch of the blended Slinkyfibre on top of the tube so that the tips extend between the junction of the hook and tube. Trim excess.

Step 6: Take the excess Slinkyfibre blend and tie in the pre-tapered butt end on top of the tube facing forward, not quite tight to the forward end of the tube.

Step 7: Attach a cream polecat zonker strip. Wrap the zonker strip forward to the middle of the tube with the hairs pointing towards the rear. Tie off and trim any excess zonker strip. Trim off the top fibers of badger and darken the bare hide with a black Sharpie or other permanent marker.

Step 8: Tear some polecat fur from the zonker hide and apply it to the thread. This may take some wax, as it can be difficult to dub on clear monofilament thread. Wrap the dubbed polecat rope around the lead eyes with figure-eight wraps until the thread wraps are covered.

Step 9: Take the pre-tapered bundle of Kinkyfibre that is hanging forward of the hook eye and reverse it. Bring your thread forward of the bundle and take turns to create a "wall" of thread that will cock the bundle rearwards towards the bend. Without

DAVE SKOK

the surface of a hook eye to help you, you may need to take one or two turns of thread over the bundle to get it to lie down properly. Whip finish twice and apply head cement.

Step 10: Serve with butter and a bib!

Lobster patterns are typically big-fish magnets as striped bass less than ten pounds usually know better than to fool with a vicious one-half-pound lobster. The strikes on these flies are usually anything but subtle. Anglers must be cautious to hold the fly line firmly when between strips; that is when most bass strike. The Slobster fly is designed to ride hook point down, so I never just crawl the fly along the bottom. The most effective retrieve is violent and erratic. One strip…pause…four strips…pause…two strips…pause…one strip…BANG! I alter that retrieve when fishing the rocky surf. The waves that crash against the rocks flow back into the ocean in series of little rivers. Bass will sometimes sit within inches of shore waiting for a tasty treat to fall back crippled in the foamy surf. A stealthy approach with a dead-drifting fly is incredibly effective in this situation.

To date, many bass over 20 pounds have been taken on the Slobster. The pattern has proven effective from the North Shore of Boston to the Connecticut shoreline, and I'm sure big bass in Maine and on Long Island would equally relish it.

Incidentally, I never tie this fly the same way twice. Any pheasant feathers and saddle hackles or many other varieties of plumage can be used. I tend to prefer darker colors, but lighter-colored feathers have been good, too. I almost always use red-dyed grizzly saddles, however, as the bass seem to dig them. Perhaps that is because red is the first color of the spectrum to turn black with the absence of light? Or perhaps not? So many mysteries!

FLAMING TUBE SQUID (ORANGE AND PURPLE)

Hook: TMC 600SP 2/0 or other short shank hook

Thread: Clear fine monofilament

Tail: Bright orange Slinkyfibre surrounded by 6 to 12 strands of orange Flashabou Mirage

Eyes: Holographic silver molded Prismatic eyes, size 10MEY (1/2-inch diameter). Use Goop or hot glue to glue eyes in place, making them adhere to the Slinkyfibre tail and the upper corner of the hook bend.

Collars: Magenta Kinkyfibre. One collar is tied mid-shank and another at the hook eye.

Finish: Head cement

FLAMING TUBE SQUID
(CHARTREUSE AND ORANGE)

Tube: Plastic 1/8-inch O.D., 1 1/4 inches long with silicone hook sleeve

Thread: Clear fine monofilament

Body: Several turns of bright-orange Finnish raccoon zonker strip, followed by a sparse collar of bright-purple bucktail, followed by one or two more turns of bright-orange Finnish raccoon zonker strip, followed by a few turns of a webby dark-purple saddle hackle

Finish: Head cement

Hook: TMC 600SP 2/0 or other short shank hook

Thread: Clear fine monofilament

Tail: Chartreuse Slinkyfibre

Eyes: Holographic silver molded Prismatic eyes, Size 10MEY (1/2-inch diameter). Use Goop or hot glue to glue eyes in place, making them adhere to the Slinkyfibre tail and the upper corner of the hook bend.

Collars: Ginger Kinkyfibre. One collar is tied mid-shank and another at the hook eye, with 6 to 12 strands of fluorescent yellow Flashabou Mirage between the collars.

Finish: Head cement

Tube: Plastic 1/8-inch O.D., 1 1/4 inches long with silicone hook sleeve

Thread: Clear, fine monofilament

Body: Several turns of chartreuse Finnish raccoon strip, followed by a sparse collar of fluorescent yellow bucktail, followed by one or two more turns of bright-orange Finnish raccoon zonker strip, followed by a few turns of a webby chartreuse saddle hackle

Finish: Head cement

FLAMING TUBE SQUID (BURGUNDY AND TAN)

Hook: TMC 600SP 2/0 or other short shank hook

Thread: Clear, fine monofilament

Tail: Burgundy Slinkyfibre

Eyes: Holographic silver molded Prismatic eyes, size 10MEY (1/2-inch diameter). Use Goop or hot glue to glue eyes in place, making them adhere to the Slinkyfibre tail and the upper corner of the hook bend.

Collars: Ginger Kinkyfibre. One collar is tied mid-shank and another at the hook eye, with 6 to 12 strands of purple Flashabou Mirage in between the collars.

Finish: Head cement

Tube: Plastic 1/8-inch O.D., 1 1/4 inches long with silicone hook sleeve

Thread: Clear, fine monofilament

Body: Several turns of fuchsia cross-cut rabbit strip, followed by a sparse collar of pale tan bucktail, followed by one or two more turns of coyote zonker strip, followed by a few turns of a webby burgundy saddle hackle

Finish: Head cement

Matt Dormer fishes the big rocks for stripers on Boston's North Shore.

DAVID SKOK

GEORGE W. (ALEC) SMITH

Bolton-LE-Sands, England

I live four miles from Lancaster, in northwest England. After spending ten years in the Royal Navy, I became a Physical Education teacher at Rishworth School near Halifax, Yorkshire, and I retired as head of Physical Education.

I am a member of the Southport Fly-Fishers. We own fishing rights to a one-mile stretch on the River Lune. I fish the Tweed, Leven, North Esk, and Nith in Scotland, and the Ribble and Hodder in England, mainly for salmon and sea trout.

I got started fly-tying 40 years ago after reading *Trout and Salmon* magazine. I have been tying flies on tubes for about five years, now. I find them easier to tie on than hooks, and my catch rate (6 to 10 salmon a season) with tubes is higher. I use a variety of tubes — aluminum, plastic, brass — depending on water conditions, from 1/4 inch long to the heavily weighted, 3-inch-long Osprey Diving Tubes.

David Hoenes of Merlin Products, 127 New Bedford Road, Luton, Beds LU3 1LF England, designed and began producing the Osprey Diving Tubes about eight years ago. They consist of a section of 5/32-inch O. D. lead tube connected to a black plastic tube of the same diameter by a clear plastic liner. The rear of the black plastic tube is machined down to accept a silicon hook sleeve. They come in several lengths, and can be cut to suit. The available weights are 1.5 gram, 2 gram, 2.5 gram, and 3.5 gram (3 inches long). A fly rod of 15 or 16 feet is advised for weights of 2 grams and up.

Osprey Diving Tubes provide a very fast sink. They swim nose down at a 45-degree angle, giving fish a full view of the fly. This also puts the hooks above the fly in the water column, and keeps them from snagging bottom. Osprey Diving Tubes can be used in most conditions, but obviously not in extreme low water. I fish them with either sink-tip or full-sinking lines. I don't false cast these flies. I water-load the rod on the back cast and push forward, nearly overhead.

Once while spin fishing in the River Bladnoch in Scotland I was having no luck with a Devon lure, even though the pool held plenty of salmon. To see what would happen, I reversed the Devon on the line, and within two casts had a salmon follow the lure. On my tenth cast a seven-pound salmon took it. It then occurred to me, why not have a few flies tied in similar fashion for just such a situation?

Clockwise from top right: Willie Gunn; Shrimp; Stoat's Tail; Shrimp Junction; Comet Variant; Alec's Backward Logie; Alec's Backward Shrimp; Alec's Backward Purple Demon; Alec's Backward Blue and Yellow

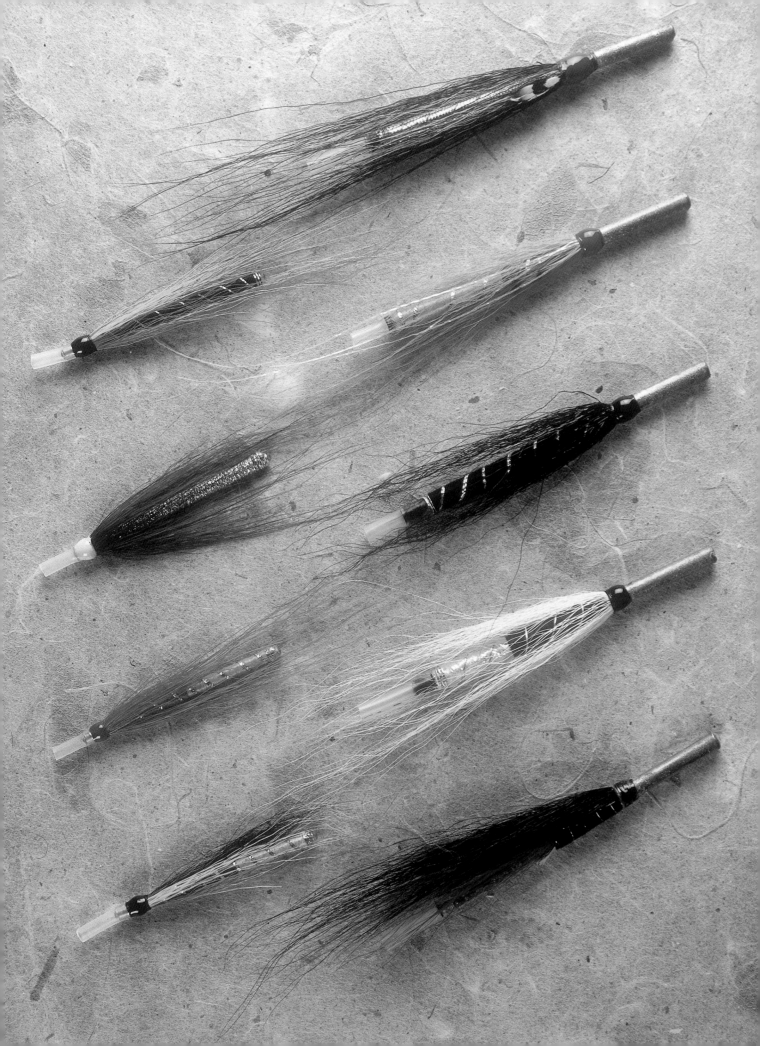

Alec's Backwards Tube Flies can be tied on aluminum, copper, brass or plastic tubes, but the reverse wings should always be lightly dressed. The flies flutter and go wild in fast or slow water, causing a disturbance that attracts fish. I dead-drift them until the swing of the cast is complete and the line is on the dangle, then I slowly work the flies back towards me, keeping the rod tip high to provide slack in case of a take.

SHRIMP

Tube: Osprey Diving Tube, 5/32-inch O. D. (3 inches long, 3.5 gram) with silicone hook sleeve
Rib: Medium silver oval tinsel
Body: 1/2 orange Glo-Brite, 1/2 red Glo-Brite
Throat: Golden pheasant tippet
Top wing: Red bucktail, long, sparse
Bottom wing: Orange bucktail, long, sparse
Topping: A few strands of pink Flashabou tied in the space between the wings
Head: Red thread
Hook: Treble or double

Step 1: Put the Osprey Diving tube on your vise. Attach oval silver tinsel with thread at the rear of the tube. Attach orange Glo-Brite and wind it forward in tight turns half the length of the body. Tie off and trim excess.

Step 2: Tie in red Glo-Brite and wind it in tight turns to the head of the fly. Tie off and trim excess.

Step 3: Wind the tinsel forward, ribbing the entire body to the head. Tie down and trim excess tinsel.

Step 4: Tie in a sparse top wing of red bucktail. It should extend 1 1/2 inch past the end of the body.

Step 5: Rotate tube 180 degrees and tie in sparse bottom wing of orange bucktail. It should also extend 1 1/2 inch past the end of the body.

Step 6: Tie a throat of golden pheasant tippet, about 3/4 inch long.

Step 7: Add a few strands of pink Flashabou between the wings. They should be a little longer than the wings.

Step 8: Make a small, neat head with thread, whip finish, and apply head cement or epoxy.

WILLIE GUNN

Tube: Osprey Diving Tube, 5/32-inch O. D. (3 inches long, 3.5 gram) with silicone hook sleeve
Rib: Fine gold oval tinsel
Body: Embossed gold tinsel
Wing: Sparse, mixed black, orange, and yellow bucktail, 1 1/2 inch longer than tube
Cheeks: Jungle cock
Head: Red thread
Hook: Treble or double

Alec casts over very low water on the River Tweed, Scotland.

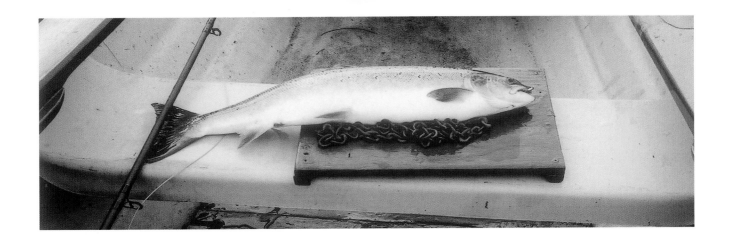

STOAT'S TAIL

Tube: Osprey Diving Tube, 5/32-inch O. D. (3 inches long, 3.5 gram) with silicone hook sleeve
Rib: Silver Lureflash
Body: Black yarn or floss
Wing: Black bucktail, 1 1/2 inch longer than tube
Head: Black thread
Hook: Treble or double

SHRIMP JUNCTION

Tube: Osprey Diving Tube, 5/32-inch O. D. (3 inches long, 3.5 gram) with silicone hook sleeve
Rib: Flat silver tinsel
Body: 1/2 pearl Lureflash; 1/2 black yarn or floss
Mid-wing: Orange bucktail, 1 1/2 inch longer than tube
Wing: White bucktail, same length as orange
Head: Black thread
Hook: Treble or double

COMET VARIANT

Tube: Osprey Diving Tube, 5/32-inch O. D. (3 inches long, 3.5 gram) with silicone hook sleeve
Rear body: Red metallic tape
Front body: Black wool
Mid-wing: Red bucktail, slightly longer than tube at rear
Beard: Yellow bucktail trimmed short
Rib: Fine silver tinsel
Front wing: Black bucktail, slightly longer than the red
Head: Black thread
Finish: The entire body is painted with clear epoxy
Hook: Treble or double

This is an autumn favorite on Scotland's River Tweed. A very productive fly.

ALEC'S BACKWARD SHRIMP

Tube: Plastic, aluminum or brass, 2 inches long, 1/8-inch O.D.
Rib: Flat gold tinsel
Body: 1/2 orange; 1/2 red floss or wool
Wing: Sparse orange bucktail, 1 1/2 inch longer than end of tube
Head: Red thread

ALEC'S BACKWARD PURPLE DEMON

Tube: Plastic, aluminum or brass, 2 inches long, 1/8-inch O.D.
Body: Silver tinsel
Wing: Mixed sparse orange and purple bucktail, 1 1/2 inch longer than end of tube
Head: White thread

ALEC'S BACKWARD LOGIE

Tube: Plastic, aluminum or brass, 2 inches long, 1/8-inch O.D.
Rib: Flat silver tinsel
Body: 1/2 yellow floss; 1/2 red floss
Wing: Mixed sparse yellow, brown and blue bucktail, slightly longer than end of tube
Head: Black thread

ALEC'S BACKWARD BLUE AND YELLOW

Tube: Plastic, aluminum or brass, 2 inches long, 1/8-inch O.D.
Rib: Silver Lureflash
Body: Black wool or floss
Wing: Sparse blue and yellow bucktail, 1 1/2 inch longer than end of tube
Head: Black thread

ANIL SRIVASTAVA

Kent, Washington

My intro-duction to fly-fishing began in high school when I tagged along to some eastern Washington lakes with a couple of friends. These guys also fly-fished Puget Sound beaches for sea-run cutthroat. When I scraped up enough money for a fly rod of my own, I christened it on a saltwater beach.

I fell hard for fly-fishing — and particularly saltwater fly-fishing — and began hanging out at my local fly shop, the Clearwater Angler, soaking up all the fly-fishing and tying information I could get. Fishing with shop employees Tony and Matt McGinnis, I learned many new skills, and I became convinced that I'd enjoy working in the industry, myself. To that end, I majored in Philosophy and minored in beach fishing at the University of Puget Sound in Tacoma.

After graduation, I was employed for several years as a part-time guide and full-time shop employee at The Mad Flyfisher in Federal Way, Washington. When that shop closed, Clark Jennings and I opened up our own store in Kent, the Puget Sound Fly Company.

The tiers who have influenced me the most are Tony McGinnis, Corey Scheuffelle, Bob Popovics, Trey Combs, Bob Clouser, Tom Wolf (See Chapter 35: Tom Wolf), Mike Duey, Mark Waslick, and Mark Mandell (See Chapter 17: Mark Mandell). Currently, the majority of my tying is for salt water and I tie almost all of my patterns on tubes.

My first flies, tied on hooks, for shallow-water salmon and cutthroat were smaller versions of popular saltwater patterns. My boxes were filled with Clouser Minnows, Deceivers, and Sea Habits. While I loved the appearance and effectiveness of these flies, I was less enamored by the tendency of their hooks to rust and dull. An accidental saltwater soaking — and subsequent destruction — of an entire fly box forced me to find an alternative. Fortunately, tube materials were available at some Northwest fly shops. When I discovered how simple the tying transition could be, I migrated from hooks to tubes. Nowadays, the patterns I prefer to tie are better suited to tubes, and in some cases can only be properly tied on a tube.

Two recurring themes in my fly-tying are the use of taper and blended colors. I achieve a life-like taper and silhouette on baitfish imitations by applying materials in different lengths, and making certain they are not cut flat or stacked. Proper taper is not just a matter of aesthetics, it affects how the fly swims and dives in the water.

Color in commercial fly patterns is usually over-simplified; with baitfish flies this translates into "green over white." A close inspection of live baits reveals a myriad of hues and shades that blend together to create the color seen from a distance. This explains why materials like peacock are so effective at imitating

Clockwise from top: Solomon Grundy; Shock & Awe (Bozo); AJS Dorado; AJS Smolt; AJS Herring; Shock & Awe (Herring)

ANIL SRIVASTAVA

attest, a sizeable portion of my year is spent at this little town. I love the wild and untamed feeling I get when fishing among the ocean swells and towering rock spires. Summer brings huge numbers of migrating coho salmon through Neah Bay. They are perfect targets for fly-fishers because they are aggressive surface-feeders. Schools of coho can be located by spotting jumping fish, flocks of diving or circling birds, or blind-casting in tide rips. If fish are on the surface, I use floating lines and poppers; if fish are down deeper, I use a high-density shooting head with a short, stout leader and a head-heavy fly such as the Shock & Awe. This outfit allows me to fish a wide variety of depths from the surface down to 40 feet. It is also ideal for the rockfish species that inhabit the Washington coast.

Fall brings "hooknose silvers," the largest coho of the season, through the Strait entrance. This is also when albacore tuna make their annual migration from Mexico to British Columbia, following the Japanese Current. Albacore fishing in the Pacific Northwest is not for the timid. Everything about it is big: the fish (20 to 30 pounds), the water (20 to 70 miles offshore), and the boats (more than 30 feet). Although this fishery has been targeted for more than half a century with live bait, it is virtually untapped by fly-fishers. The Puget Sound Fly Company has been putting together fall charters for albacore off the Oregon coast for the past few years. Many fly-fishers already have the necessary gear from their tarpon trips. A 12-weight rod, a high-density head, and an anchovy pattern Shock & Awe have proven an effective combination.

Most Northwest anglers stop fishing the salt water in the fall. Bad weather can make trips impossible or dangerous at times, but just as often, "good enough" weather allows a brief fishing window. Winter and spring are my favorite times to target rockfish and lingcod because of the low or nonexistent angling pressure. A seaworthy boat, good seamanship, and a close eye on changing conditions are all essential for a safe return home.

When I tied my flies on hooks, I had to tie twice the quantity that I do today. Rockfish and lingcod are fond of same patterns as salmon and tuna; unfortunately (for my flyboxes) they are ambush hunters and live around structure. To prevent losing all my flies to the kelp and rocks, I had to tie patterns with weed-guards. While these provided good protection against snagging, they also reduced the hook-up ratio on salmon which tend to slash and run on a fly. The solution to the problem was tube flies. By carrying an assortment of hooks, from circle or weed-guard hooks to heavy-wire tuna irons, I am able to use a single tube for a number of applications/species.

Despite claims to the contrary, I have seen rockfish become selective and difficult to catch. At times like these, good baitfish patterns fished properly can out-produce almost any other lure, bait, or fly. These aggressive fish are worthy of our respect and conservation. They can reach ages of more than 30 years and may not become sexually mature until they are five to twelve years old. I urge anglers to practice catch and release with rockfish and lingcod. Their numbers once seemed limitless in other parts of our state, and we have all seen the folly of that type of thinking.

life-like color: they contain a built-in blend of shades. However, peacock's texture, size, and color doesn't always mix well with other natural and synthetic materials. By blending many different colors and shades of the same or similar materials, I try to imitate the reflected colors seen on a peacock feather or a bait-fish's back in sunlight.

My favorite place to fish in Washington is Neah Bay, near the Pacific entrance to the Strait of Juan de Fuca. As my wife will

SHOCK & AWE

Tube: Plastic HMH 1/8-inch O.D., 1 1/2 inches long, with silicone hook sleeve. This diameter matches up with the 7/16-inch Spirit River Cross- Eyed cone; HMH 3/32-inch O. D. matches the 3/8-inch cone head

Thread: UNI-Clear fine monofilament

Beard: White yak hair or Slinkyfibre

Wing: White yak hair or Slinkyfibre topped with U. V. pearl Krystal Flash

Overwing: Yak hair and Krystal Flash, blended. My favorite blends are ("Bozo") chartreuse, Herring Back, and fluorescent fuchsia Saltwater yak hair mixed with U.V. pink and chartreuse Krystal Flash; and ("Herring") fluorescent fuchsia, Herring Back, blue and purple Saltwater yak hair mixed with Herring Back Krystal Flash

Head: Nickel Spirit River Cross-Eyed cone

Eyes: Silver Spirit River 3-D, Size 3.0

Hook: Size 4 to 4/0

Anchovy and Shock and Awe tube fly

Step 1: Before you get started, make sure the tube snugly fits through the cone head. Cut the tube to a 1 1/2-inch length and use a flame to melt a collar on one end. This forms a lip to hold the hook sleeve.

Step 2: Place the tube in your vise with the collar towards the rear and build a 1/8-inch-wide thread base 1/4 inch from the front of the tube. It is critical to leave *at least* 1/4 inch of bare tube at the front of the tube, in order to accommodate the cone head.

Step 3: Tie in 20 strands of pearl Krystal Flash, tapered with scissors or by hand, on top of the tube. These should be approximately 1 1/2 inch shorter than the finished length of the fly.

Step 4: Tie a bunch of white yak hair or Slinkyfibre on the top of the tube, slightly shorter than finished length of the fly.

Step 5: Once your yak or Slinkyfibre is attached, add another 20-strand bunch of pearl Krystal Flash on top. This should be the longest portion of the fly and extend beyond the white yak hair by approximately 1/2 inch. It doesn't matter if some of the flash fibers roll onto the sides of the fly.

Step 6: Blend a bunch of chartreuse, Herring Back, and fluorescent fuchsia Saltwater yak hair (or Slinkyfibre) and U.V. pink and chartreuse Krystal Flash; or a bunch of fluorescent fuchsia, Herring Back, blue and purple Saltwater yak hair (or Slinkyfibre) and Herring Back Krystal Flash. The bunch should be about twice the finished length of the fly. Taper both ends. Find the middle of the bunch and tie it down at that point, on top of the other materials. Half of the fibers should extend to the rear and half to the front. Be sure to leave the first 1/4 inch of the tube bare of thread.

Step 7: Cut a bunch of white yak or Slinkyfibre approximately 3 times the length of the tube and sparser than the wing. This bunch forms the belly of the fly. It should kept short to prevent hook-fouling and make the fly swim correctly. Taper both ends. As in Step 6, find the middle of the bunch, then tie it on the underside of the tube, directly beneath the tie in point of the other materials. Keep the first 1/4 inch of the tube free of thread. Again, half the hair will extend to the rear, and half to the front. At this point the fly should look like two baitfish "kissing."

Step 8: Whip finish the fly over the tie in point, leaving room for the cone head, and remove it from the vise.

Step 9: Push a Cross Eyed cone over the front of the tube. Force all of the materials that extend forward towards the rear of the fly, forming the back and belly, and filling the inside of the cone.

Step 10: Holding the cone back, carefully apply a flame to the protruding front end of the tube and melt a collar that will keep the cone in place. If you need to clear the opening at the front of the tube use a bodkin or mandrel while the plastic is still fluid.

Step 11: Finish the fly by filling the back of the cone head with 30-minute epoxy, then hang the fly vertically until it cures. Add the hook sleeve to the rear of the tube after the fly is finished.

The early cone-head tube flies that I came up with were effective, but they all suffered from the "turtle-neck syndrome" that plagues

Steven Rohrback caught this 38-inch chinook salmon on a Shock & Awe Herring in 30 feet of water on a slack tide at Tofino, British Columbia. The fish was safely released.

bead-and-cone patterns — an unattractive and unnatural gap between shoulder and head. My solution was inspired by the Atlantic salmon fly technique of reverse-tying wing material and then folding it back while over-wrapping the butts with thread. It occurred to me that the folding back could also be accomplished by the cone. The tapered inside of the cone pushes back wing fibers tied forward, filling the void behind the head. Ultimately, I began tying down both wing and belly bunches in the middle, so that materials extend forward as well as back. When the cone head is slipped on, it forces the forward-facing material to the rear, where it blends into the rear-facing material. This creates a very realistic silhouette.

Originally designed to imitate herring and candlefish in Puget Sound and Strait of Juan de Fuca, the Shock & Awe has caught over 20 species of game fish including: salmon, striped bass, albacore, roosterfish, yellowfin tuna, skipjack, dorado, rockfish, largemouth bass, lingcod, and trout. It is most effective in colors and sizes that imitate the predominant forage fish. As with all head-heavy flies, a pause between strips allows the fly to dip and dive much like an injured baitfish.

AJS HERRING

Tube: Plastic HMH 1/8-inch O.D., 1 inch long, with silicone hook sleeve. Overall length of finished sample fly is 4 1/4 inches.

Thread: UNI-Clear fine monofilament

Body: Pearl Mylar braid, 3 1/4 inches long, slipped over the tube and tied down at the front and back ends. Fray out the rest of the braid at the rear. Coat the tube with epoxy. Let cure.

Underwing: White yak hair, slightly longer than the body braid, and topped with more frayed out pearl Mylar braid, 4 1/4 inches long

Eyes: Silver 3-D stick-on, 3/16-inch diameter. Epoxy the eyes to the sides of the tube, 7/16 inch back from the front, and let dry.

Topwing: Fluorescent fuchsia, Herring Back, blue, and purple Saltwater yak hair mixed with Herring Back Krystal Flash, 4 1/4 inches long

Belly: White yak hair, 1 1/4 inches long

Finish: 5- or 30-minute epoxy

Hook: Size 4 to 4/0

This pattern is an attempt to accurately represent the silhouette and colors of the Pacific herring. The separate epoxy steps allow a realistic eye placement, while maintaining durability and a clean look. The AJS Herring is a shallow-fishing alternative to cone head and other epoxy head flies. I often slide a small, floating slider head on the leader and fish the pattern on the surface.

AJS DORADO

Tube: Plastic HMH 1/8-inch O.D., 1 3/4 inches long with silicone hook sleeve

Thread: UNI clear fine monofilament

Body: Yellow Diamond Braid, 3/4 inch long, slipped over and tied down on tube

Tail: Eight yellow saddle hackles, 6 inches long, tied four to a side, cove style. Each side is topped by a yellow grizzly saddle hackle.

Flash: Ice pearl blue and June Bug Flashabou, slightly shorter than the yellow saddles

Eyes: Yellow Mirage Dome, 3/8 inch diameter. At this point the eyes are epoxied to the sides of the tube and allowed to dry.

Belly: Yellow bucktail, sparse, 3 inches long, tied in 1/4 inch from the front of the tube

Wing: Two matched peacock swords, 6 1/4 inch long, tied cove style 1/4 inch from the front of the tube.

Finish: 30-minute epoxy

Hook: Size 2 to 4/0

The AJS Dorado is very similar in design to the AJS Herring. I tie down the peacock sword at the front of the tube. This creates a blunt head like a dorado.

A cone-head tube fly fooled this black rockfish.

AJS SMOLT

Tube: Plastic HMH 3/32-inch O.D., 1 inch long. No hook sleeve; hook eye fits inside of hard tube. The tube is barred with a black permanent marker, then covered in small pearl Mylar braid, and coated with epoxy.

Thread: UNI clear fine monofilament

Belly: White Slinkyfibre, 1 inch long, sparse

Side Flash: Rainbow Krystal Flash, 1 1/2 inches long, sparse

Wing: Olive and Shrimp Slinkyfibre, 1 1/2 inches long, sparse

Eyes: Mirage dome, 3/32-inch diameter

Finish: 30-minute epoxy

Hook: TMC 105 or Gamakatsu C14S, size 8

Other than the parr marks drawn on the tube, this is a fairly generic baitfish imitation. It's been effective off Puget Sound beaches in the spring when salmon fry migrate from fresh to salt water. I've never fished it in Alaska, but I've been told it's an effective pattern

ANIL SRIVASTAVA

there as well. *A sinking or sink-tip line and quick erratic retrieve seems to work best. If schools of smolt are being forced to the surface, I often switch to a floating line.*

SOLOMON GRUNDY

Tube: Plastic HMH 1/8-inch O. D., 1 1/4 inches long, with 3/8-inch hook sleeve

Thread: Red

Flash: Unraveled silver holographic braid, 4 inches long

Hackle: Chartreuse grizzly saddles, five or six to a side, 4 inches long

Gills: Red thread

Popper head: 1/2-inch diameter, 1 1/4 inch long. Seattle Saltwater popper head in yellow and black stripe

Mylar sheathing: Large pearl Flashabou Minnow Body. Unraveled Mylar braid extends 3 3/4 inches past rear of popper head.

Eyes: Yellow 3-D stick-on, 3/8-inch diameter

Finish: 30-minute epoxy

Hook: Size 1/0 to 3/0

Step 1: Cut the tube to length and melt a collar on one end. Slip the hook sleeve on the collar end. The overall length of the joined tubes should be at least 1/2 inch longer than the popper head.

Step 2: Tie a thread base the length of the tube.

Step 3: Approximately 1/2 inch from the rear of the tube, tie in a piece of silver holographic braid (core removed). Use a bodkin to unravel the braid, forming a flash tail.

Step 4: At the same point, tie in 8 to 12 narrow, grizzly saddle hackles, cove style. Create a thick band of red thread for gills, whip finish, and trim thread.

Step 5: Apply Zap-A-Gap to the tube and push the predilled popper head over the front until it abuts the red thread. Cut the excess tube from the front of the popper.

Step 6: Take the popper off your vise. Slide the Minnow Body over the front of the head, extending the ends of the braid to the desired length. Pull on the rear of the braid while holding the front, drawing the Minnow Body tight — this makes the braid grip the head like a Chinese finger cuff. If the fit isn't snug enough use twist ties or pipe cleaners to hold the ends tight against the edge of the popper head. Apply the 3-D eyes to the Mylar covered sides of the head.

Step 7: Put a hook in the hook sleeve so you can hold the popper. Use a craft brush to coat the head with 30-minute epoxy, then dry the fly on a wheel.

Step 8: After the epoxy has fully cured, use sharp scissors to trim the Mylar flush with the face of the popper. To prevent fraying, apply a second coat of epoxy, covering the popper face as well. Dry on wheel.

This is a very versatile popper. I've fished it in creeks in the Bahamas for tarpon and jacks, in Mexico for dorado, and in the Strait of Juan de Fuca for rockfish and salmon.

GERRIT VAN EE

Zetten, the Netherlands

I live in a suburban village with a population of 5,000. Zetten is situated in a region called De Betuwe, between the rivers Rijn and Waal, near the larger cities of Arnhem and Nijmegen. I'm a construction supervisor for a housing corporation in Nijmegen. The river Linge runs through my village, and the Rijn is two kilometers away. I fly-fish the Linge for pike, and for pike, perch and asp in the Rijn. I also fish in the Oostvoorn-semeer, the largest trout lake in Europe, which is near Rotterdam. The Oostvoornsemeer was once part of the Noordzee (North Sea); now it is a brackish-water reservoir that holds rainbow trout up to one meter (3 feet) in length.

I regularly travel to Germany to fish the Sieg, Kyll, Diemel, Isar rivers, and I spend my summer holidays mostly in Sweden and Norway, fishing the Klaralven and Nissan rivers and many little mountain lakes.

I started fishing at age eight, and I've been tying and fishing with flies for 18 years. After tying everything from dry flies to traditional salmon flies on hooks, I decided to try my hand at tube flies eight years ago. Now I tie all my large flies on tubes, and I cut the tubes from aluminum stock and line them myself.

As a member of DAAFT (Dutch American Association of Fly Tiers), I have the opportunity to meet and exchange ideas with the Netherlands' most talented fly tiers.

From top: Golden Pheasant Pike Tube Streamer; Smelt Tube Fly; Peacock Pike Tube Streamer; Stickleback Tube Fly

SMELT TUBE FLY

Tube: Aluminum 3/16-inch O. D., 1 1/2 inches (4 cm) long, with plastic liner and silicone hook sleeve. Tube is cut from aluminum stock.

Thread: UNI-Clear nylon

Belly: White Polafibre, sparse, twice the length of the tube

Lateral flash: Lavendar and aquamarine Sparkleflash, 3 1/2 inches long

Back: Olive over chartreuse Polafibre, sparse, same length as Flash

Head: Pearl Mylar braid, 8 mm

Eyes: Orange 3-D Prismatic eyes, 1/4-inch diameter

Finish: Devcon or Zpoxy epoxy

Hook: Size 1/0

Gerrit with a Oostvoornsemeer rainbow

Step 1: Put the tube on your vise, attach thread 1/8 inch from the front, and tie in the white Polafibre, spreading it 360-degree around the tube, so it is covered on all sides.

Step 2: On the top of the tube, on top of the Polafibre, tie in the Sparkleflash. Then tie in the chartreuse Polafibre, followed by the olive Polafibre. Apply a few drops of super glue.

Step 3: Slip a 1 1/4-inch-long piece of pearl Mylar braid over the head and tie it down at the front of the tube.

Step 4: Smear a thin layer of epoxy on the Mylar braid and let it cure.

Step 5: Apply the 3-D eyes, centered about 1/2 inch from the front of tube, and apply a second, heavier coat of epoxy. Put the fly on a wheel to dry

This is a good fly for sea bass along the Dutch northeast coast. I fish it on a 6- or 7-weight rod with a floating line. I prefer the Rio Windcutter with a nine-foot (3 meter) leader; tippet is 20/00 (8.2-pound test). I vary the speed of the retrieve, from fast to slow, so the fly behaves like a real smelt.

PEACOCK PIKE TUBE STREAMER

Tube: Aluminum 3/16-inch O. D., 1 1/2 inches (4 cm) long, with plastic liner and silicone hook sleeve. Keep the first 3/8 inch (1 cm) of the tube free of material so the hook sleeve can be slipped on. Tube is cut from aluminum stock. Overall length of finished fly is 4 inches.

Thread: Black

Body: Five alternating, equal bands of yellow and chartreuse wool, about 3/8 inch wide

Collars: The first yellow band is separated from the first chartreuse band by a 2-inch-long, sparse, 360-degree collar of yellow bucktail. The chartreuse band is separated from the next yellow band by a 2-inch-long, sparse, 360-degree collar of chartreuse bucktail. In front of the second yellow band is a 2 1/4-inch-long, sparse, 360-degree collar of dull orange Arctic fox with black tips, and 3 1/4-inch-long pearl Krystal flash. Ahead of the fourth band of wool is a 2-inch-long, sparse collar of natural brown Arctic fox with black tips. Ahead of the last wool section is a 2-inch-long, sparse, 360-degree collar of dark pink Arctic fox with black tips.

Wing: A pair of grizzly saddles, tied cove style

Hackle: Peacock body feather

Head: Black thread

Finish: Laquer, several coats

Hook: Size-7 treble

The bucktail and Arctic fox in this pattern are tied tightly against the wool body to make the material flare, creating volume.

I fish these streamers with an 8- or 9-weight rod. Depending on water depth, I use an intermediate or a sinking line with a 1-meter (three-foot) leader of 30/00 (10-pound-test) nylon. These lines sink

to the lake or stream bed, and the short leader makes the fly float just above the bottom to tempt pike. For tippet I use a piece of Kevlar thread about 30 cm long (12 inches) to prevent the pike's teeth from cutting off the fly. I vary my retrieve, from fast to slow.

GOLDEN PHEASANT PIKE TUBE STREAMER

Tube: Aluminum 3/16-inch O. D., 1 1/2 inches (4 cm) long, with plastic liner and silicone hook sleeve. Keep the first 3/8 inch (1 cm) of the tube free of material so the hook sleeve can be slipped on. Tube is cut from aluminum stock. Overall length of finished fly is 4 inches.

Thread: Black

Body: Five equal bands of red wool, about 3/8 inch wide

Collars: The first band is separated from the first chartreuse band by a 2-inch-long, sparse, 360-degree collar of white Arctic fox. The second band is separated from the next by a 2-inch-long, sparse, 360-degree collar of dark blue Arctic fox. In front of the third band is a 2 1/4-inch-long, sparse, 360-degree collar of yellow Arctic fox, and 3 1/4-inch-long pearl Krystal Flash. Ahead of the fourth band of wool is a 2-inch-long, sparse collar of dark blue Arctic fox. Ahead of the last wool section is a 2-inch-long, sparse, 360-degree collar of black Arctic fox.

Cheeks: Five or six golden pheasant body feathers, tied 360 degrees around the tube

Head: Black thread

Finish: Laquer, several coats

Hook: Size 7 treble

Again the bucktail and Arctic fox are tied tightly against the wool body to flare the material, creating volume.

STICKLEBACK TUBE FLY

Tube: Aluminum, heavy, 1/8-inch O. D., 1/2 inch long, with machined step at the rear for the silicone hook sleeve

Thread: UNI-Clear nylon

Body: Sparse, 2-inch-long (5 cm) tuft of red Polafibre, tied on top of the tube at a 45-degree angle, 1/8 inch from the front end. This is topped by an equal-sized bunches of white, then olive Polafibre. During the tying, moisten the material slightly and form it into the shape of a little fish.

Lateral flash: One strip of pearl Mylar tinsel, 2 inches long, tied in the middle of the body on both sides

Eyes: Orange or yellow 3-D stick-on eyes, 1/16-inch (3 mm) diameter

Finish: Devcon or Zpoxy epoxy

After tying-in the pearl Mylar strips and whip finishing, I smear on a thin coat of epoxy, forming the wide, flat head of the fly. I let it cure, then stick on the eyes, and recoat with epoxy.

I began work on this pattern after examining the stomach contents of Oosetvoornsemeer rainbows and finding both shrimp and tiny stickleback minnows. I tie this fly at a 45-degree angle to the tube because on a fast retrieve it allows me to duplicate the stickleback's unique, up-and-down darting movement. The aluminum tube supplies the fly's necessary weight; it's not there for flash.

I fish this fly early in the morning or as the sun is going down; that's when big rainbows come into the shallows of the Oosetvoornsemeer to chase down these little baitfish. I retrieve very quickly, keeping the fly 20 cm (8 inches) below the surface. I use a 6- or 7-weight rod and a floating Rio Windcutter with a 3.5-meter (10-foot) leader and a 18/00-tippet (7-pound test).

TOM WOLF

Gig Harbor, Washington

MARK MANDELL

Fly-tying has fascinated me for 30 years, not only how the fly relates to the fish, but how the fly reflects the mind of the human being behind the vise. "Everything in the world is potential fly-tying material," my good friend and mentor Mike Croft (See Chapter 9: Mike Croft) once told me. I was ogling his fly box at the time; specifically a deer-hair tube popper for coho salmon that he had made more durable by using cuttings from a pair of his wife's pantyhose.

When I started trout guiding rivers in Utah in the late 1970's to have great success all I needed to do was to copy established patterns. Nine years ago, when I began guiding Puget Sound salt water full-time — about 100 days a year — I encountered many new challenges, and there were few answers floating around. These on-the-job problems sent me back to the vise again and again, looking for solutions. After pondering a "new" pattern I'd stuck together I'd give Mike a call. "What do you think about this fly?" I'd ask. "How come nobody is using it for coho?" Mike's reply usually went something like this: "Bill Nelson started using that pattern 30 years ago when he was head guide at Quadra Island." Rather than being dismayed, I've always felt that if I have an historical foundation for my flies I'm on the right track.

One of the challenges of any kind of guiding is finding the time to tie up a dozen or so copies of a hot pattern for the next day's fishing. Barring break-offs, I've found that tube flies last longer than hook-tied flies, which means fewer need to be tied. Tubes also give me the ability to manipulate action, length, weight, and hook placement on the water, allowing quick adjustments to changing conditions — again without having to tie a different fly for each situation.

A few years ago I started tying flies on very fine-diameter Teflon tubing (1/16- to 1/32-inch O. D.) to better match the baits on which Puget Sound salmon selectively feed. The I. D. of this tubing allows me to use 8-pound and larger fluorocarbon tippets. I make hook sleeves out of 1/8-inch, clear heat-shrink tubing, fitted to the fine Teflon. The fitted heat-shrink tubing has a thin wall thickness, so it is not obtrusive.

I can be reached by phone at 253-863-0711, and email: capttwolf@comcast.net.

Clockwise from top: Weighted Sandlance; (unweighted) Sandlance; Cyclops Marabou Gurgler; Euphausid; Mini-Tube Clouser; Euphausid; Rake End Skimmer; Herring

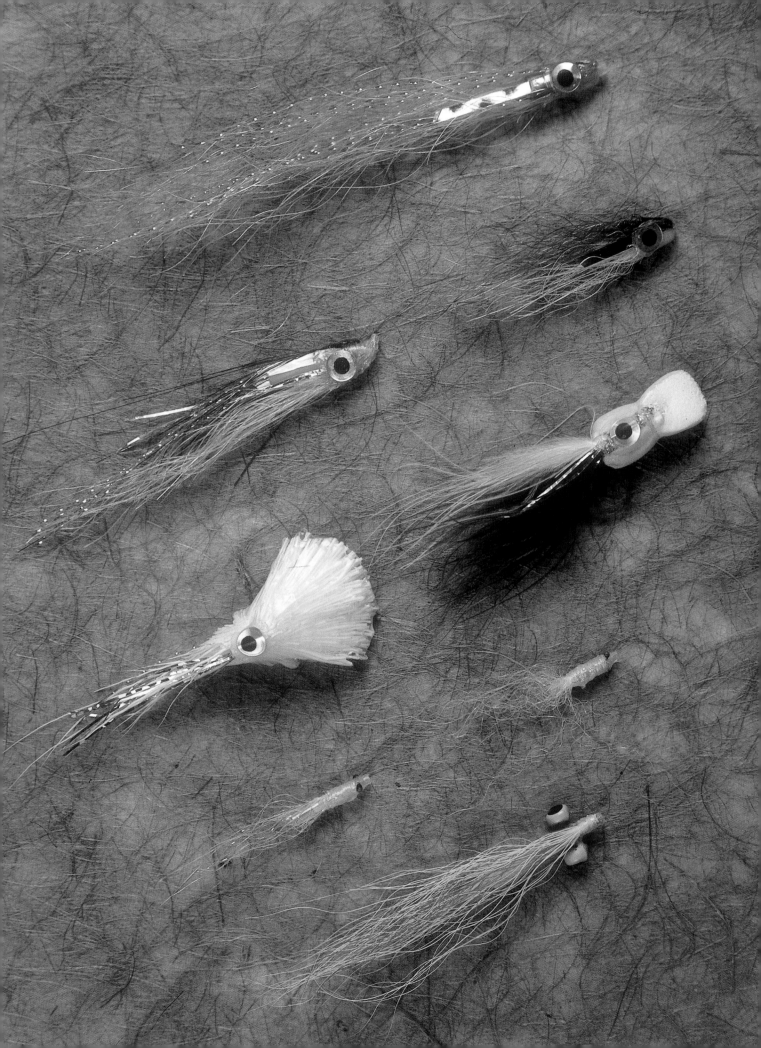

A tube fly fooled this Puget Sound sea-run cutthroat.

TOM WOLF

CYCLOPS MARABOU GURGLER

Tube: Teflon, 1/16-inch (1.5 mm) O. D., .031-mm I. D.,
    3/8 inch long on finished fly. Hook sleeve is 1/8-inch
    O. D. clear heat-shrink tubing, 3/8 inch long.
    Combined tube length on finished fly is 5/8 inch
Note: I use a longer than necessary piece of Teflon and
    when the fly is done, I cut the excess off at the nose.
Thread: Clear UNI monofilament, fine
Wing: Olive and white, or brown and white marabou,
    1 inch long and sparse
Body: Sheet foam, 1/8-inch thick, in white, brown or olive
Lateral flash: Fine, silver holographic Flashabou, two strands
    on one side, 5/8 inch long
Head: Silver Mylar Diamond Braid, 3 inches long
Eye: Silver Prismatic stick-on, size 2 1/2 or 3 (1/8-inch
    diameter)
Hook: Gamakatsu SC15, sizes 8 to 4, tin-plated, wide gap
Finish: Softex

Step 1: To prepare the hook sleeve, find a bodkin or similar tool
that matches the O. D. of the Teflon tube. Slide the end of a long
piece of clear, heat-shrink tubing onto the bodkin, close to the
handle. Use a candle flame to heat the handle end of the shrink
tube until it grabs onto the shaft. Apply light pressure by
pulling on the other end of the shrink tube while rotating the
material quickly back and forth over the flame. Putting pressure
on the tubing creates a thinner wall for the sleeve. Work back
from the handle end of the bodkin, shrinking and stretching the
tube on the full length of the shaft. Maintain a little pressure on
the tubing until it cools, then use a fingernail on the handle end
to pry the material off the shank. This produces enough material to make a number of hook sleeves.

Step 2: Cut a 3/8-inch-long piece of prepared hook sleeve and
slip it over the end of the Teflon tubing. The tubes should overlap by 1/16 to 1/8 inch. The fit should be tight. Put the joined
tubes on a push pin (mandrel), hook sleeve first, then put the pin
in your vise. Build a lip of monofilament thread over the join
area. A light touch is necessary with Teflon, as too much pressure will crush it. Whip finish but do not cut the thread. Apply
super glue to the thread wraps. The joint's strength comes from
the super glue.

Step 3: After the glue dries, add a couple more turns of thread
and begin tying in the marabou. This fly rides on its side, eye
pointed down. Tie the bunches of olive and white marabou side
by side on top of the tube. Then add the two strands of silver
holographic Flashabou.

Step 4: Tie in a 3-inch-long piece of silver Mylar braid. Wrap
the Mylar braid up the tube and back to form a 1/4-inch-long
base for the head, and tie it off at the marabou. Trim excess
braid.

Step 5: Cut sheet foam to make the popper head. The foam is 1/4
inch wide at the lip, 1 1/8 inches long, and doubled over the

initial tie in point. Trim one end of the foam strip into a point to reduce bulk.

Step 6: Rotate the tube in the vise 180 degrees. On top of the tube, tie in the narrow end of the foam strip; the tip should point towards the front of the tube. Whip finish but do not cut thread. Work the thread forward, tying over the foam to the front of the silver head base. Fold over the rest of the foam strip, and tie it down at the front of the tube. Whip finish, trim thread, and super glue the wraps. I put a tiny amount of super glue on the back of the foam head and hold it in place until it dries, this to keep an upward angle on the popper lip.

Step 7: Add the stick-on eye to the underside of the head and coat with Softex. I cover the foam with Softex as well, making it nearly indestructible. When the Softex is dry, cut the fly from the length of tube.

This is one of my favorite skating patterns for adult coho salmon; it also works well on sea-run cutthroat. It was inspired by an East Coast striped bass fly, the Gartside Gurgler. Coated with Softex, the foam head is very hard for fish to destroy, and if the leader breaks, the hook stays in the fish and the floating tube usually pops right to the surface.

When adult coho are still feeding hard, I fish this fly with a dry floating line on an 8-foot leader and 12-pound fluorocarbon tippets. When they are in a feeding frenzy on the surface, I use a clear intermediate-sink line as well. To present this pattern to feeding fish, use a slow, two-handed retrieve that creates a steady wake; a one-handed, rapid baitfish strip; and a strip-and-pause retrieve that gives fish down deeper time to come up to the fly.

I have had great success with this fly when a hooked salmon is played within casting distance from the boat for the first time. If you drop the popper close to the hooked fish and give it a few chugs, it will draw the attention of the free-swimming salmon that are following. Be ready for explosive strikes!

When I approach feeding summer sea-run cutthroat I like to use a scaled-down skater for the first few casts, then come back through the same water with a sub-surface fly.

RAKE END SKIMMER

Tube: Teflon, 1/16-inch (1.5-mm) O. D., .031-mm I. D., 3/8 inch long on finished fly. Hook sleeve is 1/8 inch O. D. clear heat-shrink tubing, 3/8 inch long. Combined tube length on finished fly is 5/8 inch. Note: I use a longer than necessary piece of Teflon and when the fly is done, I cut off the excess at the nose.

Thread: Clear UNI monofilament, fine

Body: Sparse bunch of olive green, brown, or white elk hair, 1 3/4 inch long.

Lateral flash: Fine, silver holographic Flashabou, three or four strands on one side, 5/8 inch long

Eye: Silver Witchcraft stick-on, size 2 1/2 or 3 (1/8-inch diameter)

Hook: Gamakatsu SC15, sizes 8 to 4, tin-plated, wide gap

Finish: Softex on front, top, and sides. Don't put it on the tail!

After tying the sparse bunch of elk hair on top of the tube, hair tips to the rear, trim the blunt ends into rough shape. Apply a small amount of super glue to the hair and form the skimmer head by "petting" the strands into position with a bodkin as the glue sets. When the glue is dry, fine trim the hair, then cover the head, eye, sides, and top with Softex. If fish are hitting the fly short, use a tube extension — a small length of tube with a hook sleeve — to position the hook farther back.

Sick or injured baitfish sometimes rise to the surface and skim the water on their sides. Feeding coho and sea-run cutthroat zero in on this kind of easy meal. The Rake End Skimmer pushes a little more water than the Cyclops Marabou Gurgler, cutting a wake like the bow of a boat. I fish it on a floating line and 7- to 9-foot leader, with an 8-pound fluorocarbon tippet.

HERRING

Tube: Teflon, 1/16-inch (1.5 mm) O. D., .031-mm I. D., 3/8 inch long on finished fly. Hook sleeve is 1/8-inch O. D. clear heat-shrink tubing, 3/8 inch long. Combined tube length on finished fly is 5/8 inch. Finished sample fly is 2 inches long. Note: I use a longer than necessary piece of Teflon and when the fly is done, I cut the excess off at the nose.

Thread: Clear UNI monofilament, fine

Lips: Approximately 30 strands of white yak hair, held together with spiral wraps of monofilament thread, then doubled in half and pretied in a small loop. The loop is then slipped over and super-glued to the front of the tube; the tag ends of the loop are trimmed so they taper back into the belly of the fly.

Belly: Sparse, tapered white polar bear for small flies. Yak hair for larger flies

Back: Dark green Angel Hair, sparse

Lateral flash: Fine, silver holographic Flashabou, two strands on each side, 1 1/2 inch long. Few strands of yellow Krystal Flash on each side, 2 inches long

Eyes: Silver Prismatic stick-on, size 2 1/2 or 3 (1/8-inch diameter)

Hook: Gamakatsu SC15, sizes 8 to 4, tin-plated, wide gap

Finish: Softex

I tie this pattern in sizes from 1 to 7 inches for hard-feeding, adult salmon at Neah Bay, and for fishing Baja. Having a Sharpie on hand to match the hatch for parr marks is a good idea, too.

WEIGHTED SANDLANCE

Tube: Teflon, 1/16-inch (1.5-mm) O. D., .031-mm I. D., 1 inch long on finished fly. Hook sleeve is 1/16-inch I.D., clear aquarium hose. Sample fly is 3 inches long. For larger flies I use 3/32-inch O. D. HMH plastic with silicone hook sleeve. On this pattern the hook sleeve is put on *after* the fly is tied.

Thread: Clear UNI monofilament, fine
Body: Light green over white yak hair, sparse, 2 3/4 inches long, with a few strands of either yellow, pearl, or blue Krystal Flash mixed in, to match the color of the bait.
Lateral flash: Medium silver holographic Flashabou, one strand on one side, 5/8 inch long
Eyes: Silver Prismatic stick-on, size 2 1/2 or 3 (1/8-inch diameter)
Weight: Brass bullet worm weights, from 1/32 to 1/2 ounce, depending on size of fly
Hook: Gamakatsu SC15, sizes 1 to 4, tin-plated, wide gap
Finish: Softex

I tie the body material pointing toward the front on this fly, then bend it to the rear to shape the head. A very small amount of super glue holds the material in place until the eyes are on, then the head is coated with Softex. This "bend back" method creates an empty pocket behind the eyes. A bullet worm weight can be slipped on the back of the Teflon or plastic tube, pushed into the pocket, and held in place with an aquarium hose or silicone hook sleeve. Switching out weights is easy and quick. I fish this fly on sink-tip or clear full-sinking lines, with a 3- to 6-foot leader and a 12-pound fluorocarbon tippet.

Captain Tom Wolf with a Neah Bay, Washington lingcod

KIMBAL DUNBAR

EUPHAUSID

Tube: Teflon, 1/32-inch O. D., 5/16 inch long on finished fly. Hook sleeve is 1/8-inch O. D. clear heat-shrink tubing, 3/16 inch long. Combined tube length on finished fly is 7/16 inch. Note: I use a longer than necessary piece of Teflon and when the fly is done, I cut the excess off at the nose.
Thread: Clear UNI monofilament, fine
Body: White or pink polar bear, sparse, 3/4 inch long
Eyes: Clear, 20-pound monofilament, melted
Hook: Gamakatsu SC15, sizes 8 to 6, tin-plated, wide gap
Finish: Softex

Euphausids are a prime winter food source for resident Puget Sound coho. When krill are present on the surface, salmon graze on them in large schools. Euphausid-feeding coho can be wary and hard to stay close to when tide movement starts to slow down, and on windless days. Casting too close to a school of fish will often put them down. Because of its light weight this fly stays close to the surface, even when fished on a clear intermediate-sink line. Cast it well in front of the fish to avoid spooking them and start your short-strip retrieve when the fish swim near the fly. I fish it on a 4-weight rod and a 9-foot leader with 4- or 6-pound tippet.

MINI-TUBE CLOUSER

Tube: Teflon, 1/16-inch (1.5-mm) O. D., .031-mm I. D., 3/8 inch long on finished fly. Hook sleeve is 1/8-inch O. D. clear heat-shrink tubing, 3/8 inch long. Combined tube length on finished fly is 5/8 inch. Finished fly is 2 inches long. Note: I use a longer than necessary piece of Teflon and when the fly is done, I cut the excess off at the nose.
Thread: Clear UNI monofilament, fine
Body: White under pink, under chartreuse bucktail, sparse, 2 inches long
Eyes: X-Small or Small dumb bell, yellow with black pupils
Hook: Gamakatsu SC15, size 6 to 1 for adult salmon
Finish: Super glue

This is a good Neah Bay or open-water pattern when coho are not showing on the surface. A fun way to fish it: use a 400-grain sink-tip line, strip out 15 to 30 feet, and let the fly hang while dead-drifting the boat. The action imparted by wind and waves will make fish slam the fly.

APPENDIX OF SOURCES

Bidoz
www.bidoz.com/tubes
Tubes designed by Martin Joergensen come in two sizes and are produced in aluminum (light) and brass (heavy). Extension pieces of both materials are available. Bidoz also offers tungsten tubes and Jurij Shumakov tubes.

Guideline Sweden AB
Kärrlyckegatan 29 B, S-418 78 Göteborg Sweden
Phone: +46-31-923650 Fax: +46-31-924687
Email: info@guidelineflyfish.com
www.guidelineflyfish.com
The Frödin-Norling tube system is distributed by Guideline Sweden AB. It consists of four sizes of tubing in clear, fluorescent yellow, fluorescent orange, fluorescent chartreuse, fluorescent red, and black. Michael Frödin is working on a new series of tungsten cone heads to go with the tubing.

HMH
14 Maine Street, Box 18,
Brunswick, ME 04011 USA
Phone: 800-335-9057 or 207-729-5200
Fax: 207-729-5292 Email: hmh@hmhvises.com
URL: www.hmhvises.com Contact: John Albright
HMH Rotary Tube Vise, tube-tying adapter tools, tube blanks in plastic, aluminum, and brass alloy. HMH also has a line of cone heads and plastic beads manufactured to fit the O. D. of their tubes.

Jurij (Yuri) Shumakov Tubes
www.shumakovtubes.com
A line of unique Mörrum-style tubes invented by Yuri and manufactured by Bidoz of France.

Lagartun Ltd.
16741 S. Old Sonoita Hwy., Vail, AZ 85641 USA
Contact: Ercin "Urch" Gultepe
Email: post@lagartun.com
Phone: 1-800-833-5077 Fax: 520-762-5959
Manufacturer of fly-tying materials and the Lagartun Micro Tubes.

Loop Tackle Designs
P. O. Box 195, S-18422 Akersberga, Sweden
Phone: (+46) 8 544 101 90
Fax: (+46) 8 544 101 99
Email: info@looptackle.com
URL: www.looptackle.se/eng
Manufacturer of black and silver metal bottle tubes. Distributor of custom double tube fly hooks by Mustad of Norway.

Midtgård Fluefiske
Brugata 15, NO186 Oslo, Norway
Email: dag@midtgardfluefiske.no
URL: www.midtgardfluefiske.no and
www.midgartubeflies.com
Phone: (+47) 22 17 17 34
Contact Person: Dag Midtgard
Manufacturer of tubes and cone heads, and distributor of traditional Scandinavian tying materials.

Nor-Vise
Norlander Company, P. O. Box 926
Kelso, WA 98626 USA
Phone: (360) 636-2525 Fax: (360) 636-2558
Email: norm@nor-vise.com
URL: www.nor-vise.com
Contact: Norm Norlander
Manufactures a Rotary Tube Tying vise. The web site has excellent photos and drawings.

Osprey Diving Tubes
Merlin Products, 127 New Bedford Rd
Luton, Beds LU3 1LF, England
Phone: +44 (0) 1582 737463
Manufactures lead-weighted diving tubes.

Partridge of Redditch, Limited
Bordesley Hall, Alvechurch, Worcestershire
B4B 7QB, England
Phone: 44 1527 597 222
Fax: +44 (0) 1527 597 111
Email: hooks@partridge-of-redditch.com
URL: www.partridge-of-redditch.co.uk
Manufacturer of many styles of hooks, including a line of single and treble hooks designed for tube flies.

Renzetti, Inc.
8800 Grissom Pkwy, Titusville, FL 32780 USA
Phone: (321) 264-7705 Fax: (321) 264-5929
URL: www.renzetti.com
Manufacturer of the Renzetti Tube vise.

Rooney Tube Works
1041 E. 12th St., Lafayette, OR 97127 USA
Phone: (503) 691-1485
Email: sales@rooneytubeworks.com
URL: www.rooneytubeworks.com
Contact: Tanya Rooney
Manufactures linerless tubes in plastic and brass.

Rudi Heger, GmbH
Traun River Porducts
Haupstr.4, D-83313 Siegsdorf, Germany
Phone: (+49) 08662/7079
Fax: (+49) 08662/2711
Email: rudi-heger@online.de
Sells tube-fly tools, and tubes in aluminum, copper, plastic, and machined tubes in aluminum, brass, and tungsten.

Seattle Saltwater
P.O. Box 3727, Crested Butte, CO 81224
Phone: (970) 349-6715
Email: seattlesaltwater@msn.com
Manufacturer of the Seattle Saltwater tube-fly vise; kits and materials for tube flies; and permanently multicolored, foam popper heads.

Spirit River, Inc.
423 Winchester St., , Roseburg, OR 97470
Offers EZE-Release hooks and tubes, cone heads, machined eyes.

The Canadian Tube Fly Company
4214 40th Avenue
Edmonton, Alberta, Canada T6L 5T4
Phone: (800) 572-7493
Email: canadiantubeflies@shaw.ca
URL: www.canadiantubeflies.com
Contact: Stewart Anderson
Specializes in tube flies for salt- and freshwater species, distributor of tube-tying supplies.

The Fly Co.
Noerbaekvej 12, Hammershoe
DK-8330 Tjele Denmark
Email: info@flyco.dk
URL: www.flyco.dk
Distributor of the HC Danish Tube tying tool and specialty tubes for tying.

Upton Distributors
Aurora Australia/Talon Australia
P. O. Box 6402,
G.C.M.C. QLD 4217 Australia
Phone: 07 55 740 047
Contact: Barry Ryan
Fly-tying materials.

INDEX

A

Abraham's 80 Percent Sailfish Fly, 38, *39*, 40, 41
AJS Dorado, 158, *159*, 162
AJS Herring, 158, *159*, 162
AJS Smolt, 158, *159*, 162, 163
Akroyd, 12, 16
Alaska, 68, 70, 71, 72
Albright, John, 127
Alec's Backward Blue and Yellow, 154, *155*, 157
Alec's Backward Logie, 154, *155*, 157
Alec's Backward Purple Demon, 154, *155*, 157
Alec's Backward Shrimp, 154, *155*, 157
Alevras, John, 8, *9*, 10, 11, 12, 13
Anchor River, Alaska, 72
Anchovy, (comparison photo with Srivistava tube fly) *161*
Andersen, Rex, 14, *15*, 16, 17, 18, 19, 20
April Point Lodge, Vancouver, B.C., 48
Apte, Stu, 38
Atlantic salmon, 16, 17, 20, 21, 22, *23*, 29, 32, 36, 42, *43*, 44, 45, 63, 76, *77*, 90, *91*, 92, 93, 94, 100, *101*, 102, 103, *104*, 105, 106, 107, 114, *115*, 136, *137*, 138, 139, 140, 141, 142, 143, 154, *155*, 156, 157
Aurora, 8, *9*, 11
Australia, 73, 75

B

BC Minnow, *26*, 27
B/W, *30*, 31
Baby Bunker, *128*, 129, 130, 131
Baby Lobster – Rhea, 32, *33*, 34, 36, 37
Baja California, 46
Ballyhoo, 38, *39*, 41
Bart's Basic Baitfish – Rhea, 32, *33*, 37
Bart's Basic Baitfish – Tarpon, 32, *33*, 37
Bates, Joseph, 12, 75
Bauman, Jack, 66
Beast Master General, 127, 129
Bedford, Jim, 109
Bell, Graydon, 21, 22, *23*, 24, 80
Belly Gunner, 136, *137*, 141
Beis Fly Variation, 29, *30*, 31
Berger, Bob, 32
Bernd's G. P., 100, *101*, 102
Bidoz, Andre Fournier, 60
Big Meal Streamer, 51, *52*, 53
billfish, 38, *39*, 40, 41, 54, *55*, 144, *145*, 146, 147
Billfish popper double-hook rig, 41
black bass, 86, 89, *133*, 134, 135, *159*, 161
Black and Silver Tempeldog, *104*, 105, 108
Black Back Shiner, 122, *123*, 125
Black Back Shiner Variant, 122, *123*, 125, 126
Black, Bill, 25, *26*, 27, 28
Black Boss, 76, *77*, 79
Black Doctor, 16
Black Green Highlander Tempeldog, *104*, 105, 107
Black Ice, 64, *65*, 66
Black Karup Marabou *30*, 31
Black Pyramid, 136, *137*, *140*, 141
black rockfish, 49, 120, *133*, 134,

135, *159*, 160, 161, 162, 163
Black Sheep, (Kristinsson) 76, *77*, 78; (Shumakov) 136, *137*, 143
Black's Foam Ant, *26*, 27
Blades, Bill, 13
Blados, Captain Joe (Crease Fly), 129
Blanco-Concepcion, Robin, 82, 85
Blood Dog, *23*, 24
bluefish, *96*, 98, 99
Blue Fly, *30*, 31
Bonde Larsen, Ken, 29, *30*, 31, 86
bonefish, *15*, 18, 19, 32, *33*, 34, 35, 36, 37,
Bonefish Bob's, 32
Bonito, 41
bottle tubes, 8, *9*, 16, 29, *30*, 33, 34, 37, 60, *61*, 62, 70, 76, 100, 138, 139
Brazil, 86, *87*, 88, 89
Bullard, Betsy, 38, 84,
Butorac, Joe, 13, 59

C

Call of the Sea, 100, *101*, 102
candlefish, 46, *47*, 48, 50
catfish, giant European, 51
Catherwood, Bill, 127
Cerdas, Captain Jeremias, 62
Chandler, Bart, 32, *33*, 34, 35, 36, 37
Chandler, Leon, 136
Chapman, Phil, 148
char, 71
Chemelko, Danny, 40
chunking, 56
Clegg, Thomas, 12
Close, George, 66
Clouser, Bob, 28, 85, 158
Clouser Minnow, 28, 80, *81*, 84
Coal Car, 64
coho (silver) salmon, 48, 50, 64, *65*, 66, *69*, 70, *81*, 85, *133*, 134, 135, 158, *159*, 160, 161, 162, 163, 168, *169*, 170, 171, 172
Cold Wind, 8, *9*, 10
Colored junction tubes, (photo) 111
Combs, Trey, 158
Comet Variant, 154, *155*, 157
Concepcion, Abraham, 38, *39*, 40, 41
cone heads, (Norling/Frödin plastic tube system) (photo)105, 106, 107, 161
Conehead Rubber Leg Muddler, *26*, 27
Cone-head weights, 106
Conomo Special, *96*, 97, 99
Convert-A-Damsel, *110*, 112
Convert-A-Hex, *110*, 111, 112
Convert-A-Stone, *110*, 112
Convertible Tube Fly, 109
Costa Rica, 38, *39*, 40, 54, *55*
Crab spawn, 48
Croft, David, 12, 42, *43*, 44, 45
Croft, Mike, 46, *47*, 48, 49, 50, 132, 168
Croft's (Mike) Italian Glass Minnow, 46, *47*, 49
Croft's (Mike) Marabou Candlefish, *47*, 48
Croft's (David) Original Buoyant Flies, 42, *43*, 44, 45
Croft's (Mike) Sardina, *47*, 50
Croft's (Mike) Slider, *47*, 49
Curcione, Nick, 127

Cyclops Marabou Gurgler, 168, *169*, 170, 171
CZCDNTM, 60, *61*, 63

D

Dahlberg, Larry, 73
Dapper Dan, 118, *119*, 121
Dam, Royce, 66
Denmark, 14, 16, 29, 60, 100
Derrick's Sculpin, 118, *119*, 120
Devon minnow, 12, 42, 44
Dolly Varden, 70, 72
Don Gallo, 80, *81*, 82, 83, 84
dorado, *33*, 37, *55*, 56, 57, 80, *81*, *159*, 161, 163
double hooks, for bonefish, 32
Duey, Mike, 158
Dustball Tube, 60, *61*, 62, 63
Dusty Miller, 16

E

East Cape, Baja California, 54
Easy Silver Doctor, 14, *15*, 19
Egg-Sucking Black Leech (Rothermel), 122, *123*, 125
Egg Sucking Leech (Bill Black), *26*, 28
Ellidaar River (Iceland), 76
England, 21
Essex River (Massachusetts), 99
Euphasid, 168, *169*, 172
Eye Candy, 64, *65*, 67
EZE-Release Half 'N' Half, *26*, 27
EZE-Release hook 25, 27, 28

F

F-Boss, 76, *77*, 79
Ferguson, Bruce, 13
Fetcher, Captain Ray, 51
Fiery Brown Special Turbo, *30*, 31
Fire Woman, 114, *115*, 116, 117
First Edition, 64, *65*, 67
Fish Me Spey, 64, *65*, 67
Flaming Tube Squid, 148, *149*, (Orange and Purple)152, (Chartreuse and Orange; Burgundy and Tan) 153
Flats, *15*, 18, 19, 32, *33*, 34, 35, 36, 37, 38
Flexo, 56
Flickering Ember, 14, *15*, 19
Floss tags 17
Frank's Jig Fly, *110*, 111, 113
French, Jerry, 8
Freight Train, 64
Frödin, Michael, 100, 105, 138
Fulsher, Keith, 8

G

Garry Dog, 12
Gartside, Jack, 127, (Floating Minnow) 129, (Gartside Gurgler) 171
Gentle Surgeon, 32, *33*, 36
Glasso, Syd, 8
Gmundner Traun River (Austria), 51
Go-Go Girl, 68, *69*, 71
Golden Light, 90, *91*, 94
Golden Pheasant Pike Tube Streamer, 164, *165*, 167
Golfito Sailfish Rancho, 38, 41, 83, 84
Gort, John, 13
GP Wanted, 136, *137*, 143
Graesser, Neil, 12
Great Lakes, 64, 66, 109, 113
Green Butt Skunk, 64
Green Highlander Variation, *30*, 31
Grey Ghost, 64
Grey Tempeldog, *104*, 105, 107

Griffin, Berney, 132
grouper, 86

H

Haas, Ed, 73
Hairy Mary, 12, 64
Hale, J. H., 90, 92
Half-inchers, 107, 138, 139, 140, 141, (photo of Shumakov tubes) 142
Heger, Rudi, 51, 52, 53
Herd, Andrew, 12
herring, 46, *47*, 48, 50, 80, *81*, 96, 99, 158, *159*, 162, 168, *169*, 171
Hill, Fred, 12
HMH Tube Fly tool, 17
Homer, Alaska, 72
hooks, 10, 14, 16, 18, 19, 21, 25, 27, 32, 35, 40, 41, 63, 66, 70, 73, 100, (double and treble hook weights)106, (free swinging)107, 112, 116; 146
Huchen, 51
Humphreys, Joe, 127
Hylander, Peter, 38, 54, *55*, 56, 57, 58, 59

I

Iceland, 76,
Intruder flies, 8
Islamorada, Florida, 32

J

jacks, 36, 41, 86, 163
Jewel Fly/California Sardine, 144, *145*, 146, 147
Jewel Fly/Green Mackerel, 144, *145*, 147
Jewel Fly/Mediterranean, 144, *145*, 147
Jewel Fly/Pink Squid, 144, *145*, 147
Jewel Fly/Slimey Mack, 144, *145*, 147
Johnson, Les, 13, 68, 109
Johnson, Tim, 64, *65*, 66, 67
Joergensen, Martin, 60, *61*, 62, 63, 86
Jorgensen, Poul, 8, 68, 127

K

Kachemak Bay, Alaska, 72
Kamchatka, 68, 71, *137*, 138, 139, 140, 141, 142, 143
Kenai Peninsula, 72
Kenly, Bob, 68, *69*, 70, 71, 72, 86, 122
king (chinook) salmon, 48, 64, *65*, 70, *159*, 160, 162, 163
Kingfish, 86
Kingston, Nick, 73, *74*, 75, 80
Koch, Ed, 127
Kola Peninsula, *137*, 138, 139, 140, 141, 142, 143
Kolander, Michael, 136, *137*, 143
Kreh, Lefty, 28, 85
Kurtz, Kevin, 38

L

Lady Amherst, 14, *15*, 16, 17
Lake Michigan, 64, 66
lake trout, 66
largemouth bass, 24, *159*, 160
Lax-a Angling Club, 76
leaders 8, 18, 24, 31, 34, 41, 51, 66, 70, 141, 160, 166, 167, 168, 171, 172
Leah Marie, 118, *119*, 121
Lefty's Deceiver, 80, *81*, 83,
Leon, Scott, 146